Assessing Teacher Dispositions

This book is dedicated to our parents, spouses, and children (both human and canine). Doris and Jerome Rothgesser and Rita and William Lang inspired us with their wisdom and gave us the ability to think logically and write clearly and the conviction to do so. Jim, Debbie, and Jerome gave us the encouragement and support to work through the endless hours it takes to produce a detailed work. JJ, Jazzy, and Zoom Zoom sat on our laps and kept us calm—those little puppies who, like validity, never left our sides.

Assessing Teacher Dispositions

Five Standards-Based Steps
to Valid Measurement
Using the DAATS Model

Judy R. Wilkerson
William Steve Lang

Foreword by Richard C. Kunkel

CORWIN PRESS
A SAGE Publications Company
Thousand Oaks, CA 91320

For information:

Corwin Press
A Sage Publications Company
2455 Teller Road
Thousand Oaks, California 91320
www.corwinpress.com

Sage Publications Ltd.
1 Oliver's Yard
55 City Road
London EC1Y 1SP
United Kingdom

Sage Publications India Pvt. Ltd.
B 1/I 1 Mohan Cooperative Industrial Area
Mathura Road, New Delhi 110 044
India

Sage Publications Asia-Pacific Pte. Ltd.
33 Pekin Street #02-01
Far East Square
Singapore 048763

Printed in the United States of America

Library of Congress Cataloging-in-Publication Data

Wilkerson, Judy R.
Assessing teacher dispositions: Five standards-based steps to valid measurement using the DAATS model / Judy R. Wilkerson, William Steve Lang.
    p. cm.
Includes bibliographical references and index.
ISBN-13: 978-1-4129-5367-2 (cloth : alk. paper)
ISBN-13: 978-1-4129-5368-9 (pbk. : alk. paper)
1. Teachers—United States—Attitudes. 2. Teachers—United States—Psychology.
3. Teacher effectiveness—United States. I. Lang, William Steven. II. Title.

LB1775.2.W55 2007
371.1—dc22   2006102789

This book is printed on acid-free paper.

07   08   09   10   11   12   10 9 8 7 6 5 4 3 2 1

Acquisitions Editor:	Faye Zucker
Editorial Assistant:	Gem Rabanera
Typesetter:	C&M Digitals (P) Ltd.
Cover Designer:	Lisa Miller

Contents

List of Tables, Figures, and Boxes

CHAPTER 6. DAATS STEP 4—DECISION MAKING AND DATA MANAGEMENT   121

Boxes

CHAPTER 9. LEGAL AND PSYCHOMETRIC ISSUES   231

Boxes

List of Abbreviations and Acronyms

AACTE: American Association of Colleges of Teacher Education

ACEI: Association of Childhood Education International

AERA: American Educational Research Association

APA: American Psychological Association

CF: conceptual framework

ESE: exceptional student education

ETS: Educational Testing Service

HEA: Higher Education Act

IEP: individual educational plan

INTASC: Interstate New Teacher Assessment and Support Consortium

IR: Institutional Report

IRA: International Reading Association

KSDs: knowledge, skills, and dispositions

LEA: local education agency

LEP: limited English proficiency

NAEYC: National Association for Education of Young Children

NBPTS: National Board for Professional Teaching Standards

NCATE: National Council for Accreditation of Teacher Education

NCLB: No Child Left Behind

NCME: National Council for Measurement in Education

NCSS: National Council for Social Studies

NCTAF: National Commission on Teaching and America's Future

NCTE: National Council for Teachers of English

NCTM: National Council of Teachers of Mathematics

NRC: National Research Council

SCDE: school, college, or department of education

SEA: state education agency

SPA: specialty professional association

TEAC: Teacher Education Accreditation Council

TWSM: Teacher Work Sample Methodology

VRF: validity, reliability, and fairness

Disposition Assessments Aligned With Teacher Standards (DAATS) Steps and Worksheets

DAATS STEP 1: ASSESSMENT DESIGN INPUTS

DAATS Step 1A: Define the purpose(s) and use(s) of the system.

DAATS Step 1B: Define the propositions or principles that guide the system.

DAATS Step 1C: Define the conceptual framework or content of the system.

DAATS Step 1D: Review local factors that impact the system.

Worksheets

Worksheet #1.1: Purpose, Use, Propositions, Content, and Context Checksheet

Worksheet #1.2: Purpose, Use, Content, and Draft

Worksheet #1.3: Propositions

Worksheet #1.4: Contextual Analysis

DAATS STEP 2: PLANNING WITH A CONTINUING EYE ON VALID ASSESSMENT DECISIONS

DAATS Step 2A: Analyze standards and indicators.

DAATS Step 2B: Visualize the teacher demonstrating the affective targets.

DAATS Step 2C: Select assessment methods at different levels of inference.

DAATS Step 2D: Build an assessment framework correlating standards and methods.

Worksheets

Worksheet #2.1: Organizing for Alignment (Version 1)

Worksheet #2.1: Organizing for Alignment (Version 2)

Worksheet #2.2: Visualizing the Dispositional Statements

Worksheet #2.3: Selecting Assessment Methods for INTASC Indicators

Worksheet #2.4: Assessment Methods for INTASC Indicators: Blueprint

Worksheet #2.5: Cost-Benefit and Coverage Analysis of Assessment Methods

DAATS STEP 3: INSTRUMENT DEVELOPMENT

DAATS Step 3A: Draft items and directions for each instrument.

DAATS Step 3B: Review items for applicability to values, domain coverage, and job relevance.

Worksheets

Worksheet #3.1: Creating Scales

Worksheet #3.2: Creating Questionnaires, Interviews, or K–12 Focus Group Protocols

Worksheet #3.3: Creating an Affective Behavior Checklist

Worksheet #3.4: Creating an Affective Behavior Rating Scale

Worksheet #3.5: Creating a Tally Sheet for Affective Observation

Worksheet #3.6: Checklist for Reviewing Scale Drafts

Worksheet #3.7: Review Sheets for Questionnaires and Interviews

Worksheet #3.8: Review Sheets for K–12 Focus Group Protocols

Worksheet #3.9: Checklist for Reviewing Observations and Behavioral Checklists

Worksheet #3.10: Coverage Check

Worksheet #3.11: Rating Form for Stakeholder Review

DAATS STEP 4: DECISON MAKING AND DATA MANAGEMENT

DAATS Step 4A: Develop scoring rubrics.

DAATS Step 4B: Determine how data will be combined and used.

DAATS Step 4C: Develop implementation procedures and materials.

Worksheets

Worksheet #4.1: Explanation of Dichotomous Scoring Decisions

Worksheet #4.2: Rubric Design

Worksheet #4.3: Sample Format for Candidate/Teacher Tracking Form

Worksheet #4.4: Format for Data Aggregation

Worksheet #4.5: Sample Disposition Event Report

Worksheet #4.6: Management Plan

DAATS STEP 5: CREDIBLE DATA

DAATS Step 5A: Create a plan to provide evidence of validity, reliability, fairness, and utility.

DAATS Step 5B: Implement the plan conscientiously.

Worksheets

Worksheet #5.1: Assessment Specifications

Worksheet #5.2: Analysis of Appropriateness of Decisions for Teacher Failures

Worksheet #5.3: Analysis of Rehire Data

Worksheet #5.4: Program Improvement Record

Worksheet #5.5: Expert Rescoring

Worksheet #5.6: Fairness Review

Worksheet #5.7: Analysis of Remediation Efforts and Equal Opportunity (EO) Impact

Worksheet #5.8: Psychometric Plan Format

Foreword

For over thirty years, colleagues and I have been working to design, develop, and implement systems of assessment that can be used by those involved in teacher education to do two things: (1) help us improve our programs in a thoughtful and data-based way and (2) help us account for our actions and programs through student performance in a convincing, evidence-based way.

This book, written by Wilkerson and Lang, was designed and written to assist with these important tasks. It was written from the knowledge of educational and psychometric policy and driven by many years of valued learning by its authors.

I clearly recall discussions about how important it was to assess what we do in teacher education at national professional meetings, college faculty meetings, and in graduate classes at universities across this country. I recall, in the 1960s, we were all talking about Bloom's taxonomy and levels of questions used in the classroom. We felt that in general, the cognitive domain was measurable. However, the common statement mentioned then and today whenever someone mentioned David Krathwohl's Affective Domain was, "Oh, that's important but we can't measure that." Both topics were seen as important in teacher education, but few of us had the knowledge and skills to assess them, especially when considering validity and reliability.

This book is an important course correction to that drift. Yes, the cognitive domain is important and it can be measured, and YES, we can measure the affective domain with validity and reliability as well.

Wilkerson and Lang clearly are responding to national attention to this important topic brought by the National Commission on Teaching and American Future, the National Council for Accreditation of Teacher Education, the Council of Chief State School Officers' through their work with the Interstate New Teacher Assessment and Support Consortium (INTASC) Principles, along with the National Board for Professional Teacher Standards system.

We have watched work in many states, such as Connecticut, California, Ohio, Indiana, and Florida, establish standards and methodologies to assess these standards in teacher preparation. This is neither a new topic nor one that has been viewed as fact and conclusively solved.

As of late, the continued growth of attention to standards in the dispositional realm has compounded this task. In the early years of INTASC and the 1980s redesign of the National Council for Accreditation of Teacher Education (NCATE), I clearly remember discussions that used language of dispositions and affective interest in evidence of teacher competencies in areas other than cognitive knowledge.

I recall the zeal of those who mocked up the first draft of dispositions for INTASC principles. Many of them were also involved in the 1980s redesign of NCATE and the zeal was ever present because of the importance of this task to our nation and its schools.

NCATE and many state program reviews now focus on a professional education unit assessment system. As more and more teams apply these standards with academic rigor, increased attention is focused on the important qualities of validity and reliability in the unit assessment system.

A clear example of this is found in the mid 1990s work in Indiana. A quality group of educational stakeholders, banded together through the Indiana Professional Standards Board, wanted dispositions to be an important part of their standards, assessment, and program review. I remember long and hard conversations with Dr. Marilyn Scannell (Executive Director of the IPSB), and Phil Metcalf of the Indiana State Teachers Association, who was the Chairman of the Board at that time. This discussion was very sensitive and important in regard to strenuous standards and assessment development in a state with a sizable population of quality educators and citizens with generally conservative beliefs. This was only one example of many meetings across the country with strong teacher association leadership demanding solid educational standards for program reviews. The big question then, and still remaining today in professional standards development is, "How might such standards be addressed and how might this be done in a valid and reliable way?" Wilkerson and Lang clearly contribute a solid response to that question.

In *Assessing Teacher Dispositions: Five Standards-Based Steps to Valid Measurement Using the DAATS Model*, the authors have recognized this history and worked with many stakeholders in Florida and around the country. They have had their fingers and toes stepped on from time to time, and through perseverance have produced a publication that offers a valid step-by-step procedure which is based on sound principles of measurement, program evaluation, accreditation, and public policy.

This book is being published at a time when there is a strong backdrop of public interest, public policy, and even public demand that all call for the evidence of important outcomes as critical to our nation and its schools. No Child Left Behind (NCLB), a bipartisan national policy framework, calls for increased attention to assessing teacher competency and doing so with strong research-based methods.

Along with a primary focus on testing the students of our nation's teachers, *Assessing Teacher Dispositions: Five Standards-Based Steps to Valid Measurement Using the DAATS Model* is being published at a time when the U. S. Government also shows a strong interest in the topic of quality teacher preparation. Witness the presence of The Institute of Education Science and the National Institute for Child Health and Human Development, both with increased attention to the importance of individual student data guiding decisions on instruction at all levels.

Wilkerson and Lang give us a solid foundation and strong design to help think through the use of data collected on teacher preparation program graduates that impact the entire national mosaic. Our nation is growing in its agreement that every child must be taught by a quality teacher. There is a vitally important link between teacher preparation and the performance of those teachers and their students. This book provides a strong underpinning to both improve teacher competencies and to prove those competencies in both the cognitive and affective areas.

I strongly believe you will agree with these hopes when you read Wilkerson and Lang's *Assessing Teacher Dispositions: Five Standards-Based Steps to Valid Measurement Using the DAATS Model* and follow the clear steps it proposes.

Richard C. Kunkel
Professor, Educational Leadership and Policy Studies
Former Executive Director, National Council for Accreditation of Teacher Education

Preface

Across the nation, those who prepare teachers are struggling with questions about how to assess teacher affect or dispositions. In its seminal 164-page report on American schooling, *No Dream Denied: A Pledge to America's Children* (NCTAF, 2003), the National Commission on Teaching and America's Future (NCTAF) began its work with a chapter titled "What Still Matters Most: Competent, *Caring*, Qualified Teachers in Schools Organized for Success." The operant word here for this book is **"caring."** That chapter begins with a quotation from Sharon M. Draper, a National Board Certified Teacher and National Teacher of the Year in 1997:

> A child, unlike any other, yet identical to all those who have preceded and those who will follow, sits in a classroom today—*hopeful, enthusiastic, curious.* In that child sleeps the vision and the wisdom of the ages. The touch of a teacher will make the difference. (p. 5, emphasis added)
>
> —Sharon Draper, NBPTS Teacher and Teacher of the Year
> National Commission on Teaching and America's Future, 2003

The quote was taken from a book titled *Teaching From the Heart.* In that description of a child, it is dispositions that come first and wisdom last. In this book, our readers will find that we, too, place dispositions first, with knowledge and skills second. Teachers who want to teach well are more likely to teach well than those who do not care. Teachers who do not care either about children or about the profession of teaching will certainly not teach well.

We use as our basis for defining dispositions the standards articulated by the Council of Chief State School Officers, *The Model Standards for Beginning Teacher Licensing, Assessment and Development,* developed by the Interstate New Teacher Assessment and Support Consortium (CCSSO, 1992). In those standards, the authors concluded,

> . . . to eventually become an expert practitioner, beginning teachers must have, at the least, an awareness of the kinds of knowledge and understandings needed—as well as resources available—to develop these skills; must have some capacity to address the many facets of curriculum, classroom, and student life; and must have the *dispositions and commitments that pledge them to professional development and responsibility.* (p. 11, emphasis added)
>
> —Interstate New Teacher Assessment and Support Consortium, 1992

The above citations serve as a backdrop for this book. We focus on the affect, or dispositions, of teachers—the "caring" word of NCTAF, operationally defined by INTASC in terms of "professional development and responsibility."

All too often in education, we spend an inordinate amount of time planning instruction and then dealing with assessment as an afterthought. We then limit that assessment, already handicapped, to knowledge and skills, setting dispositions even further aside. Here, we will reverse the tradition.

We believe it is critically important that teacher preparation and staff development programs offered in colleges and school districts assess teacher candidates and teachers using systematic processes based on recognized teacher standards, that they identify the assessments needed to ensure that teachers have met those standards, and that they develop instruction targeted at helping teachers succeed in demonstrating the standards. This holds true for both competencies and dispositions. We will propose a comprehensive planning process, rooted in the standards of teaching, as the key to successful assessment. This process allows professional educators to *commit* to excellent assessment through effective planning in order to focus their vision of high-quality teaching.

The model described in this book is aimed at protecting children from unqualified teachers, regardless of entry route. We believe that it is possible to define the critical values of teaching, based on standards. These values can be assessed using tried and tested techniques of assessment that have withstood the test of time. If we plan and implement this well the public can count on each of us to do our jobs and have confidence that teachers can do their jobs.

The assessment model in this book should work equally well for teachers at all levels in their careers. Unlike skills, values may or may not increase with experience. Some teachers will become more committed, some less, to the skills of teaching. Consequently, the DAATS model can be used at any stage in a teacher's career, although the book is written to be linked to NCATE accreditation. The model would work well for annual evaluations of teachers and for National Board Certification; the NBPTS and INTASC standards are not all that dissimilar!

The book is divided into nine chapters, with the assessment core in Chapters 3 through 7. We begin with two introductory chapters, which are targeted at practitioners who are unfamiliar with what dispositions really are and how to measure them. In the first chapter, we define dispositions as a construct and write about why we should measure them. In the second chapter, we link the taxonomy created by Bloom and Krathwohl, specifically the affective domain, to the teaching profession. We describe a teacher's dispositions related to planning in each of the five levels of the affective domain. We demonstrate how the NCATE rubric is based on the taxonomy, noting that the linkage may have been unintentional. We then present a summary and a set of examples of the available literature-based methods for measuring dispositions.

The heart of this book is the five chapters in the middle (Chapters 3 through 7), which establish the steps and substeps of the DAATS model—Disposition Assessments Aligned With Teacher Standards. The model calls for clearly delineating the assessment design inputs, planning with a continuing eye on valid assessment decisions, instrument development, decision making and data management, and credible data. In each of these five chapters, readers will be presented with the following:

- A quick summary or refresher of where we have been so far

- An introduction to the DAATS step to set the stage

- "Before Moving On . . ." Questions to invoke early thinking about the content of the chapter

- A detailed discussion of how to implement the step, with examples and important points in highlighted text

- An alignment of the steps with the "gold" standard of assessment design (AERA, APA, NCME *Standards for Educational and Psychological Testing,* 1999)

- A "Wrap-Up" summary of the chapter

- "Story Starters" for preparing readers to answer the "nay-sayers" in their departments

- Activities, worksheets, and/or examples to work through the model

- Terms from our glossary at the end of the book, interspersed throughout each chapter

After the step-by-step discussion of our model, we conclude with two more chapters. Chapter 8 provides some technical information on a measurement model that can provide useful information for individual teacher diagnostics; validity, reliability, bias studies; gain score calculations; rater adjustments; and further research. Chapter 9 discusses legal challenges that are tied to a failure to attend to psychometric integrity. There we include a fictitious case study in which the teacher first wins and then loses her case, as her program shifts from a nonscientific approach to a scientific one to measure her dispositions. We also include three recent legal cases won by the teacher candidates and lost by their universities.

Throughout the book, we help readers address the need for assessment credibility from a psychometric standpoint—as a matter of integrity. We understand and acknowledge the fear of high-quality assessment that exists in our society, so we have attempted to write in an easy style, using humor as a tool. Even our technical chapter is intended to be as user-friendly and as to-the-point as we can make it. But our message is, we hope, very clear. We maintain throughout the book that it is important to make sure that we are truthfully measuring what we intend to measure and what we need to measure (validity), that we do so in a trustworthy and consistent way (reliability), and that our instruments and procedures are fair and unbiased (fairness).

This book is based in part on our work with partnering institutions in the development of our own set of disposition assessment instruments. We have used this model and our instruments to identify teachers who need help with their dispositions and teacher candidates who should not be allowed to enter the profession.

Audiences that may find this work useful include all those involved in assessing teachers and prospective teachers:

- Teacher educators (college of education and school district based) preparing teachers through traditional or alternative routes

- Colleges of education preparing for accreditation and program approval

- School system administrators responsible for evaluating teachers and providing professional development activities for them

- State department personnel seeking to improve their oversight of certification preparation programs and requirements

- National policymakers who want every child to learn

- Graduate students learning about measurement and program evaluation

- Measurement professionals who want to work with teacher educators
- School board members or elected officials who want to understand what a valid and reliable, performance-based teacher assessment system can be

Although this book is not written specifically for teachers, its practical discussions, worksheets, and assessment design techniques can be useful to classroom teachers hoping to create their own instruments to help diagnose affective problems in their own classrooms. Readers interested in measuring teacher competencies are referred to the companion book, *Assessing Teacher Competency: Five Standards-Based Steps to Valid Measurement Using the CAATS Model.*

—Judy R. Wilkerson & William Steve Lang
February 2007

Acknowledgments

It is difficult to mention all the contributors to this book, but we will attempt to thank a few. We gratefully acknowledge the staff of the American Association of Colleges of Teacher Education, particularly Judy Beck and Brinda Albert, who have supported our workshops offered over the last 5 years at the Association annual meetings, where we learned from our hundreds of eminent colleagues and "students."

Our journal editors gave us a forum for our ideas and the wisdom of peer reviewers: Gene Glass of *Educational Policy Analysis Archives;* Larry Rudner of *Practical Assessment, Research, and Evaluation;* and Richard Smith of *Journal of Applied Measurement.* John Mike Linacre, author of *Winsteps and FACETS* software, was always there for us when we needed advice on data analysis advice and has been our guide in learning the Rasch model.

We would like to say thanks to our research partners: Ivory Toldson of Southern University, Nelly Hecker of Furman University, and Larry Daniels of the University of North Florida.

The authors also thank the American Educational Research Association, the American Psychological Association, and the National Council for Measurement in Education for permission to reproduce selected Standards from the *Standards for Educational and Psychological Testing.* Copies of the book may be ordered at their Web site http://www.apa.org/science/standards.html.

We also thank the Council of Chief State School Officers for permission to reproduce the Interstate New Teacher Assessment and Support Consortium (INTASC) Principles from their *core standards* in our discussion. Copies of the INTASC core standards may be downloaded from the Council's Web site at http://www.ccsso.org.

We appreciate very much the permission granted to use the NCATE *unit standards and program standards* from the National Council for Accreditation of Teacher Education. NCATE can be contacted at http://www.ncate.org, where a copy of their Standards may be downloaded or ordered for purchase.

The authors thank the editor of *Education Policy Analysis Archives* for permission to reproduce portions of material previously printed as an article in the journal, an open-access, refereed education journal available at http://www.epaa.asu.edu.

Finally, and most important of all, we would never have had the courage to engage in this project without our tireless and talented Corwin Executive Editor, Faye Zucker, and all of the wonderful Corwin Press staff.

Corwin Press gratefully thanks the following reviewers for their contributions to this book:

Marilyn Troupe, Director, Division of Educator Preparation
Education Professional Standards Board, Frankfort, KY

Martha Gage, Director, Teacher Education and Licensure (TEAL)
Kansas State Department of Education, Topeka, KS

About the Authors

 **Judy R. Wilkerson** is Associate Professor of Research and Assessment at Florida Gulf Coast University, where she teaches graduate and undergraduate courses in measurement, research, and evaluation. As in this book and all of her research, she focuses her efforts with students on providing a highly pragmatic approach, based in theory, with the goal of instilling a commitment in them to assess K–12 learning. Her PhD is in Measurement and Research from the University of South Florida, where she served for 15 years as Director of Program Review, leading college and university efforts in accreditation. Her career has been dedicated to standards-based assessment of programs and teachers, beginning with the creation of an evaluation model for accreditation in 1987, which she implemented in several states. Beginning in 1990, for 15 years, she served as the primary accreditation consultant for higher education to the Florida Department of Education, where she drafted the standards for the initial approval of teacher education programs, designed the program approval process, and provided technical assistance to colleges of education in evaluation of teachers and programs statewide. She has consulted nationally on NCATE accreditation and worked with state associations of teacher educators on accreditation-related issues. She has also consulted with school districts in Florida on assessment systems for teachers. She was lead designer of the assessment system for the Florida Alternative Certification Program, now used in over 40 of the 68 school districts in the state.

 **William Steve Lang** is Associate Professor of Educational Measurement and Research at the University of South Florida St. Petersburg, where he teaches graduate courses in measurement, statistics, and research. He, too, focuses his teaching on making meaningful and pragmatic uses of the disciplines he teaches. He earned his PhD from the University of Georgia in 1984. He has taught as a public school teacher in South Carolina and Georgia and as a college faculty member in South Carolina, Georgia, and Florida. He has published on a variety of applications in educational testing and works extensively with the Rasch model of item response theory. He began working extensively with Judy when she joined the faculty of the St. Petersburg Campus in 2001. Since that time, they have collaborated in all aspects of their research and service efforts with the Florida Department of Education, Florida school districts, and teacher education programs nationwide. They are working together to build two teacher assessment scales—one on teacher dispositions, the subject of this book, and another on competencies. Their work in both areas is standards driven.

1

What Are Dispositions, and Why Should We Measure Them?

It's so hard when I have to, and so easy when I want to.

—Annie Gottlier

*D*ispositions, or affect, form a different construct than knowledge and skills, as was so effectively noted by Benjamin Bloom (Bloom & Krathwohl, 1956) decades ago. In this chapter, we will describe the importance and challenge of measuring dispositions in both preservice and inservice contexts and from several national perspectives. We will review the requirements in teacher education for measuring dispositions, and we will examine the relationship between knowledge, skills, and dispositions. We will focus on some pitfalls in the NCATE description of the process. We will conclude with some activities that should help assessors articulate their own beliefs about affective measurement and experience the measurement of dispositions using an affective technique (Thurstone Agreement Scale) that demonstrates the process.

Throughout the book, we will provide some user-friendly definitions, along with "guiding questions" to help you use the terms in practice. Our first term, "dispositions," is provided in the next section.

THE IMPORTANCE OF MEASURING DISPOSITIONS

Much time is spent on ensuring that teachers—both preservice and inservice—have the knowledge and skills that they are supposed to have. In teacher preparation programs, faculty score tests and exams and evaluate assigned projects. In district-based alternative certification programs and in performance appraisal systems for certified teachers, school system personnel review lesson plans and other work products. Both preservice and inservice teachers are observed in the classroom to provide more data on their teaching abilities. States often require a certification exam to provide information on whether or not the teacher has the knowledge and, to some extent, the skills to be admitted into the profession.

None of these measures, however, tell the assessor *directly* whether or not the teacher has the dispositions—values, beliefs, and attitudes—needed to be a good teacher. While we might infer that the teacher who is doing a good job is doing so because of high values and strong commitment, this inference can easily be misguided if we fail to check specifically for dispositions. Suppose the teacher knew the assessor was coming and just put on a good show for the visit. While we all know in our hearts that without the appropriate dispositions, teachers will not be good teachers, we are often far too ready to just assume that the dispositions are there or can be witnessed from observations of the teacher.

We believe that this is a serious problem facing the K–12 education system. Much can go wrong if we lack confidence that the teachers we are assessing have the values we hold to be important. Here, in Box 1.1, are some examples of how we can ensure the acquisition of skills but can still have teachers who are likely to be ineffective in the long run.

⸮ ——— Disposition ———

We will use the word "disposition" in this book to mean teacher affect—attitudes, values, and beliefs that influence the application and use of knowledge and skills. We will aim at determining whether or not the teacher has reached the "valuing" level in the Bloom and Krathwohl taxonomy. Our focus will be on standards-based, skill-related values, aligned with the INTASC Principles.

Guiding Question: "What does the teacher believe to be important about teaching and being a good teacher? How is he or she likely to act?"

> **Box 1.1. Examples of Assessing Standards-Based Skills Without Attending to the Accompanying Beliefs**
>
> - *Planning:* Reviews of completed work and on-site visits in the classroom help decision makers feel confident that the teacher has acquired the proper planning skills to succeed with children's learning. But the teacher may think planning is a waste of time and just "wing it" in the classroom most of the time when no one is watching.
>
> - *Diversity:* Teachers may have successfully modified instruction for special needs children but may not value the needs of these children enough to help them when they are in their own classrooms, expecting the exceptional student education (ESE) children to just get by.

- *Reflective Practice:* If candidates write a reflection on the 50 pieces of evidence in their portfolios and become very good at it (and very tired of it), how reflective will they be in their own classrooms? Will they use portfolios to help children learn?

- *Assessment:* We teach teachers to assess each child's learning and the learning of the group as a whole, but will they look at individual and group learning for diagnostic and remediation purposes when in their own classes? Will they be satisfied with the test at the end of the chapter in the teachers' guide and discontinue thinking about innovative approaches focused on critical and creative thinking when rushed to get everything else done?

These examples and questions demonstrate why it is important to spend some significant time and effort on measuring dispositions. If we do not attempt to project whether the skills will continue to be applied in the "real" world, after teachers graduate from their college preparation or district-based preparation programs, then we have partially failed in our obligation to produce highly qualified teachers. Without assessment of dispositions, there is no way to program or predict improvement of dispositions, either individually or in aggregate, among the teacher candidates we see. There are many very bright teachers who attempt to teach—and fail miserably because they do not have the values and commitment it takes.

THE CHALLENGE

In January 2003, the National Commission on Teaching and America's Future (NCTAF) released its second report on the challenges faced by children in the schools. Titled *No Dream Denied: A Pledge to America's Children,* the report continues the work previously written in *Doing What Matters Most: Investing in Quality Teaching* (NCTAF, 1997) and provides a discussion and a set of recommendations on building quality teacher preparation, accreditation, and licensure efforts as the foundation upon which the nation needs to rest its hopes for change.

The Commission had the wisdom to say that we have defined good teaching based on a decade of policy development, experience, research, and classroom practice that has resulted in consensus. This consensus is articulated by both the Interstate New Teacher Assessment and Support Consortium (INTASC, 1992) and the National Board for Professional Teaching Standards (NBPTS, 1986), with the former defining good teaching at the beginning level and the latter defining it at the advanced or accomplished level. In its discussion of accountability for teacher preparation at the federal, state, and local levels, the Commission advised that documentation efforts need to include the extent to which graduates have mastered the qualities of a highly qualified beginning teacher. It defined those qualities in a paragraph that provides a useful synopsis of the INTASC Principles and NBPTS *Propositions.* We quote this below, with our own emphases added to facilitate the distinction between cognitive (knowledge and skills) and affective (dispositions) domains. We will use italics for the cognitive and bold italics for the affective.

Great teachers *have a deep understanding* of the subjects they teach. They *work* with a firm **conviction** that all children can learn. They *know and use* teaching skills and a complete arsenal of assessment strategies to *diagnose and respond* to individual learning needs. They *know how to use* the Internet and modern technology to *support* their students' mastery of content. They are **eager** to *collaborate* with colleagues, parents, community members, and other educators. They are **active** learners themselves, **cultivating** their own professional growth throughout their careers. They **take on** leadership roles in their schools and profession. Finally, they *are models,* instilling a **passion** for learning in their students. (NCTAF, 2003, p. 19)

Words like "conviction," "eager," and "passion" imply something very different from words like "know and use," "diagnose and response," and "support." The second set of words are the cognitive (knowledge- and skill-based) ones, and these words are the typical focus of most teacher assessment systems. While we, as teacher educators, spend countless hours determining whether or not a teacher can write a good lesson plan (skill assessment), we rarely ask for that teacher's thoughts about a picture of a scantily clad, inappropriately dressed teacher (disposition assessment).

WHAT ARE STANDARDS-BASED DISPOSITIONS?

In this book, we limit our discussion to beginning teacher assessment and the INTASC Principles (Council of Chief State School Officers [CCSSO], 1992). There are 10 Principles, each of which contains a statement (the Principle, or standard) accompanied by three subsets of indicators, divided into knowledge, dispositions, and performances (skills). Note that the cognitive (knowledge and performances) and affective (dispositions) domains are clearly differentiated and split. The complete set of INTASC Principles can be viewed online at http://www.ccsso.org/content/pdfs/corestrd.pdf. We provide a list of the indicators for dispositions as an appendix to the book (see Resource B). Some examples of dispositional indicators from the INTASC Principles help to clarify what we are really looking for in terms of the skills-based standards. A few indicators are given in Box 1.2, with our comments about them.

Indicators

Indicators are statements or subparts that give specific examples or meanings to standards. We would call them "substandards," but that might be misinterpreted!

Guiding Question: "What are the details of the standards that help me visualize what the standard is intended to mean?"

Box 1.2. Examples of INTASC Disposition Indicators

- **Indicator**: The teacher realizes that subject matter knowledge is not a fixed body of facts, but is complex and ever evolving. He or she seeks to keep abreast of new ideas and understandings in the field.

Comment: This teacher is the lifelong learner who seeks to keep abreast of new knowledge as a matter of choice.

- **Indicator:** The teacher is sensitive to community and cultural norms.

  Comment: This key word here is "sensitivity." The sensitive teacher will look for opportunities to incorporate community or cultural experiences into teaching and will avoid inappropriate materials or comments—by choice.

- **Indicator:** The teacher understands how participation supports commitment and is committed to the expression and use of democratic values in the classroom.

  Comment: This key word here is "commitment." This teacher will actively look for opportunities to involve the students in classroom management and activities—again by choice.

- **Indicator:** The teacher values both long-term and short-term planning.

  Comment: This key word here is "values." This teacher will avoid arriving in class without a good set of lesson plans and may make many sacrifices of his or her own time to plan adequately. There might even be a planner on the desk!

- **Indicator:** The teacher is committed to using assessment to identify student strengths and promote student growth rather than to deny students access to learning opportunities.

  Comment: This key word here is "commitment." This teacher assesses on a continuous basis, looking for opportunities to identify student strengths and weaknesses and make frequent adjustments.

- **Indicator:** The teacher values critical thinking and self-directed learning as habits of mind.

  Comment: This key word here is "values." This teacher asks lots of questions, not just the ones in the lesson plan, and finds many opportunities for children to explore on their own.

- **Indicator:** The teacher respects the privacy of students and confidentiality of information.

  Comment: This key word here is "respects." This teacher guards student privacy and grades carefully. The gradebook is nowhere in sight for prying eyes. Papers are folded to hide grades when returned.

Clearly, many of the values in Box 1.2 can be observed. The key is to figure out which ones need to be observed, what to look for during an observation, which ones to assess through written documents, and which ones require new and different methods. The point is that most observation instruments used in districts and schools do not currently explicate the specific behaviors to be watched, even though many observers think they can "catch" attitudes while looking for skills. Using the INTASC indicators listed above can help us write the observable behaviors for such a process. Here are a few that can be assessed relatively easily through *systematic* observation:

- Introduction of materials beyond the scope of the textbook
- Visible lesson plan that frames instructional delivery

⸮ ─────────── Construct ───────────

The concept or characteristic that a test or assessment system is designed to measure. In this work, we name it "teacher performance."

Guiding Question: "What's the big-picture idea of what we are assessing?"

?

- Verbal and nonverbal encouragement to children asking thoughtful questions
- Gradebook out of sight and grades on papers hidden

Like all good assessment, we have to operationally define the construct and how we will measure it!

HIERARCHICAL RELATIONSHIPS AMONG KNOWLEDGE, SKILLS, AND DISPOSITIONS

We see a relationship between knowledge, skills, and dispositions in the INTASC Principles that some readers do not recognize. It is important to internalize this relationship as a foundation for the design of dispositional measures. It can help assessors acquire the cognitive understanding and affective values they need to move toward a more comprehensive and meaningful approach to teacher assessments.

Let us look at a subset of the indicators for the INTASC Principle on Planning (#7), in Box 1.3, with the verbs emphasized in bold italics.

Box 1.3. INTASC Knowledge, Skills, and Dispositions: An Example of the Hierarchical Relationship

Principle #7: The teacher plans instruction based upon knowledge of subject matter, students, the community, and curriculum goals.

Selected Indicators:

- The teacher **knows** when and how to adjust plans based on student responses and other contingencies. (Knowledge)
- The teacher **believes** that plans must always be open to adjustment and revision based on student needs and changing circumstances. (Dispositions)
- The teacher **responds** to unanticipated sources of input, **evaluates** plans in relation to short- and long-range goals, and systematically **adjusts** plans to meet student needs and enhance learning. (Skills)

INTASC identifies specific indicators for knowledge, disposition, and skill. They are not aligned or ordered, simply listed in clusters: first, knowledge, then disposition, then performances. NCATE *Standards* use the term "skills" instead of "performances," and we will do the same in this book. They are essentially synonymous in our view. It requires some analysis to align the indicators as we did above, but this is not always necessary. We do so for demonstration purposes to show that they are different. Nonetheless, as one explores the indicators, it is clear that a relationship such as the one in the example above exists between and among many of them.

Note that INTASC places dispositions in the middle of the sequence, whereas NCATE refers to dispositions last in its triumvirate of knowledge, skills, and dispositions. Either way, skills that are not valued are not likely to be used. For us, the important point is just that. Dispositions may very well be the most important element in the assessment system. Without commitment to the skills espoused in the INTASC Principles themselves, which are drawn from the literature on teacher effectiveness, little else matters. ***We do what we value***. We can know how to do something but not want to do it—and so we do not do it! Skills and dispositions are different, but symbiotic, constructs.

REMEMBERING BLOOM

For those still doubting that dispositions provide for a different construct than knowledge and skills, we remind readers that Bloom and Krathwohl's original taxonomy addressed three domains, one of which was affect. Most readers can recite the cognitive (knowledge and skills) domain easily, but they are not able to do the same for the affective (dispositions) domain elaborated by Krathwohl, Bloom, and Masia (1964) more than 40 years ago. We have long known that cognitive and affective objectives are different (Anderson & Krathwohl, 2001; Bloom & Krathwohl, 1956; Krathwohl et al., 1964).

In this taxonomy, there is again a hierarchy, but here it relates to the degree of internalization of affect. In Chapter 2, we will elaborate on the Krathwohl taxonomy for affect, and then we will describe some methods for assessing affect. For now, we hope this brief reminder has served as an "ah-hah" moment, as we attempt to raise your commitment to the need to assess dispositions.

DISPOSITIONS AND ACCREDITATION: REQUIREMENTS AND DEFINITIONS

We mentioned above that NCATE requires the measurement of dispositions as part of its accreditation requirements for teacher education programs. We will now provide a little more detail on that requirement, pointing out some lack of clarity or inconsistency in the language of the standards that could lead to confusion if not recognized.

The first NCATE (2002) standard, titled, "Candidate Knowledge, Skills, and **Dispositions**" (emphasis added), is cited in Box 1.4.

Box 1.4. NCATE Standard 1

Candidates preparing to work in schools as teachers or other professional school personnel know and demonstrate the content, pedagogical, and professional knowledge, skills, and ***dispositions*** necessary ***to help all students learn***. Assessments indicate that candidates meet ***professional, state, and institutional standards***.

Note that dispositions are clearly included in the NCATE Standard 1 and that assessments are required to be linked to professional standards. So, standards are nested within the standards, and dispositions are of weight equal to that of knowledge and skills. The "Supporting Explanation" for this Standard, in Box 1.5, links NCATE and INTASC together as the standards "of reference" in the statement, making it clear that the INTASC Principles should be used as a major basis for designing assessment systems.

Box 1.5.   NCATE Standard 1—Supporting Explanation

NCATE and INTASC expect teacher candidates to demonstrate knowledge, skills, and dispositions[11] to provide learning opportunities supporting students' intellectual, social, and personal development. (p. 18)

---

[11]This list is based on the standards of the Interstate New Teacher Assessment and Support Consortium (INTASC). The complete INTASC document includes knowledge, dispositions, and performance related to each principle. It is available on the Web site for the Council of Chief State School Officers (CCSSO): http://www.ccsso.org/intasc.html.

Validity

Validity is the extent to which assessment measures are truthful about what they say they measure or the degree to which evidence and theory support the interpretations and use of a test or assessment process.

Guiding Question: "Does this test really measure what it says it measures? Does the assessment system provide adequate coverage of the standards?"

Reliability

Reliability is the degree to which test scores are consistent over repeated applications of the process and are, therefore, dependable or trustworthy.

Guiding Question: "If a student took the same test again under the same conditions (or a similar version of the test), would he or she score the same score?"

To meet the NCATE standard, then, we need to start by defining our construct of dispositions, so that we know what we have to assess. The two places to start are with the INTASC Principles, which define the content for us, and an understanding of what dispositions are—and are not! As in all good measurement, we need to adequately cover the construct and not limit our efforts to piecemeal attempts and inadequate content. This will be a big focus for us in the DAATS process and the steps-based chapters that follow, and we will call it "validity." Even though terms like "validity" and "reliability" can be scary if associated with some bad experience you had in a college course, it is important that we be precise and consistent with our decisions and results. In this book, we will provide some practical advice on how to do this.

For now, let us look at some definitions and conflicts that can prevent good coverage of the dispositions construct and impede the validity of decisions we make about teachers and teacher candidates. There are many definitions of dispositions that we could cite. We will provide three: one from the literature, a standard dictionary definition, and the NCATE definition.

Katz (1993) helps us to see that dispositions are both voluntary and a habit of mind, outside our conscious control, with the definition provided in Box 1.6.

Box 1.6.   Dispositions: A Definition From the Literature

A pattern of behavior that is exhibited frequently and in the absence of coercion and constituting a habit of mind under some conscious and voluntary control, and that is intentional and oriented to broad goals.

Our dictionary definition, in Box 1.7, comes from the *Merriam-Webster Online Dictionary* (2006) and adds to our understanding not only mood but also a tendency to act in certain ways.

Box 1.7.   Dispositions: A Dictionary Definition

A prevailing tendency, mood, or inclination; temperamental makeup; the tendency of something to act in a certain manner under given circumstances.

NCATE (2002) provides the definition of "dispositions" in its glossary, shown in Box 1.8, introducing ethics and some specific examples of dispositions important for teachers.

Box 1.8.   Dispositions: An NCATE Definition

The values, commitments, and professional ethics that influence behaviors toward students, families, colleagues, and communities and affect student learning, motivation, and development as well as the educator's own professional growth. Dispositions are guided by beliefs and attitudes related to values, such as caring, fairness, honesty, responsibility, and social justice. For example, they might include a belief that all students can learn, a vision of high and challenging standards, or a commitment to a safe and supportive learning environment. (p. 53)

The first conflict we face in the NCATE *Standards* appears in this definition. Mention of the INTASC Principles and what they represent in terms of skill-based values (e.g., commitment to critical thinking, planning, assessment, and so on: INTASC Principles 4, 7, and 8) *is missing in the definition*. Only learning environment (INTASC Principle 5) is mentioned. This happens despite the footnote (from p. 18) referenced in Box 1.5 above. For valid measurement of dispositions, assessors need to take the definition as well as the "Supporting Explanation" and its footnote into account, and that means all of the INTASC Principles. Also note here that the definition includes ethics as one of three sources of behavioral influence. It is not exclusive. The importance of this point will be highlighted in the next two sections.

MEASURING DISPOSITIONS: SOURCES OF CONFUSION

Conflicts and confusion about what dispositions are and how they should be measured has roots in the literature. For example, Usher, Usher, and Usher (2003) appropriately define teacher dispositions as including empathy, the views of others, the views of self, authenticity, and meaningful purpose and vision; however, they continue to conclude inappropriately that such definitions of this construct cannot be measured: "They [the dispositions] are not directly observable, and they are not directly linked to certain behaviors. . . . Thus, they are not readily assessable using the instruments of measurement that have become rather standard in the social sciences" (p. 5).

Unfortunately, writings such as this have become a kind of cop-out for those who do not truly believe that dispositions are important enough to spend the time it takes to determine whether or not teachers have them. They may also be the source for confusion in the NCATE *Standards.* In the "Supporting Explanation" for Standard 1, NCATE (2002) continues with the statement, shown in Box 1.9, which closely parallels the Usher et al. (2003) statement.

Box 1.9. NCATE Standard 1—More From the Supporting Explanation

Candidates for all professional education roles develop and model dispositions that are expected of educators. The unit articulates candidate dispositions as part of its conceptual framework(s). The unit systematically assesses the development of appropriate professional dispositions by candidates.[14] Dispositions are not usually assessed directly; instead they are assessed along with other performances in candidates' work with students, families, and communities. (p. 19)

---

[14]Codes of ethics may be helpful in thinking about dispositions and are available from a number of professional associations, including the National Education Association (NEA).

The confusing issues that we see in the above explanation from NCATE are as follows:

1. NCATE suggests that institutions focus their measurement of dispositions on the conceptual framework. Given the examples provided in the first excerpt from the "Supporting Explanation," which include honesty, fairness, social justice, and so on, this causes institutions to focus most heavily on their own conceptualizations of what they need to measure, adding on INTASC Principles at a secondary level (see Box 1.9). In this book, we will encourage colleges and districts to merge and align their values, as expressed in a mission statement or a conceptual framework and the INTASC dispositional indicators, with national standards coming first and predominating, as a matter of validity and legal safety.

2. There is some overlap between dispositions and ethics, but they are *not* the same thing. Referring institutions specifically to the NEA Code of Ethics in the footnote (Box 1.9) rather than the INTASC Principles is somewhat

misleading. Referencing both in different footnotes (Boxes 1.5 and 1.9) makes matters even worse. That will be the subject of the next section.

3. Dispositions can be measured directly, and this has been done for decades. There is much literature about affective measurement, and many viable instruments are available. We will address the literature in the next section of this chapter and the methodologies in Chapter 2. To us, this is the most disturbing part of the NCATE "Supporting Explanation." When we combine this narrowed focus on the dispositions to be measured with a method that confuses affective and cognitive measurement techniques, we end up with mush.

Institutionally defined dispositions, such as commitment to social justice, can be assessed readily and early in a teacher's career, even at the point of admission to a program. These attitudes may also later be linked to INTASC Principles that target how teachers treat individual children and work with colleagues. They should not, however, be used to the exclusion of the other aspects of the INTASC Principles to which they are not readily linked.

In this book, we will focus on measuring the INTASC disposition indicators. We will occasionally incorporate some samples from representative conceptual framework values at the institutional and school district levels. We also encourage institutions and districts to look for early and broad-based measures if that is something in which they are interested. See the work of Wasicsko (2004), for example. Our predominant approach, however, will remain a standards-based one, and we will use scientifically based, proven methodologies of measuring affect. These techniques are not fads; they have withstood the test of time for decades.

MEASURING DISPOSITIONS: MORALS, ETHICS, OR STANDARDS BASED?

In recent years, the American Association of Colleges of Teacher Education (AACTE) has spent considerable time on the moral basis for teaching through the work of its Task Force on Teacher Education as a Moral Community (TEAM C), working in collaboration with the Character Education Partnership (see http://www.aacte .org/programs/standards_practice/practice_scholarship.htm).

A recent publication from AACTE also linked the measurement of dispositions with moral education and assessment (Sockett, 2006). In that publication, NCATE President Arthur Wise introduced the book, describing the NCATE process "as unleashing a search by all institutions for the moral and ethical foundation of the profession of teaching" (Sockett, 2006, p. 5). A search of the NCATE *Standards* document, however, yields not a single use of the word "morals." As measurement professionals, we are uncomfortable with this shift away from a series of 10 standards (the INTASC Principles) toward a single facet of them—ethics. For most assessment purposes, a standard or a construct can be "deconstructed" into subcomponents (Briggs & Wilson, 2004). Clearly, a subcomponent or facet resulting from this deconstruction process should not become the overarching focus of the measurement process.

Nonetheless, given the NCATE "Supporting Explanation" that references codes of ethics and morals as useful sources of information for how to define teacher dispositions, we will provide three definitions and discussions on these two related terms taken from the online research literature and encyclopedias.

Velasquez, Andre, Shanks, and Meyer (2006), from the Markkula Center of Applied Ethics at Santa Clara University, provide us with the first of our definitions in their online discussion on the meaning of ethics, shown in Box 1.10.

Box 1.10. Literature-Based Definition of Ethics

What, then, is ethics? Ethics is two things. First, ethics refers to well-based standards of right and wrong that prescribe what humans ought to do, usually in terms of rights, obligations, benefits to society, fairness, or specific virtues. Ethics, for example, refers to those standards that impose the reasonable obligations to refrain from rape, stealing, murder, assault, slander, and fraud. Ethical standards also include those that enjoin virtues of honesty, compassion, and loyalty. And, ethical standards include standards relating to rights, such as the right to life, the right to freedom from injury, and the right to privacy. Such standards are adequate standards of ethics because they are supported by consistent and well-founded reasons.

Second, ethics refers to the study and development of one's ethical standards. As mentioned above, feelings, laws, and social norms can deviate from what is ethical. So it is necessary to constantly examine one's standards to ensure that they are reasonable and well-founded. Ethics also means, then, the continuous effort of studying our own moral beliefs and our moral conduct, and striving to ensure that we, and the institutions we help to shape, live up to standards that are reasonable and solidly based.

For encyclopedia definitions of "ethics," we turn to two sources. First, the *Columbia Encyclopedia Online* provides the definition in Box 1.11.

Box 1.11. Encyclopedia-Based Definition of Ethics

In philosophy, the study and evaluation of human conduct in the light of moral principles. Moral principles may be viewed either as the standard of conduct that individuals have constructed for themselves or as the body of obligations and duties that a particular society requires of its members. (*Columbia Encyclopedia Online*, 2001–2005)

Wikipedia's online definition of "ethics" incorporates "morality," and we provide this source's definition of both terms in Box 1.12.

Box 1.12. Encyclopedia-Based Definitions of Ethics and Morality

Ethics (from the Ancient Greek "*ethikos*," meaning "arising from habit"), a major branch of philosophy, is the study of value or quality. It covers the analysis and employment of concepts such as right, wrong, good, evil, and responsibility. It is divided into three primary areas: *meta-ethics* (the study of what ethicality is), *normative ethics* (the study of what ethical truths there are and how they are known), and *applied ethics* (the study of the use of ethical knowledge). (*Wikipedia*, 2006)

> **Morality** refers to the concept of human ethics which pertains to matters of good and evil—also referred to as "right or wrong," used within three contexts: individual conscience; systems of principles and judgments—sometimes called moral values—shared within a cultural, religious, secular, Humanist, or philosophical community; and codes of behavior or conduct.
>
> Personal morality defines and distinguishes among right and wrong intentions, motivations or actions, as these have been learned, engendered, or otherwise developed within each individual. (*Wikipedia*, 2006)

Ethics and morality, then, are all about knowing the difference between right and wrong and avoiding "wrong" actions that can be harmful to others. Clearly, it is important that teachers avoid harming children by doing evil things, and, clearly, the newspapers are filled with stories of teachers who do not act morally. Clearly, it is important for us to be on guard, trying to prevent teachers from entering or remaining in the profession if they are going to harm children. We believe, however, that there is much more to dispositions than this. We also know that finding the secret pedophiles and other obviously immoral teachers is not an easy task and certainly not one that will be evident through a routine classroom observation! The trouble with basing our dispositions assessment systems on a definition of morality is threefold:

1. Morals and ethics, or the lack thereof, are hard to spot unless an egregious error is openly committed, and this is rare.

2. Some religious overtones associated with moral and character education are not clearly supported dimensions of morality for all members of society. Some religions, for example, are adamantly opposed to homosexuality and various sexual practices, whether they are practiced privately or not. Others would believe that such practices, practiced at home and behind closed doors, are not related to teacher effectiveness.

3. Focusing on morality and ethics, rather than skill-based standards, is shortsighted, bordering, in our view, on the *real* immoral action, letting unmotivated teachers into the profession because of a failure to recognize the codependence of knowledge, skills, and dispositions.

The confusion about dispositions—both what they are and how to measure them—has caused a series of challenges that are likely to continue (Wilkerson, 2006). In 2005, Le Moyne College was forced by the New York District Court of Appeals to take back a student whom they had dismissed for advocating for corporal punishment and against multicultural education in a classroom management plan (Jacobson, 2006). Washington State University, Brooklyn College, and the University of Alaska have also been legally challenged on their procedures related to dispositions assessments (R. Wilson, 2005).

We conclude that if we use the standards as a definition of the construct, rather than codes of ethics from professional or church-affiliated organizations, we stand a better chance of avoiding lawsuits, the wrath of the public, and the other consequences of failing to cover the spectrum of teacher attitudes and values associated with a highly skilled professional. Our challenge becomes, then, how we identify, diagnose, and even dismiss a teacher whose values are clearly violations of standards-based dispositions. Advocacy for corporal punishment and denial of the importance of multicultural education, for example, are serious dispositional deficits that can be assessed in appropriate ways to protect K–12 children (INTASC Principles 5 and 3, respectively).

DIFFERENT CONSTRUCT, DIFFERENT ASSESSMENTS, SIMILAR ASSESSMENT DESIGN PROCESS

Competencies, or knowledge and skills, make up a construct different from dispositions. As a result, the same instruments, as conceived for skills, cannot serve both purposes. However, some instruments, such as the observation form or process, can be modified to add dispositional components. New ones can also be created. In general, the same basic, standards-based design process can be used to design both types of measures.

In this book, we will extend our previous work (Wilkerson & Lang, 2007), which outlined a step-by-step process for measuring teacher competence in the skill-based areas, to the measurement of teacher dispositions. Both are important! In our competency-based process, we proposed a five-step design model, which we called *Competency Assessments Aligned With Teacher Standards,* or CAATS. In this book, we propose a parallel five-step design model, *Disposition Assessments Aligned With Teacher Standards,* or DAATS.

We approach this work with the same framework we proposed for competencies: The problems in teacher assessment are largely a function of designing systems without adequate evidence or operational understanding of standards. We reiterate that decisions about entrance into the profession have to be based on a demonstration of standards, and these decisions need to be valid. As measurement professionals, we believe that the greatest challenge to those assigned the responsibility of ensuring both teacher competence and teacher dispositions is to design systems with a constant eye on validity and utility. Reliability is important, too, but more difficult in this context.

The INTASC Principles (or national standards) teacher assessment form the core of this approach from a content or construct perspective. The INTASC Principles provide indicators of knowledge, dispositions, and performances (skills) and are, therefore, appropriate for measuring both skills in our CAATS model and dispositions in this DAATS model. The statements of the Principles themselves and the dispositions indicators are included at the end of this chapter for reference and design purposes. Use of these indicators provide built-in construct validity for what we intend to measure. These Principles are also required as part of teacher education accreditation through NCATE.

As we did with the CAATS model, we will also again apply the accepted standards of the profession for assessment, the *Standards for Educational and Psychological Testing* (AERA, APA, and NCME, 1999). These standards provide the requirements for valid, reliable, and fair assessment. A merger of these two sets of standards establishes a stronger opportunity to measure teacher dispositions with confidence, precision, and accuracy.

V WRAP-UP

We have made the case that measuring knowledge and skills is different from measuring dispositions or affect, as did Bloom and Krathwohl about four decades ago. We have reviewed our context, as established by NCTAF, INTASC, NBPTS, and NCATE. We have thought about the relationship among knowledge, skills, and dispositions, considering the extent to which they are codependent. We have discussed the relationship of morals and ethics to dispositions, and the pitfalls of focusing too heavily on a philosophical discussion of morals and ethics to the exclusion of skills-based and standards-based dispositions.

DAATS ACTIVITIES

DAATS CHAPTER 1—ACTIVITY #1

Questions for Exploration

Explanation:

You can use the following questions to examine some important issues that will help frame the assessment design process. These questions should be addressed by school leaders.

1. What disposition measures are currently being used (or have recently been used) in your department or district?

2. Does your state mandate disposition assessment?

3. Are faculty and administrative personnel aware of the requirements and importance of disposition assessment?

4. Do you have any faculty or district-level support for creating disposition measures?

5. What resistance can you identify to measuring dispositions in your department?

6. Should disposition assessment include ethics and morals, and, if so, to what extent?

DAATS CHAPTER 1—ACTIVITY #2

What Have You Noticed?

Explanation:

1. Convene your faculty and/or leadership team and read the following statement to them:

   Visualize a great teacher. Let your mind wander through your experiences with that teacher. What do you see him or her doing? What makes this teacher great? Is it knowledge? Skill? Disposition? All three? Can you pinpoint anything specific that is a window onto that teacher's heart and soul? Run through the 10 INTASC Principles and decide whether you think the teacher was intensely committed to, or passionate about, any of them. Write it down for later.

2. Have the faculty report out and tally the number (and percentage) of faculty members who visualized something for each of the INTASC Principles. You could use this chart:

INTASC Principle	Faculty Visualizations of Dispositions
#1	
#2	
#3	
#4	
#5	
#6	
#7	
#8	
#9	
#10	

3. Repeat the process for the **BAD** teacher!

DAATS ACTIVITIES

DAATS CHAPTER 1—ACTIVITY #3

Assessment Belief Scale

Explanation:

You can use this scale to "take a dispositions assessment temperature check" in your school. If many faculty members get low scores, assessment literacy is a problem you will face throughout this process. Some staff/faculty development may be a problem. Check out some of the writings of Rick Stiggins and Jim Popham on this topic. After you score yourself, tally the scores of the group. You may want to plan a discussion of the results.

    We provide the scoring key here, but it should not be distributed to the faculty in advance!

   Agree: 3, 5, 6–7, 10, 11, 14, 15

   Disagree: 1, 2, 4, 8, 9, 12, 13, 16

Please go to the next page to complete the survey.

DAATS CHAPTER 1—ACTIVITY #3

Beliefs About Assessment

Name: _____

Please decide whether you agree or disagree with each of the following statements about assessment. Circle your answers: "A" for "agree" and "D" for "disagree."

1	A	D	Assessing teacher skills is more important than assessing teacher dispositions.
2	A	D	It's impossible to determine whether a teacher will become a great teacher without measuring his or her dispositions accurately.
3	A	D	Just about everyone has had the experience of watching a bad teacher who has a bad attitude.
4	A	D	The best teacher educators can monitor teacher values informally and do not need formal measures. They can tell!
5	A	D	Even the most experienced teachers need to constantly monitor their performance for the attitudes and values their students will perceive.
6	A	D	It's virtually impossible for a college or district to measure teacher dispositions without planning systematically how to do so.
7	A	D	A great way to keep track of bad attitudes is to keep a file of "incidents" in the main office.
8	A	D	Good principals believe that education would improve if we just focused on teaching performance and stopped worrying about other things like student perceptions of their teachers.
9	A	D	I am looking forward to measuring teachers' morals and ethics. That is the most important part of dispositions.
10	A	D	If given a choice between spending my time on designing a performance task and designing an attitude scale, I would spend my time on planning the attitude scale.
11	A	D	Disposition assessment is one of the most rapidly developing areas of education, and good teacher educators keep up with new developments.
12	A	D	Disposition assessments should be used only when we think a teacher has a bad attitude.
13	A	D	Disposition assessment is a waste of time, so let's just get something simple and be done with it.
14	A	D	I'm in charge of this program, so I had better start thinking about what dispositions are really important to good teaching.
15	A	D	If you ask a teacher the right question, you can get good information about what he or she believes and values.
16	A	D	Disposition assessments are kind of flakey, so I don't like to use them.

DAATS ACTIVITIES

DAATS CHAPTER 1—ACTIVITY #4

Cognitive, Affective, and
Psychomotor Objectives and Assessments

Explanation:

Convene your faculty and assign them to work groups, one for each component of Bloom's taxonomy. Have them develop assessments for each level of Bloom's taxonomy to support the learning outcome. You can continue this activity with new outcomes related to your curriculum. Report out.

Learning Outcome: Demonstrate play of a team sport (e.g., volleyball).

Taxonomic Level	Objective	Assessment
Cognitive	Learn the rules.	
Affective	Exhibit sportsmanship and teamwork.	
Psychomotor	Serve and return the ball.	

DAATS ACTIVITIES

2

Methods for Assessing Dispositions

If you don't like something, change it; if you can't change it, change the way you think about it.

—Mary Engelbreit

In this chapter, we outline a conceptual framework for measuring teacher dispositions and provide a brief description of the literature on measuring teacher dispositions, noting that it is sparse but evolving. We revisit Bloom's taxonomy, looking at the affective domain in some depth, providing examples of teacher dispositions matched to the levels of the domain. We then describe some strategies available for measuring teacher dispositions based on the more general field of affective measurement, providing examples of items for each instrument type and comparing the affective and cognitive domain methodologies. We conclude with a discussion of the importance of inference and increasing levels of confidence in making valid decisions about teacher dispositions.

A CONCEPTUAL FRAMEWORK FOR MEASURING DISPOSITIONS

Just as we expect teachers to have some theoretical underpinnings for selecting and applying their teaching methodologies, teacher educators and professional development personnel need to have theoretical underpinnings for how they measure teachers in both

♀——— Content Domains ———

Content domains consist of each grouping of standards that have been aligned because they are similar and convey the same basic set of ideas. In the case of disposition assessment, they might include indicators from INTASC and indicators of locally defined values.

Guiding Question: "Does this set of standards and indicators hang together to form a logical body of content that can be assessed?"

?

♀— Construct Underrepresentation —

Construct underrepresentation occurs when we do not have enough data to make a decision about the construct because we haven't sampled well.

Guiding Question: "Do I have enough stuff to make a confident decision?"

?

♀— Construct-Irrelevant Variance —

Construct-irrelevant variance is any extraneous factor that distorts the meaning or interpretation of a score. A common form of this variance is measuring the wrong thing.

Guiding Question: "Have I mixed some other stuff that's not useful into the decision I am trying to make?"

?

the cognitive and affective domains—a conceptual framework. Here, we will address four areas of the conceptual framework that need to be driven by theory and the wisdom of practice:

- *Construct definition:* When measuring anything—knowledge, skills, dispositions, or any trait whatsoever—it is critical to start with a clear statement of that which we intend to measure. In this case, our construct is teacher dispositions. The standards regarding teacher effectiveness, whether they are from NCATE, INTASC, NBPTS, national speciality professional associations, other national agencies, state educational agencies, local educational agencies, or colleges or departments of teacher education, provide the starting points for articulating the content that helps shape the construct. Once the standards, indicators, or behaviors from these sources are identified and combined, we have what we can call a "content domain." This is how the construct is operationally defined into what can be observed and measured. To make useful measures, we make sure we cover the content and only the content, avoiding both construct underrepresentation and construct-irrelevant variance. We avoid delving into related tangents or breaking down every concept into impractical minutiae. By doing so, we help to provide evidence of content validity.

- *Instrument design:* When measuring knowledge and skills, cognitive measurement methodologies apply (e.g., tests and product or performance tasks). When measuring dispositions, we need to use scales and interviews and other appropriate techniques. The literature provides support for selecting and applying the correct methodologies for the correct purposes in both domains, cognitive and affective.

- *Data analysis:* No matter what we count or measure, we need to figure out some way of expressing the results in quantitative terms. It is usually better to say how many times something happened than to say that it happened "frequently." Your vision of frequently may be very different from mine, but "three times" is three times for all of us. Once we can say it happened three times, then we can determine if three times is just right, too much, or too little. So, sometimes, we can report just the number of points on a test or the number of pounds on a scale. The more sophisticated our needs, though, the more sophisticated our techniques need to be. At a minimum, we will need frequencies and percentages in lieu of qualitative descriptions like "sometimes." As we move into more sophisticated applications, it becomes useful to select a measurement methodology (i.e., classical test theory or item response theory). Item response theory provides distinct advantages for the situation we face here, and we will devote a later chapter (Chapter 8) as a primer for those who want to "go the extra mile." Some will be happy to stop with the frequency count or raw score, and that is okay.

- *Decision making:* The accepted standards of the profession for measurement are contained in the *Standards of the Educational and Psychological Testing* (AERA, APA, and NCME, 1999). These standards should be applied in the design and validation of any instruments in order to ensure validity, reliability, and fairness of decisions made about candidate knowledge, skills, and dispositions. In high-stakes decision making, a cut-score methodology also needs to be selected. (In this book on dispositions, cut-score setting is less important and, therefore, beyond the scope of this work. Please see our work on competency assessment, CAATS, for a discussion of cut scores.)

Content Validity

Content validity is a form of validity evidence that ensures that the test measures the construct comprehensively and appropriately and does not measure another construct instead of, or in addition to, the construct of teacher performance on the job.

Guiding Question: "How do I know that the decisions I will make about teachers will be based on adequate coverage of the construct of teacher performance and nothing else?"

The elements of the conceptual framework are woven through this book, serving as a framework for the book as well. We discussed the standards, or the beginning of construct definition, in the previous chapter, and we will continue with that thread in Chapters 3 through 5. Chapter 5, though, focuses most heavily on instrument design. Data analysis and decision making provide the underpinnings for Chapters 6 and 7. As a conceptual framework, these four elements or strands will stay with us throughout this journey.

We now turn to the literature on measuring teacher dispositions, which also serves as a framework for the procedures outlined herein.

MEASURING TEACHER DISPOSITIONS: THE STATE OF THE ART

The published literature on measuring teacher dispositions is sparse. This is probably at least in part because of the general assessment illiteracy that pervades our culture (Popham, 2004; Stiggins, 2000). A study by Schulte, Edick, Edwards, and Mackiel (2004) confirms that little guidance is provided about measuring teacher dispositions. There is instead much in the literature that is skill based rather than values based (Darling-Hammond, 2000). There are some exceptions: Wasicsko's (2004) "20-Minute Hiring Assessment," Holt-Reynolds's (1991) biographical and metaphorical assessments, and several discussions of portfolios applied to disposition assessment; all are cited in Schulte et al. (2004).

The Schulte team developed and validated a Teacher Disposition Index (TDI) that is similar in some ways to one of the instruments we describe and model in this book. The TDI appears to be the first scale developed using the INTASC Principles to define the construct. There are many differences, though, and chief among them is the limitation to a single instrument item type. Just as in cognitive assessment, multiple measures are necessary to increase decision-making confidence.

We note, however, that the field is beginning to grow quickly. Measuring dispositions was a popular topic at the annual meetings of the American Association of Colleges of Teacher Education (AACTE) in recent years. Processes described in the workshops and sessions at the conference included attention to critical incidents, accountability, policy, moral dimensions and/or social justice, alignments, reflection, and teacher effectiveness, as well as our focus on scaling and looking at validity and reliability. There are others, too, of course. Hence measuring dispositions is clearly an evolving and timely topic.

We retrieved and reviewed a sample of 22 NCATE institutional reports available online in 2005 to illustrate the manner in which institutions are addressing this requirement. We summarize our findings about the number of institutions and components of their responses in Table 2.1.

Table 2.1. Sample of Institutional Reports Analyzed for Descriptions of the Disposition Assessment Construct, Type of Data Produced, and Use of Data

Unit Description of Disposition Assessment Construct	Number of Institutions
• Stated use of INTASC Principles as at least one basis for measuring	2
• Stated use of conceptual framework as a basis for measuring and/or identified a specific construct (e.g., "teacher as decision maker," "collaboration, responsibility, reflective capacity," "moral compass")	2
• Based assessment on constructs not clearly defined or relevant (e.g., "behavior and dress code," "handbook")	15
• Described specific instruments without stating construct	2
Primary Type of Disposition Data Produced	
• Observations and/or interviews	8
• Referral sheets, communication of concerns sheets, etc.	3
• Review of written work (e.g., journals, portfolios)	7
• Self-screening devices and self-assessments	5
Use of Disposition Data	
• Candidate removal from program	6
• Program refinement	2
• Remediation	2

NOTE: The institutions reviewed remain anonymous.

None of these reports, however, appear to show a systematic approach to measuring teacher dispositions that takes full advantage of the literature and strategies available for affective measurement, the standards for educational measurement, and/or the depth and breadth of the 10 INTASC Principles.

BACK TO BASICS: BLOOM AND KRATHWOHL

The literature on affective measurement has in its roots the taxonomy developed by Krathwohl, Bloom, and Masia (1956). The well-known cognitive domain of the Bloom and Krathwohl taxonomy, which includes, of course, knowledge, comprehension, application, analysis, synthesis, and evaluation, was edited and republished again by Anderson and Krathwohl (2001). However, the affective domain was not reworked in that latter book.

We remember that the cognitive domain, as defined in this taxonomy, is hierarchical, with the authors proposing that one had to know before one could comprehend, comprehend before applying, apply before analyzing, and so on. The hierarchical relationship became questionable at the end of the taxonomy, with debate over the relationship between synthesis and evaluation. Nonetheless, the concept of a hierarchical relationship has withstood the test of time, as has the importance of using the taxonomy to develop tests and alternative assessments. What teacher preparation program omits this step? As a prerequisite for measuring teacher dispositions, then, it is useful to provide a brief synopsis of the affective domain, as originally conceptualized. Like the cognitive domain, it, too, contains hierarchical levels:

- *Receiving:* attends, becomes aware of an idea, process, or thing
- *Responding:* makes response at first with compliance, later willingly with satisfaction
- *Valuing:* accepts worth of a thing, prefers it, consistent in responding, commitment
- *Organization:* organizes values, determines interrelationships, adapts behavior to value system
- *Characterization:* generalizes value into controlling tendencies, integrates these with total philosophy

The Bloom and Krathwohl taxonomy, then, begins with awareness, just like the NCATE rubric for the dispositions element of Standard 1. In Table 2.2, we work through the NCATE rubric, applying the taxonomy. Certainly, intuitively, we would hope that teachers are aware of the values they should have, and this is exactly what NCATE requires, at its most basic level. Keywords used in the analysis of the NCATE rubric are emphasized with bold italics, and our taxonomic classification is at the end of each row in brackets and in boldface.

Table 2.2. Taxonomic Analysis of NCATE Dispositions Rubric	
NCATE Rubric for Dispositions	*Comparison to the Bloom and Krathwohl Taxonomy*
Unacceptable: Candidates are ***not familiar*** with professional dispositions delineated in professional, state, and institutional standards. They do not model these dispositions in their work with students, families, and communities.	These candidates have not reached the lowest level of the taxonomy—receiving; they are ***unaware*** of the values teachers should have; hence, they cannot model them in their work with constituents. **[Not Receiving]**
Acceptable: Candidates are familiar with the dispositions expected of professionals. Their work with students, families, and communities *reflects* the dispositions delineated in professional, state, and institutional standards.	These candidates are aware (receiving) of dispositions required of teachers and have reached the level of responding or valuing the dispositions enough to reflect them in their day-to-day practice. If they do so some of the time, they are probably responding; if the dispositions are evidenced in a ***consistent*** way, they are at the valuing stage—where we would want them to be at a minimum. **[Responding or Valuing]**
Target: Candidates work with students, families, and communities in ways that reflect the dispositions expected of professional educators as delineated in professional, state, and institutional standards. Candidates *recognize* when their own dispositions may ***need to be adjusted*** and are able to develop plans to do so.	These candidates are able to self-assess and ***adapt*** their behavior to the value system. They are at the level of organization. They may even reach the characterization stage, integrating their values into their own philosophy as controlling tendencies, which could be evident in their plans for adjustment. **[Organization or Characterization]**

We will take this analysis one step further before moving on to methodologies. We will characterize a teacher on these levels for the INTASC Principle of Planning (#7).

- *Receiving:* The teacher who is not yet at the receiving level is unaware that planning is important. He or she will not attempt to plan and probably has not yet attempted writing a lesson plan or has found the experience to be boring or distasteful. At the receiving level, the teacher knows that planning is important and is beginning to think about doing it.

- *Responding:* This teacher is emotionally ready to plan and attempts to do so. He or she recognizes the importance but does not yet place much value on it, getting by with little extra effort or schedule alterations. When time permits, this teacher plans but is easily distracted.

- *Valuing:* This teacher derives some satisfaction from a well-written lesson plan and is uncomfortable if asked to approach a class without a lesson plan. This teacher would work extra hours to be sure to be prepared. He or she might run out of time, though, and still arrive in class with sparse notes or no clear plan in mind if other aspects of life and scheduling interfered. This is the *bare minimum* of what we would want for a teacher.

- *Organization:* This teacher plans the daily schedule in such a way as to ensure that planning time is carefully guarded and used wisely. This teacher never enters the room without a plan. The Internet and other sources would serve as valuable resources for expanding lessons from the school curriculum whenever time permits. We would be so happy if every teacher hit this target!

- *Characterization:* This teacher plans all aspects of the day and all parts of life. He or she helps others to plan as well. This teacher would lobby effectively at the school level for planning time and rewards for planning. This teacher uses the Internet widely, subscribes to journals, and wakes up early in the morning thinking about ways to improve planning. We would be even happier with this teacher, but he or she could be approaching a dangerous level of planning. This could be the teacher who overplans and burns out. A teacher at this level could be a major asset but may need to be watched as a high risk for retention.

AVAILABLE METHODS FOR MEASURING DISPOSITIONS OR AFFECT

Thurstone Agreement Scales

A scale similar to a Likert except that respondents are forced to "agree" or "disagree" only. There is no place for "strongly" or "neutral." This is often called "forced choice." It is easier to interpret.

Guiding Question: "Do they agree or disagree with a statement without copping out with a 'don't know' response?"

A number of demonstrated methods are available for affective measurement, and, as with cognitive assessments, multiple measures help to increase the confidence in decisions made. Hopkins (1998) provides a useful list and discussion of affective measures, which are organized and summarized below with relevant references to the affective assessment literature. We also provide some illustrative examples for each methodology.

Selected-Response Methods

Selected-response methods provide self-reported information that is based on the selection of a chosen response from a predetermined pair or set of responses for each item. As with traditional testing approaches in cognitive assessment (e.g., true/false, multiple-choice), there is an opportunity for guessing or faking the response. Here, the respondent indicates a level of agreement, importance, or some other value-laden judgment for specified characteristics (e.g., a belief in children's capacity to learn). Scales are an important method for measuring affect in this way (Anderson, 1988a).

Scale items are among the more difficult to write but the easiest to score. Four types of scales are generally used: Thurstone agreement scales (Anderson, 1988b; Thurstone, 1928); Likert scales (Anderson, 1988c); rating scales (Wolf, 1988b); and semantic differential scales (Phillips, 1988). Thurstone scales, as recommended herein, take more time to create but provide data that are the easiest to aggregate and interpret. Descriptions and examples of each scale type (Thurstone, Likert, rating, and semantic differential) are provided in Table 2.3.

Likert

A scale that is typically four or five points and asks respondents to "agree" or "disagree" or to do so "strongly." The midpoint may be "neutral" or may be missing; missing is preferred.

Guiding Question: "How much do respondents agree or disagree on an item?"

Rubric

A rubric is a set of scoring guidelines that facilitate the judgment-making process. They typically include a set of criteria and a mechanism (rating scale or checklist) to determine and record levels of quality.

Guiding Question: "How will I decide whether teachers did the task well or not?"

Table 2.3. Descriptions and Examples of Various Types of Scales			
		Examples	
Type of Scale	*Description*	*Scale Points*	*Items*
Thurstone Attitude	A set of statements is provided to respondents. They must agree or disagree with the statements, which typically number at least 20 to 45. Statements provide for a range in the attribute being measured.	1 = agree 0 = disagree	All children can learn. (A) If I give them my best, *most* children can learn when given enough help. (D)
Likert Scales	The same kinds of statements are provided to respondents as with Thurstone; however, in a Likert scale, respondents indicate their agreement with statements on a 5-point scale, ranging from "strongly agree" to "strongly disagree."	5 = strongly agree 4 = agree 3 = neutral 2 = disagree 1 = strongly disagree	All children can learn. If I give them my best, *most* children can learn when given enough help.

(Continued)

(Continued)

Type of Scale	Description	Examples	
		Scale Points	**Items**
Rating Scales	These scales are very similar to Likert scales but allow for more flexibility in the response options (e.g., a range from "like me" to "not like me" or "very important" to "not important"). Some rating scales define only end points, with only numbers in between anchors such as "dull" to "stimulating."	4 = critically important 3 = very important 2 = somewhat important 1 = not important	All children should learn. I should give them my best, and if I do, most children will learn.
Semantic Differential Scales	These scales are similar to rating scales but often omit the numbers, leaving blanks instead between bipolar adjectives.	5 = critically important 1 = useless	I should give them my best, and if I do, most children will learn.

? ———————— Interview ————————

A set of questions typically asked orally of one person at a time.

Guiding Question: "How can I find out what he or she believes using interactive communication?"

?

? ———————— Focus Group ————————

Meetings of 5 to 7 persons designed to put respondents at ease in talking about important issues. Prompting questions cause the group to respond and interact with each other, building consensus or difference among group members to give a truer picture than would be available from working with one person at time.

Guiding Question: "What do the kids say their teacher believes and values?"

?

Constructed-Response Methods

Constructed-response methods provide self-reported information written without predetermined choices. In the cognitive domain, constructed-response options include written short-answer or essay questions or an oral presentation. In the affective domain, the appropriate methods include questionnaires (Wolf, 1988a); interviews (Miller & Cannell, 1982); and focus groups (Flores & Alonso, 1995). Each of these methods is often assessed using rubrics.

Items in this category are easier tocreate, but scoring becomes more subjective and, therefore, more complex. Rubrics, examples, and training are often necessary for reliability. Results for written questionnaires and oral interviews can be similar, although the possibility for cheating or copying is more prevalent in written questionnaires. Focus groups with K–12 students, however, are best accomplished through the interview process and make faking or cheating very difficult.

In the description and examples in Table 2.4, the first two types of instruments are self-report instruments, but the third introduces other evidence about the teacher's values—given by the children. Progressing through the three types of instruments in this category, we are able to obtain more and more useful data for spotting teacher strengths and weaknesses as the analysis becomes more and more difficult. In this last example, assessors have to sort out group interaction or bias from real issues, making this last instrument the most difficult to use and the one that requires the most training; it leads to the highest inference level of the three but often the most useful information about the teacher.

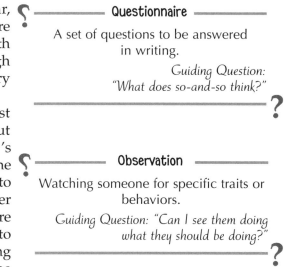

Questionnaire

A set of questions to be answered in writing.

Guiding Question:
"What does so-and-so think?"

Observation

Watching someone for specific traits or behaviors.

Guiding Question: "Can I see them doing what they should be doing?"

Table 2.4. Descriptions and Examples of Constructed-Response Methods		
Type	*Description*	*Example*
Questionnaires	Respondents are asked a predetermined set of questions, the responses to which often require analysis, training, examples of responses, and rubrics. The questions are designed to elicit a high level of specificity to help ensure that the "correct" response is not given with a yes/no answer and to help sort out cheating and faking from genuine commitment. The assumption here is that if teachers can describe the behavior in some detail, they are probably telling the truth and value the disposition enough to have it be a part of their work life.	Describe the last time you talked to a colleague about a problem with a student. What did the colleague recommend? What did you do? Did it work? Would you go back to that colleague again for advice?

NOTE: If teachers don't value the advice of colleagues, they won't seek it. |
| Interviews | The same type of questions used in a questionnaire can be administered orally. The advantage is that the teacher can't check with others and fake a response as easily. The disadvantage, of course, is time. Interviews take longer. | Same questions and same assumption as for the questionnaire. |
| Focus Groups | Questions are written for children to answer in a small group, and several can answer at the same time. These questions elicit data about how children perceive the teacher as a window onto the teacher's beliefs. Yes/no answers are acceptable in some instances. | Does your teacher listen to everyone in the class? Does he or she become impatient when you do not understand? |

? ─── Behavior Checklist ───

The list of attributes, traits, or behaviors that are observed over time. Someone who has special knowledge of the teacher (e.g., principal, mentor, supervising professor, parents) evaluates the teacher on the basis of experience over time. Typically, a yes/no checklist is used, but a rating scale can be used as well.

Guiding Question: "What can we tell over time about the teacher's beliefs?"

?

Observed Performance

Observation assessment is another excellent source of data (Stalling & Mohlman, 1988). Included in this group are direct observations in the classroom, behavioral checklists (completed after multiple observations and products have been analyzed), and event reports. Event reports provide a unique approach, used to record (and hopefully remediate) ineffective behaviors.

Since observations are required in all settings—teacher training through traditional and alternative routes as well as ongoing performance appraisal systems for fully licensed or certified teachers—an observational process that targets attitudes is feasible if collective-bargaining agreement issues can be resolved. The difficulty here, as in the other methods, is to ensure that affect, not skill, is the construct evaluated. This is particularly difficult in observations.

The type of observation will depend on who the observer is and how frequently he or she can observe. Single or small sets of observations, such as those provided by a university supervisor, mentor teacher, or principal, can provide one level of data. Overall frequency impressions from someone very familiar with the teacher's performance, such as a cooperating teacher in the room on a daily basis, can provide another.

Although not a formal part of the literature on affective measurement, one additional strategy that can work is to keep a record of events that occur that are triggers for concern about dispositions. This type of observation is of particular use in teacher assessment, and we call it the "disposition event report." In Table 2.5, we describe each instrument type and give examples.

Table 2.5.	**Descriptions and Examples of Observational Methods**	
Type	*Description*	*Examples*
Observations	One or more performances can be evaluated in person in the classroom, looking for specific affective characteristics that are rated or counted.	Frequency count (tally) of teacher recognition of majority and minority children.
Behavioral Checklists	Items may be the same as the types on the observation instrument, but an overall impression of frequency is provided. Comparison of parent, peer, and supervisor viewpoints is a valued reporting method with checklists.	3 = frequently 2 = occasionally 1 = rarely Recognition of minority children.
Event Report	The event report is completed on an ad hoc basis when a person in authority (professor, mentor, principal) observes (or learns of) an action on the part of the teacher that is inappropriate. The report is used only for serious incidents, needs to be documented carefully, and should include follow-up between the author and the teacher to attempt to remediate the problem. Disciplinary action may be a part of the reporting system, depending on the gravity of the event. Disposition event reports could also be used to describe extremely positive events, but this is rare.	Racist remark, physical contact with a child, cheating, classroom management plan that indicates disdain for multiculturalism or beliefs in corporal punishment, written reflection that indicates "all students are dumb" or "certain students are incapable of learning," continuous late arrival for class, continuous inappropriate dress.

Projective Techniques

Projective techniques (Walsh, 1988) are the last of the methods useful for measuring dispositions, but they are also the most difficult of the strategies. Rorschach and thematic apperception tests (see Table 2.6) are the most common examples. Respondents are provided a picture designed to evoke a reaction. Training and scoring procedures are helpful to interpret results, but responses are so outlandish that often, common sense prevails.

❓ ────── Thematic Apperception Test ──────

A projective technique that allows for a wide range of possibility and interpretation in how the examinee responds to stimulus cards, and the examiner interprets the results. This technique is useful to find patterns of response that surface without direct prompting.

Guiding Question: "What does this person believe or feel that he or she is not directly saying or doesn't know how to say?"

❓

Table 2.6. Description and Example of Thematic Apperception Technique

Type	Description	Example	Sample Responses
Situational Analysis Test (technically known as a Thematic Apperception Test)	Teachers are shown a picture and asked to say what they see. The interviewer records their reactions, searching for evidence of teaching values in their responses.	Teacher is shown a picture of a young woman dressed in a very short skirt with a low-cut blouse and body jewelry. The prompt is "Tell me about this teacher." Most teachers would discuss the clothing, but if not, an additional prompt might be necessary. A teacher with appropriate values would question the attire; a teacher with inappropriate values would admire it.	Acceptable answers: "She shouldn't be teaching in that attire—not professional." "She has an effect on the high school kids dressed like that." Unacceptable answers: "She has a good sense of fashion." "She teaches little ones who won't look up her skirt or down her blouse."

The idea here is only to remind teacher assessors that effective assessment techniques already exist for creating affective measures. While some are easier to use, just as true/false items are easier to write and score than essays, there is much to be said for using multiple measures at increasing levels of inference to increase the confidence we have in our decisions. A brief discussion of inference follows.

THE IMPORTANCE OF INFERENCE IN MEASURING DISPOSITIONS

In assessing knowledge and skills, we gain confidence that we have measured well when we progress through a series of well-designed, progressive measures. After instruction, we might ask the student to answer multiple-choice, sentence completion, or matching questions correctly and then use that knowledge in an applied setting. Let us look at a familiar example from knowledge and skills: lesson planning and delivery.

Most teacher educators intuitively follow this model of measuring the ability to plan. Most start by asking students to define the levels of Bloom's cognitive taxonomy, and they may also ask teacher candidates to classify a set of verbs and objectives (test). Next, the teachers will be expected to use the taxonomy in writing a lesson plan (a written product), which they may even be asked to deliver (observation of a skill).

In this series of three assessments—test, written product, and observation of a skill—the knowledge and skills applied by both the teacher and the professor or trainer become increasingly complex. Teachers can guess the answers on tests, which teacher trainers can machine score. Teachers have lots of time to develop lesson plans, which they can copy from each other or borrow from the Internet. These are more difficult to score, though, than paper-and-pencil tests, requiring a higher level of judgment and expertise on the part of the teacher trainer. When the teachers are in front of a classroom, however, having to make decisions affecting lesson delivery, both the task and the judgment of the task become the most complex. As the judgments become more difficult, our confidence about the teacher candidate's ability increases, as illustrated in Box 2.1.

Box 2.1. Moving Up the Confidence Ladder

- At the knowledge and rudimentary skill level, if teacher candidates get good scores on the **multiple-choice test**, we have **limited confidence** that they know how to plan. While that test requires **little judgment to score**—a computer can do it—inference and confidence are both low.

- We have **more confidence** about the ability of a teacher to plan once we see a **lesson plan**, but with this added complexity (and inference) comes the **need for some evaluative criteria** from which to make judgments. It also requires someone who knows a good lesson plan when he or she sees it and a little training on what the assessment author expects the candidate to do. We can no longer give it to a student assistant or support person to grade.

- Moving up to the top of the confidence/inference ladder, when the **lesson is delivered** and observed in a real classroom, we need a **well-experienced observer who can make quick decisions**, taking into account many complex factors. However, there is no substitute for this observation in terms of our **high level of confidence** about the teacher's ability. No principal would evaluate a teacher based solely on a lesson plan.

In measuring dispositions, it is important to think about a variety of techniques that fit the need for confidence, so that decision makers can move up the confidence ladder (see Box 2.1), but, as with skills, the higher up the confidence ladder, the more complex the judgment-making process. The techniques described in the previous section show increasing inference levels and increasing confidence levels. In the pages that follow, as we describe some methods of affective measurement applied to teacher assessment on the INTASC dispositional indicators, we will maintain the focus on increasing levels of inference and confidence.

Table 2.7 summarizes examples, methodologies, scoring ease, and confidence levels for each of the competency levels in the cognitive domain.

Inference Levels

Inference levels are controlled by the level of difficulty in making a decision or judgment. They range from no judgment (low inference), as in a correct/incorrect response, to extensive judgment, requiring professional expertise to interpret a response.

Guiding Question: "How hard will it be to make a decision about the teacher's level of commitment, or how much subjectivity is there in this decision?"

Table 2.7. Summary of Competency Levels, Examples, Methodologies, Scoring Ease, and Confidence Levels in the Cognitive Domain

Competency Level	Example	Methodology	Scoring Ease	Confidence Level
Knowledge and Rudimentary Skill	Classify objectives according to Bloom's taxonomy.	Multiple-choice test	Easy to score (machine)	Limited confidence—but could have guessed
Initial Skill Use	Write a lesson plan.	Product	Medium difficulty in scoring (beginning teacher or graduate assistant)	Increased confidence—but could have copied
Experienced Skill Use	Deliver a lesson plan and modify, based on student reactions.	Performance	Difficult to score with much happening concurrently (experienced assessor—faculty, master teacher, or building administrator)	Most confidence—cannot be faked

Most of us would not dream of being satisfied with the multiple-choice test as a means for determining the ability of the teacher to plan and carry out a lesson. We acknowledge all of the difficulties inherent in the observation of a lesson performed—time, resources, difficulty—but that does not stop any teacher preparation program or school-based performance appraisal system personnel from going the "extra mile." As we consider the relative importance of dispositions, it becomes equally apparent that we need to have a high level of confidence in the inferences we make about teachers' beliefs, attitudes, and values. As with skills, the higher up the confidence ladder, the more complex the judgment-making process and the more costly in terms of resources and time. This is illustrated in Table 2.8.

Table 2.8. Summary of Competency Levels, Examples, Methodologies, Scoring Ease, and Confidence Levels in the Affective Domain				
Affective Level	*Example*	*Methodology*	*Scoring Ease*	*Confidence Level*
Receiving	Agree/Disagree: All children can learn.	Scale	Easy to score (machine)	Limited confidence—but could have guessed
Responding or Valuing	Describe a recent conversation with a colleague.	Questionnaire	Medium difficulty in scoring (beginning teacher or graduate assistant)	Increased confidence—but could have copied
Organization	How do you typically plan your days and spend your time?	Interview	Medium difficulty in scoring (leader)	Increased confidence—but still can be faked
Organization	What does your teacher do to help you keep your things organized? Does she encourage you to use a planner?	Focus group	Difficult to score with much happening concurrently (experienced assessor—faculty, master teacher, or building administrator)	Most confidence—cannot be faked
Characterization	What impact does the teacher have on planning in the school?	Interview with supervising teacher or principal	Difficult to score. Must determine whether response is part of a pattern of daily life	More confidence than is likely to be obtained

V WRAP-UP

In this chapter, we have applied the idea of starting with a conceptual framework to the development of affective measures—always a useful place to start. The literature on assessment of teacher dispositions, with some examples from "NCATE Institutional Reports," was described and noted as being sparse. We turned to Bloom and Krathwohl for guidance on how to define the dispositional or affective construct, and we saw how the taxonomy fits the NCATE rubric on the element of Standard 1, addressing dispositions. Then, we looked at methodologies in the measurement literature designed for affective measurement as applied to this evolving context of teacher dispositions. These methodologies paralleled cognitive measurement in terms of ease of use, difficulty of scoring, and confidence of decision making. They included selected-response items (four types of scales), constructed-response methods (questionnaires, interviews, and focus groups), observed performances (observations and behavioral checklists), and projective techniques (thematic apperception tests). We provided examples of item types and noted the importance of using multiple measures in all measurement—cognitive as well as affective.

DAATS CHAPTER 2—ACTIVITY #1

Questions for Exploration

Explanation:

Convene your faculty and/or leadership team and have each person answer these questions and then report out. Debate the issues.

1. Of the four different types of scales presented in this chapter, which one do you like best? Do you use any of these types of scales in your current work? How do you tend to analyze them? What helps you in the analysis?

2. Discuss the pros and cons of using questionnaires with your teachers. Will they tell you the truth, or will they fake their answers to make you happy?

3. How do you feel about what K–12 children have to say? Do their views and perceptions count? What would you think if a group of four children said to you: "Our teacher doesn't like us very much. She is always yelling at us." Or "My teacher never calls on the girls."

4. What would you do if you showed a teacher the following picture and the teacher said, "Boys just aren't as creative as girls. This poor teacher is having such a hard time with him. That's why I would rather teach girls."

DAATS ACTIVITIES

DAATS CHAPTER 2—ACTIVITY #2

Bloom and the INTASC Principles

Explanation:

Convene your faculty and assign them to nine work groups, one for each INTASC Principle except #7 on planning. Have them complete the taxonomy chart with a description of a teacher at each level of the taxonomy for the INTASC Principle assigned. Report out.

INTASC Principle:_____

Affective Taxonomic Level	*Description of Teacher at This Level*
Receiving: attends, becomes aware of an idea, process, or thing.	
Responding: makes response at first with compliance, later willingly with satisfaction.	
Valuing: accepts worth of a thing, prefers it, consistent in responding, commitment	
Organization: organizes values, determines interrelationships, adapts behavior to value system	
Characterization: generalizes value into controlling tendencies, integrates these with total philosophy.	

DAATS CHAPTER 2—ACTIVITY #3

Field Work

Explanation:

Have your faculty try out these two affective assessment examples personally. Then, convene the group for a discussion of what they found.

Part A

Ask a teacher you know the following questions:

How have you kept abreast of current developments in your field? For example, did you attend any workshops, subscribe to any journals, read or buy a new book? If so, describe something you learned.

Did the teacher give you a vague or a specific response? Do you believe the teacher is enthusiastic about learning more about his or her subject area or not? How could you tell?

Part B

Go to a K–12 classroom and ask five children in a single classroom the following questions:

1. *Does the teacher ask you to help decide about classroom rules?*
2. *Does the teacher consider your feelings and ideas when he or she makes decisions about things that happen in school?*
3. *Does everyone have a role in taking care of the classroom?*

Did you pick up any useful information about whether the teacher is committed to the expression and use of democratic values in the classroom (INTASC Principle #5, third disposition indicator)?

DAATS ACTIVITIES

DAATS CHAPTER 2—ACTIVITY #4

Review Your Feelings

Explanation:

At the end of a faculty meeting, ask your faculty to review the questionnaire they completed in Chapter 1 for Activity #3. Talk about whether or not their feelings have changed, based on this chapter. Tabulate and share the results of the first and second administration of the questionnaire.

Question #	First Administration: Number of Correct Responses	Second Administration: Number of Correct Responses
1		
2		
3		
4		
5		
6		
7		
8		
9		
10		
11		
12		
13		
14		
15		
16		

Where We Have Been So Far

In our first two chapters, we defined dispositions in ways that clearly differentiate them from skills. We noted the relationship between them, but we also focused on how far greater minds than our own have separated the two—Benjamin Bloom to be chief among them. We also talked about how critically important dispositions are. We do what we value! We showed ways to measure dispositions, commenting on how different the methodologies are from cognitive assessment. We showed you how there is a hierarchy among knowledge, skills, and dispositions, attempting to convince you that without dispositions, knowledge and skills do not really matter. Teachers simply won't apply the skills they have if they believe them to be unimportant.

Measuring dispositions is about doing what is right. This is not to be confused with measuring teachers' morals. Just the opposite. It is incumbent upon us, as trainers of teachers—from a moral perspective—to ensure that teachers value the skills they have, so that we can have confidence in their desire to apply those skills in the classroom. If they fail to use the skills we have so carefully taught them, then they will harm children.

3

DAATS Step 1

Assessment Design Inputs

The true teacher defends his pupils against his own personal influence.

—Amos Bronson Alcott

In this chapter, we present the first of the five steps of the design model for building assessment systems. We call the model "Disposition Assessment Aligned With Teacher Standards," or DAATS. This chapter, and the four that follow it, will each present one step of the model and some worksheets to help you work through implementation of the model at your institution or school district.

To start the design process in a way that is likely to yield valid and useful results, it is important to analyze relevant inputs. All assessment processes and instruments are only as good as their utility for making necessary decisions. Assessment design, therefore, begins with a clear articulation of the reason(s) or purpose(s) of the assessment and the anticipated results or use(s) of the data we hope to obtain. After all, if we don't have a clear vision of why we are assessing or what

> **DAATS Step 1: Define purpose, use, propositions, content, and other contextual factors.**

we will do with the results, we are wasting a lot of time and energy on a useless process. We all have certain beliefs about teaching and assessment, and those beliefs need to be articulated and agreed upon in the form of propositions to avoid misunderstandings and conflicts as we progress through the process. We then need to ensure that we collect the right data and enough to serve the purpose and use the results for effective decision making in accordance with our values about what is important and how it can be measured. We do that by deciding what content (including standards) we will embed in our assessment system. What we will eventually do with teachers' scores and the things we actually want to know about all need to be planned in advance. Our planning efforts need to be conducted on the basis of our own strengths, weaknesses, resources, and barriers—our own contexts. The more complex or important (high stakes) the use of the assessment, the more planning we need to do. This is the essence of DAATS Step 1.

In this step, then, we will do four things, each of which is a substep of DAATS Step 1:

DAATS Step 1A: Define the purpose(s) and use(s) of the system.

DAATS Step 1B: Define the propositions or principles that guide the system.

DAATS Step 1C: Define the conceptual framework or content of the system.

DAATS Step 1D: Review local factors that impact the system.

Before Moving On . . .

1. Since you are reading this book, you probably expect to use the disposition assessments to make decisions about certification or progression in a teacher's career. Correct? Do you want to do more? If so, jot down some ideas about what you want from these instruments.

2. Do you believe that teachers should be denied certification or lose their jobs if they do not have the vital dispositions needed for teaching? If yes, what are some of those dispositions? Does ethics predominate, or should a teacher be denied a job if he or she thinks planning is not important? What about critical thinking? Diversity? Assessment? If not, why not?

3. Think of parallel certification for doctors, pilots, and lawyers. What would you think of a doctor who didn't think it was important to keep up with new developments? What about a pilot who goes drinking before the flight? Do those professionals deserve a license? Now, answer question Number 2 again in light of "protecting the public from harm."

4. On a scale of 1 to 10, with 10 being high, how important is assessment of dispositions? Justify your answer.

5. Every group has an expected troublemaker. In your department, who (or what) are you most worried about when you think about assessing teacher dispositions? Who (or what) will be your greatest help? How will you combat the evil and profit from the good?

6. Think back over your career and/or schooling and remember an experience you had when you were unclear why you had to do something. You couldn't figure out the purpose or how what you did would affect you. How did you feel?

7. In your mind, does the term "highly qualified" apply to dispositions as well as knowledge and skills?

WHY ARE PURPOSE, USE, PROPOSITIONS, AND CONTENT SO IMPORTANT?

Without a clear understanding of the fundamental conceptual inputs to the assessment system, progress can be hindered while we spend many hours and resources chasing rainbows. You can imagine how sloppy a system becomes if you attempt to assess dispositions with anything less than a clearly defined process.

By beginning with purpose, use, propositions, and content, we also begin to construct an assessment system that meets standards of validity. As the importance of our instruments increases in terms of uses for decision making (i.e., high-stakes decisions such as counseling out of a program or firing), so does the importance of making sure we are measuring the right things in the right ways (i.e., interpreting our results or scores correctly). We can be less concerned or rigorous in terms of validity about an informal observation used for counseling only than we should be about a disposition event reporting system or the accumulation of evidence across multiple instruments for high-stakes decisions. The concepts of purpose, use, propositions, and content are all highly interrelated. We will define each of these terms as we progress through this chapter.

Ingersoll and Scannell (2002) use the words "truthfulness" and "trustworthiness of data" to describe validity and reliability. If, in fact, as ethical practitioners, we recognize the utility of these descriptors, then it becomes incumbent on us to try to gather evidence of validity and reliability in appropriate ways. We will discuss some options for how to do this both judgmentally and empirically in the chapter on DAATS Step 5. For now, suffice it to say that we are setting you up for success in DAATS Step 5 and we are beginning that process here in this chapter on DAATS Step 1. We are on the path to psychometric integrity, and we begin by defining why and what we are assessing in our own local contexts.

DAATS STEP 1A: DEFINE THE PURPOSE(S) AND USE(S) OF THE SYSTEM

In this context, we will use "purpose" as the reason we create an assessment or an assessment process. The purpose will drive everything else, including the extent to which we worry about issues like validity.

There are many reasons to assess, and we have to identify them very early in our process. Sometimes we want to make decisions only about individual teachers; other times we want to look at the results for many teachers in a group (program or school). Typically, when we are looking for decisions at the individual level, we hope for the opportunity to diagnose and remediate. At the group level, however, the focus may be on ensuring that we are "on track" and finding and fixing aspects that are not as good as expected for the benefit of future teachers. These purposes have different implications for how we structure the assessment and decision-making process. Some purposes for assessing dispositions, then, are as follows:

> **Purpose**
>
> The purpose is the reason for establishing an assessment system. It is the end (not the means).
>
> *Guiding Question: "Why are we assessing our teachers?"*

- Certify or license a teacher
- Ensure a common set of values in a population

- Improve the performance of individual teachers
- Improve teacher-training programs
- Impact the value systems of children (e.g., motivation to learn)
- Receive national accreditation or state program approval
- Encourage teachers to seek NBPTS certification
- Conduct research on teaching
- Justify funding of programs
- Select teacher candidates for admission
- Demonstrate effectiveness of licensure or graduation decisions

The main purpose for most teacher educators is most likely to be the identification of candidates or practicing teachers with dispositional problems that could impact their roles with children. In this case, a severe problem could lead to denial of a certificate. Box 3.1 gives an example of a purpose statement that is typical for certification or licensure decisions. It can be used for assessors making such a decision either in colleges of education or school districts. In fact, it is likely to be the fundamental purpose driving your system. You could write other purpose statements for anything on the list above or anything else, for that matter, but this is the one we think is the most important.

Box 3.1. Sample Statement of Purpose #1

To protect the public from unqualified practitioners by determining whether the teachers assessed have demonstrated the essential dispositions, as defined in the standards of _____. These dispositions are necessary for safe and appropriate practice and certification in the State of _____.

In the context of continuing professional development, a different purpose might drive the system—one of teacher improvement at the individual level. Such a purpose is modeled in Box 3.2. Regardless of where you start in terms of purpose, the uses of the data are driven by the purpose(s), and everything else must flow from there.

Box 3.2. Sample Statement of Purpose #2

To provide diagnostic information to teachers to help them improve attitude, values, and beliefs that might diminish students' opportunities to learn.

In the context of program evaluation, yet another purpose statement can be written, as modeled in Box 3.3. It, too, will require different implementation strategies, since program evaluation will require mechanisms to aggregate the data across students. A decision on this purpose, early in the process, can avoid much grief later when personnel cannot "pull things together." That is when we hear moans and groans such as "I have so much data, but I don't know what to do with it!"

Box 3.3.   Sample Statement of Purpose #3

To provide diagnostic information at the unit (or program or district) level to identify areas of weakness in admission of candidates, instruction, or hiring so that the program can be improved and better teachers developed.

Thus the uses of the data are likely to include decisions about the candidate or teacher as well as program quality. In terms of candidate or teacher evaluation, assessors need to decide whether they will deny graduation to candidates or let teachers go if they repeatedly demonstrate affective deficits. In terms of program evaluation, the assessors can also use the data as a self-check when the data are aggregated in ways that allow assessors to pinpoint areas in which they can improve programs. Dispositions are rarely taught formally, so affective measures may clearly point to values that need to be taught (e.g., working with colleagues). The uses of the data may be high stakes or low stakes. The higher the stakes, the more serious we have to be about validity and reliability. Some sample uses are shown Table 3.1, where we also classify the uses by whether or not they are high stakes.

> **Use**
>
> The use of the system is the decision or set of decisions to be made about teachers. It defines what will be done with the data collected.
>
> *Guiding Question: "What decisions will we make with our data?"*

Table 3.1. Sample Uses of Data and the Stakes	
Entry into the profession (graduation and licensure)	High stakes
Continuation in the profession (rehire)	High stakes
Advising or remediation only	Low stakes
Program improvement	Low stakes

If the usage decision includes the possibility of denying graduation or rehire (high stakes), then the assessment developers need to spend much more time on designing their system to ensure that it has psychometric integrity. Step 5 of the DAATS model will be particularly important to these users. For those who intend to provide only informal feedback to teachers, then the low-stakes nature of the system allows for much slack in its design. By making the usage decision early in the process, assessors have the opportunity to think about how comprehensive their approach should be.

AERA, APA, and NCME *Standards* (1999)
and DAATS Step 1A

Standard 1.2:

The test developer should set forth clearly how test scores are intended to be interpreted and used. The population(s) for which a test is appropriate should be clearly delimited, and the construct that the test is intended to assess should be clearly described.

Standard 3.2:

The purpose(s) of the test, definition of the domain, and the test specifications should be stated clearly so that judgments can be made about the appropriateness of the defined domain for the stated purpose(s) of the test and about the relation of items to the dimensions of the domain they are intended to represent.

Standard 13.1:

When educational testing programs are mandated by school, district, state, or other authorities, the ways in which test results are intended to be used should be clearly described. It is the responsibility of those who mandate the use of tests to monitor their impact and to identify and minimize potential negative consequences. Consequences resulting from the uses of the test, both intended and unintended, should also be examined by the test user.

Discussion

These standards give some flavor of the importance of clear statements about purpose and use in the psychometric requirements.

NOTE: Emphases added for clarity.

DAATS STEP 1B: DEFINE THE PROPOSITIONS OR PRINCIPLES THAT GUIDE THE SYSTEM

It is hard to imagine the teacher who has not written a statement of philosophy at one point in his or her training or career. Values clarification is a starting point for much of our work. In assessment design, such clarification is, again, a starting point. Here, we will call it "propositions" or "principles" that guide the system. Examples of the types of propositions that might guide a disposition assessment system are provided in Box 3.4. They are adapted from similar statements in the AERA, APA, and NCME *Standards* (1999).

Box 3.4. Examples of Propositions Statements That Guide a Dispositions Assessment System

- Certain dispositions or affective traits are critical to effective teaching.
- These dispositions can be identified and measured.
- National standards and local missions and values contribute to the identification of these dispositions.
- Measures of affect can be developed on the basis of the standards identified and appropriate test construction theories.
- Teachers with high scores on affective measures are likely to be better teachers who can have a higher impact on K–12 learning.
- Teachers with low scores on affective measures are likely to be poorer teachers who may cause harm to children.

—————————————————— **Proposition** ——————————————————

Propositions are what we believe to be true that influences the way we will develop and use the assessments. They are the agreed-upon "givens" we hold to be self-evident. They are based on our values and beliefs about teaching and assessment.

Guiding Question: "What are the fundamental truths about teaching and assessment that guide our thinking?"

AERA, APA, and NCME *Standards* (1999)

Narrative Discussion of Propositions Relevant to DAATS Step 1B

The decision about what types of evidence are important for validation in each instance can be clarified by developing a set of propositions that support the proposed interpretation for the particular purpose of testing. For instance, when a mathematics achievement test is used to assess readiness for an advanced course, evidence for the following propositions might be deemed necessary: (a) *that certain skills are prerequisite* for the advanced course; (b) that the *content domain of the test is consistent with these prerequisite skills*; (c) that test scores can be generalized across relevant sets of items; (d) that test scores are not unduly influenced by ancillary variables such as writing ability; (e) *that success in the advanced course can be validly assessed*; and (f) *that examinees with high scores on the test will be more successful in the advanced course than examinees with low scores on the test.* . . . The validation process evolves as these propositions are articulated and evidence is gathered to evaluate their soundness. (pp. 9–10)

Discussion

Examples from the discussion of propositions from the AERA, APA, and NCME *Standards* served as a basis for the examples we created above.

NOTE: Emphases added for clarity.

STEP 1C: DEFINE THE CONCEPTUAL FRAMEWORK OR CONTENT OF THE SYSTEM

With the knowledge of why a set of assessments is needed, it is time to begin thinking about what important aspects of the teacher disposition construct will be assessed in the instruments to be built. A preliminary step that can prevent much worry and aggravation later is to identify all the content-related inputs in the system. Since this is a standards-based system, it makes sense to start with the standards as our beginning for defining content. While we do not have to determine how we will measure the selected content at this point (that is part of Step 2 of the DAATS model), we do need to know which standards form our inputs and get a general sense of their scope. We also need to think about the relationships between external standards and internal values and beliefs (the local conceptual framework or mission).

ⓟ—— **Conceptual Framework** ——

The conceptual framework is the content and philosophy that guide teaching and assessment. It is drawn from standards, research, professional experience, and vision.

Guiding Question: "What do I want to include in my system? Any standards?"

When we described the conceptual framework in the previous chapter and talked about defining the construct and its content, this is what we had in mind. At its most simplistic level, the construct is teacher dispositions, with the content articulated in the INTASC Principles.

The required standards will vary, depending first and foremost on the state in which the institution or district is located. In some states, such as Wisconsin, there are state-developed standards for dispositions. Other states, such as Florida, do not have specific requirements for measuring dispositions, although teacher preparation programs must show evidence of demonstration of appropriate dispositions to meet accreditation standards. A few of the specialty professional associations (SPAs) affiliated with NCATE,

ⓟ—— **Content** ——

The content is the set of topics or matter with which we are going to work. Content includes, at a minimum, the standards for teaching, as well as any locally defined expectations. The content defines precisely what material will be assessed and requires good sampling procedures once defined.

Guiding Question: "What will we assess?"

such as the National Council for Teachers of English (NCTE), claim to have dispositions embedded in their standards, although this is sometimes debatable. In sum, in one way or another, all states, districts, and colleges appear committed to the concept that all children can learn, and this is, in itself, a value-laden statement. It takes belief.

Many institutions and school districts are also deeply committed to values as part of their institutional missions. In these cases, there is often a core set of values that need to be integrated with national standards. Two examples of locally defined values that impact teacher behavior and dispositional assessment are "a commitment to social justice" and "a commitment to Baldridge quality improvement." Many teacher preparation institutions have adopted the principles of social justice; the "Baldridge criteria" are used in our local school district, Pinellas County Schools, in Florida (see Baldridge National Quality Program, 2006). We often see these commitments to values without clear definition of purpose or measures.

It can be very helpful to add your own value system, especially if, for example, you want to add to the critical standards. INTASC Principle #3, for example, addresses diversity but does not specifically look at economically disadvantaged backgrounds. You might believe that teachers need to take special care of populations from such backgrounds as part of your commitment to social justice. If that is the case, your conceptual framework, or content of the system, would specify indicators that lead to items in your instruments. To the extent that we can associate or align values and items, as with the standards, above, the safer we are in terms of asking the items and making decisions about teachers using them. Assessors can write their own indicators, or, better yet, they can expand on existing indicators wherever possible. In Box 3.5, we provide an example of two locally derived indicators, the INTASC linkage and a survey item.

Box 3.5.   Example of a Locally Developed Indicator

Disposition: Social Justice

INTASC Linkage: Diversity (Principle #3)

Original INTASC Indicator: The teacher respects the different economic and social backgrounds of each child and takes responsibility to provide a fair and adequate opportunity for all students—including proactive accommodation or recognition of the needs of economic deficits.

Expanded INTASC Indicator: The teacher makes students feel valued for their potential as people and helps them learn to value each other *regardless of the socioeconomic status of the students and their families.*

Survey Item: I'm sorry some students suffer by living in negative circumstances, but my job is really to teach the lessons! (answer—hopefully—"DISAGREE")

Since there are no corollary dispositional standards for NBPTS, the INTASC Principles can be applied for all levels of teaching, from precertification through career advancement. Values can be very high from the early stages of training and remain at this level throughout a career—or even regress, based on real-world experiences and disillusionment. The instrumentation does not need to change to meet our target over time. This may be different from the cognitive domain, where we expect teachers to continue to learn about their disciplines and hone their skills in the classroom.

The list in Box 3.6 provides some choices about sources of disposition content.

Box 3.6.   Sources of Content for Dispositions

- INTASC Principles
- National Professional Association Standards
- State Standards
- College Conceptual Framework
- District Standards or Mission
- School Mission and Values Statement

Whether institutions and districts choose standards or mission-based values, the specific indicators of those values need to be clearly set forth. The INTASC disposition indicators are a sufficient set for those standards. However, locally defined values, such as social justice, would need to be operationally defined in terms of *indicators* or *behaviors* or *criteria* that can be observed as the basis for instrument development. If faculty cannot visualize what a teacher exhibiting the value looks like, then it cannot be measured. For example, how is "lifelong learner" visible unless one follows the graduate for a lifetime?

Let's start putting purpose, use, and content together. Table 3.2 aligns some common purposes with potential uses and content at the standards level.

Table 3.2. Aligning Purpose, Use, and Content in a Standards-Based Context		
Purpose	*Use*	*Content*
Certify or license a teacher	Decision about acceptance or denial of entry into the profession via program completion (traditional or alternative routes)	Standards (e.g., INTASC Principles)
Ensure a common set of dispositions in a population (e.g., reflective practice)	Decisions about program structure (e.g., course content, sequence, and grades/credits)	Locally defined unit/district standards (e.g., conceptual framework, goals, or mission)
Improve the performance of teachers	Decisions about strengths and weaknesses of individual teachers related to eligibility to continue in program or job	Minimal scores on standards-based assessments and/or no indicators of serious ethical deficits
Improve teacher training	Decisions about strengths and weaknesses of programs to identify needs for program changes	Aggregated data on standards. Objectives or standards for a course or training materials
Receive national accreditation	Decisions about compliance with standards	Accreditation standards

Assessment designers will need to develop a unified approach, but it may have different subapproaches or paths to fit each set of requirements. At times these paths will converge, but at other times they will diverge. These paths, or subsystems, will be based on different purposes and will lead to different decisions using different content and standards. A college or district, for example, may determine that all of its program completers are qualified (certification decision) but there is still ample room for improvement (program evaluation decisions).

AERA, APA, and NCME *Standards* (1999)
and DAATS Step 1C

Standard 1.2:

The test developer should set forth clearly how test scores are intended to be interpreted and used. The population(s) for which a test is appropriate should be clearly delimited, and *the construct that the test is intended to assess should be clearly described.*

Standard 3.2:

The purpose(s) of the test, definition of the domain, and the test specifications should be stated clearly so *that judgments can be made about the appropriateness of the defined domain for the stated purpose(s) of the test and about the relation of items to the dimensions of the domain* they are intended to represent.

Standard 14.8:

Evidence of validity based on test content requires a thorough and explicit definition of the content domain of interest. For selection, classification, and promotion, the characterization of the domain should be based on job analysis.

Standard 14.14:

The content domain to be covered by a credentialing test should be defined clearly and justified in terms of the importance of the content for credential-worthy performance in an occupation or profession. A rationale should be provided to support a claim that the knowledge or skills being assessed are required for credential-worthy performance in an occupation and are *consistent with the purpose* for which the licensing or certification program was instituted.

Discussion

Note the strong linkages between purpose and content in these Standards. Of particular importance here, though, is that Chapter 14 of the AERA, APA, and NCME *Standards* sets the stage for using content validity studies correlating tasks and job performance as the major form of validity evidence if we do a good job here in the definition of content (and the conceptual framework).

NOTE: Emphases added for clarity.

DAATS STEP 1D: REVIEW LOCAL FACTORS THAT IMPACT THE SYSTEM

Once the purpose(s), content, use(s), and propositions are determined, it is important to analyze all the local factors that would impact the system, such as resources, faculty resistance or cooperation, time available, and NCATE status. In the case of measuring dispositions, contextual factors for the institution or district may include a variety of local issues, chief among which is the degree of commitment to assessing dispositions in the institution or district. Critical here is determining the affect of the faculty. Do they think measuring dispositions is important? If not, the measures developed will probably be low inference and low confidence and will not be taken too seriously or generate much improvement for candidates or programs.

> **Context**
>
> The context defines and describes the conditions that surround us and influence our work. They may be institutional, state, or national. Some contextual factors are helpful, and some are not.
>
> *Guiding Question: "What are the factors that will help or hinder implementation of the envisioned assessment system?"*

We have previously discussed the importance of inference and the types of measures available. We also provided a belief scale about dispositions (Chapter 1, Activity #3). This should be helpful to institutions and districts as they gauge their own values and the time they are willing to commit to dispositions measurement. The extent to which they develop their own instruments will also be contingent on the personnel resources available locally.

We strongly recommend the use of psychometricians to develop these instruments when the consequences are high stakes (failure to graduate or be rehired). Disposition assessment development is more difficult than developing competency-based tasks, such as lesson plans and classroom management plans, because most faculties have less experience with these instruments.

AERA, APA, and NCME *Standards* (1999)
and DAATS Step 1D

Standard 6.3:

The rationale for the test, recommended uses of the test, support for such uses, and information that assists in score interpretation should be documented. *Where particular misuse of a test can be reasonably anticipated, cautions against such misuses should be specified.*

Discussion

Context is an appropriate place to define who can and cannot participate in this assessment system, ensuring fairness for all involved.

NOTE: Emphases added for clarity.

In summary, there are three contextual factors to consider:

- Structural elements of the conceptual framework (e.g., mission and goals)
- Resources available to support instrument development and assessor (faculty and district personnel) training
- Individuality and willingness to dedicate the time necessary to assess and make decisions based on the data

∇ WRAP-UP

In this short chapter, we studied the first of five steps of a design model for disposition assessments aligned with teacher standards. We noted that unless the assessors are careful about defining the purpose, use, propositions, and content of the system within the context in which they operate, the design process will be seriously flawed from the start and the validity of decisions made about teachers will be questionable and dangerous.

The key aspects of purpose, use, propositions, and content are as follows:

- *Purposes* will vary, based on need. Institutions and districts may have dual or triple purposes, such as teacher certification, program improvement, teacher or pupil growth, and/or fulfillment of mission. Each purpose and use is conceptualized and evaluated separately as a matter of validity.

- *Uses* also dictate what will be done with the data. Some examples of decisions are to certify a teacher or allow him or her to graduate, identify program weaknesses and improve a program, identify weaknesses and make improvements in unit-defined areas of importance (e.g., conceptual framework or mission), and just advise teachers who are having dispositional difficulties.

- *Propositions* are based on values and what we believe in. They are part of the underlying framework that drives the system, just as our personal philosophy causes us to act the way we do.

- *Content* can be defined in many ways, but in the case of accreditation, it is reasonable to be consistent with NCATE Standard 1 in terms of the type of information we need to gather, and that means the INTASC dispositional indicators. Institutional or district values can be added to these. Given the lack of dispositional indicators in the NBPTS standards, the INTASC Principles are equally useful for accomplished teachers and novices.

- *Context* also sets the stage for us. External factors cause us to have the strengths (or weaknesses) to do (or not to do) what we plan to do.

We conclude this chapter with some simple statements of minimum requirements from our perspective. Table 3.3 provides our summary recommendations to users about purpose, use, propositions, content, and context.

Table 3.3. Summary Recommendations for Purpose, Use, Propositions, Content, and Context	
Purpose	At a minimum, the system ensures teacher commitment to learning by all children, using the skills acquired in teacher training, in order to protect the public from unqualified practitioners.
Use	The data from the system are used as intended, but, at a minimum, to determine who should be allowed to teach and who should not.
Propositions	At a minimum, teacher dispositions are critically important and need to be assessed so that we have confidence that teachers will do what we want them to do because they believe it to be important.
Content	The INTASC dispositional principles and institutional or district values are the core of the assessment design process.
Context	Assessing teacher dispositions is like swimming upstream. Most folks don't recognize its importance or feasibility.

Story Starters

Starter #1:

Professor/Teacher Tiredovitawl stomps into your office and says,

"I'm sick to death of all of this accountability stuff [not really the word he or she chose], and I'm going to teach what I want. I certainly do not need to be bothered with assessing teacher dispositions. I can tell a flake or pervert when I see one. I have tenure, and you can't make me."

You say . . .

Starter #2:

Mrs. Kidzstink was certified in the glorious state of Hellacious. She passed the certification exam, but she really does not like children, hates planning, and believes the assessments in the curriculum are more than adequate. She thinks that assessment is basically a waste of time. She is deeply committed to teaching the "3 Rs" and nothing else. What should you do about her?

Starter #3:

Mr. Righteous was seeking a teaching license 100 years ago. He successfully passed an examination of his morality after questioning by members of a local school board. He agreed to start teaching every day with an appropriate devotional. He would not date nor be seen with a female companion (except at Sunday school) unless she was unmarried and at least 16 years old, until such time as he was married. His contract contained a morality clause that he would be fired if observed violating this rule. After a trial of 2 years, the school district would provide Mr. Righteous a permanent teaching certificate for the state. How can school districts separate cultural norms from teaching competence—or can they? What cultural aspects of your current time and place are included in teacher standards for your state and local school districts?

DAATS STEP 1—WORKSHEET #1.1

Purpose, Use, Propositions, Content, and Context Checksheet

Explanation:

Complete this worksheet as your starting point for designing a disposition assessment process. Check all that apply and add your own as needed. Consider this as a rough draft.

Purpose:

_____ Ensure a common set of values in a population

_____ Improve the performance of individual teachers

_____ Improve teacher-training programs

_____ Impact the value systems of children (e.g., motivation to learn)

_____ Receive national accreditation or state program approval

_____ Encourage teachers to seek NBPTS certification

_____ Conduct research on teaching

_____ Justify funding of programs

_____ Select teacher candidates

_____ Demonstrate effectiveness of license or graduation decisions

_____ Other _____

_____ Other _____

Use:

_____ Advising or remediation only (low stakes)

_____ Program improvement (low stakes)

_____ Entry into the profession (graduation and licensure—high stakes)

_____ Continuation in the profession (rehire—high stakes)

_____ Other _____

_____ Other _____

(Continued)

DAATS WORKSHEETS

(Continued)

Content:

_____ INTASC Principles

_____ Locally defined values

_____ State, district, and school standards

_____ National professional association standards

_____ Other _____

_____ Other _____

Propositions or Principles:

_____ Certain dispositions or affective traits are critical to effective teaching.

_____ These dispositions can be identified and measured.

_____ National standards and local missions and values contribute to the identification of these dispositions.

_____ Measures of affect can be developed based on the standards identified and appropriate theories of affective measurement.

_____ Teachers with high scores on affective measures are likely to be better teachers who can have a higher impact on K–12 learning.

_____ Teachers with low scores on affective measures are likely to be poorer teachers who may cause harm to children.

_____ Other _____

_____ Other _____

Context:

Faculty support level _____

Fiscal resources available _____

Personnel resources available _____

Time available _____

NCATE status _____

Other _____

DAATS ACTIVITIES

DAATS STEP 1—WORKSHEET #1.2

Purpose, Use, and Content Draft

Explanation:

Write out a formal statement of your purpose(s). For each purpose, also write out a statement of how you will use the data and what the content of the assessment system will be. These should now be aligned. (Feel free to borrow from ours!) You may have more than three; use as many worksheets as you need or develop your own format.

	Set #1	*Set #2*	*Set #3*
Purpose: *Why are we assessing our teachers' dispositions?*			
Use: *What decisions will we make with our data?*			
Content: *What will we assess (e.g., standards)?*			

DAATS WORKSHEETS

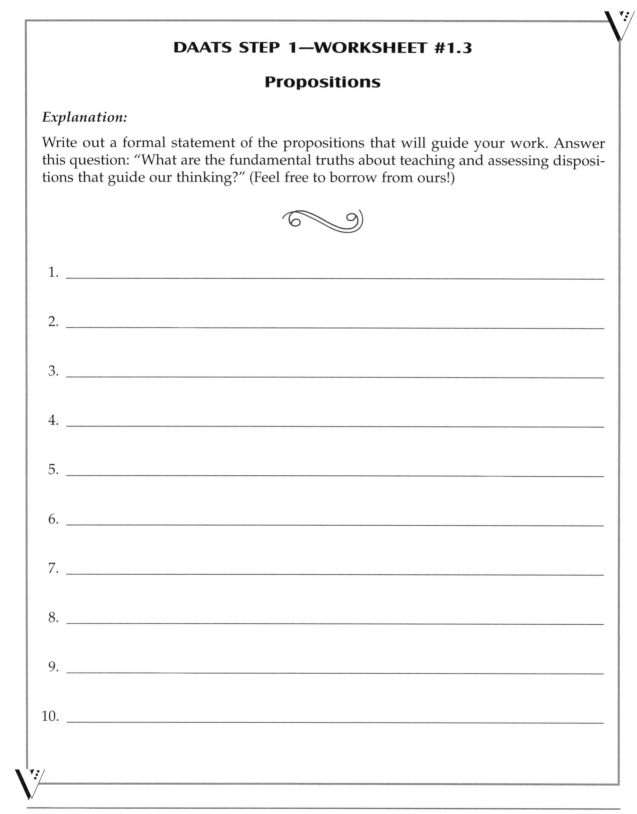

DAATS STEP 1—WORKSHEET #1.3

Propositions

Explanation:

Write out a formal statement of the propositions that will guide your work. Answer this question: "What are the fundamental truths about teaching and assessing dispositions that guide our thinking?" (Feel free to borrow from ours!)

1. _____

2. _____

3. _____

4. _____

5. _____

6. _____

7. _____

8. _____

9. _____

10. _____

DAATS STEP 1—WORKSHEET #1.4

Contextual Analysis

Explanation:

Write out a formal statement of the context within which your assessment process will be built. Answer this question: "What are the factors that will help or hinder implementation of the envisioned assessment system?"

Factors that help:

_____

_____

_____

_____

_____

_____

Factors that hinder:

_____

_____

_____

_____

_____

_____

DAATS WORKSHEETS

Where We Have Been So Far

In the last chapter, we discussed Step 1 of the DAATS model, which centers around assessment design inputs. These inputs include ***purpose, use, propositions***, and ***content*** as the primary inputs, moderated by other ***context*** factors. We also talked a little about ***validity***, reminding our readers that decisions based on assessments can be valid only if made for the purposes for which they were intended. That took us into the realm of using the data. We noted that there are many possible purposes for an assessment system and the use has to be adjusted to accommodate all purposes. We concluded that for the system to have meaning and utility, the data have to be used for appropriate decisions, given the purpose(s) of the system. If the data are useless or if the data are used for the wrong purpose, the system will not lead to valid decisions about teachers.

We ended DAATS Step 1 with a recognition that we do not work in a vacuum; our belief system, as articulated in propositional statements, and our local context influence everything we can and cannot do. We concluded that our "prime directive" (for those who remember *Star Trek*) and the primary focus of this book is the high-stakes purpose of an assessment system—protecting the public from the unqualified practitioner. Such was our "Lesson #1" on validity.

4

DAATS Step 2

*Planning With a Continuing
Eye on Valid Assessment Decisions*

To be upset over what you don't have is to waste what you do have.

—Ken Keyes, Jr.

When we face our task of assessment design with integrity, we soon come to realize that the concept of validity is the most important thing we need to think about. Like a little puppy, it never leaves our side. Sadly, most measurement textbooks leave us hanging and frustrated by offering little practical advice about how to achieve validity—just a bunch of definitions and formulae. In this chapter, we will continue to tackle the problem head-on and hands-on.

> **DAATS Step 2: Develop a valid sampling plan.**

In the last chapter, we introduced the notion of content—the "what" of the assessment process, comprised of state and national standards (especially the INTASC Principles), as well as our own beliefs and values. All of this makes up the first part of a conceptual framework that includes assessment along with philosophy (or propositions or values). In this chapter, we look at what we do to move through these aspects of our conceptual framework as connected to the assessment system and its instruments. We now leave the world of broad-based planning and enter the world of the nitty-gritty details. Step 2 of our DAATS model is all about alignment and the sampling that results from that alignment. It is really the centerpiece or heart of both the model and the system. Miss this step, and nothing else we do will ever really matter.

In this step, we will do four things:

DAATS Step 2A: Analyze standards and indicators.

DAATS Step 2B: Visualize the teacher demonstrating the affective targets.

DAATS Step 2C: Select assessment methods at different levels of inference.

DAATS Step 2D: Build an assessment framework correlating standards and methods.

Before Moving On . . .

1. Have you thought about a conceptual framework (CF)? If so, what's in it? Does it include dispositions that can be aligned with standards? If not, do you plan on developing one? Does your vision of a CF incorporate what others have said (standards as well as research literature) or just what you think is important?

2. What does a "committed" teacher look like when standing in front of a group of students? Jot down what you see "in your mind's eye."

3. Are the instruments you are currently using to assess teacher dispositions more informal or more formal in nature? Do you think you have a good balance to use for decision making about your purpose? Are some missing? Or are they lumped together in one area (e.g., caring) or one time period (e.g., internship or observation time)? Are your assessments predominantly observational?

4. If you plan on using assessments to evaluate programs or units instead of just individuals, how does your CF aggregate the data? Are the different assessment instruments organized to fit together? Are your instruments planned to demonstrate growth of students?

DAATS STEP 2A: ANALYZE STANDARDS AND INDICATORS

All Those Indicators

As we noted previously, there are often multiple sets of standards that need to be used in the disposition assessment system. These may include those of the assessor's institution, school, district, or state, and they all should have all been located in DAATS Step 1C (content). In a standards-based system, we have to start with the standards and indicators. But what do we do with them once they are all located? We need to align them. In essence, we have to pick them apart and then put them back together again in a meaningful way, so that we can use them efficiently and effectively. Obviously, the fewer the standards sets, the easier the task of blending them into one composite set with which we can work! In many instances, we will have to align INTASC Principles only with local values.

In teacher preparation programs, most institutions have found that there is extensive, and frustrating, overlap between and among the sets of knowledge and skill-based (cognitive) standards. In many cases, the state has reworked the national standards, doing little more than wordsmithing. This is the point in time to *compare* and *contrast* the standards. The commonalities are often more frequent than the differences. The same values appear over and over—for example, the belief that all children can learn and that improving program quality is critical to improving the quality of individual teachers. Organizations that want to conserve their energy and make maximum use of their time will begin by aligning internal and external standards with each other. Often, they will find the time well spent. The frustration resulting from duplication is offset by obtaining a richer set of indicators and seeing how they complement each other.

In Table 4.1, we have aligned selected indicators from three sources with three INTASC Principles. We have created and alphabetized a set of "base standards," which are little more than key words that help us remember the main thrust of each principle. This is particularly useful in working with competencies, where there are often many sets of standards. If it becomes a habit, then using the same set of base standards works well for dispositions, too— hence our choice to do so here. It certainly works well to leave the INTASC Principles in their original order, if that is your preference. The state's standards, if there are any, are a third option for organizing the alignment chart. The framework built into the INTASC Principles is "Knowledge, Skills, and Dispositions."

> **— Alignment —**
>
> Alignment is a judgmental process by which we analyze two sets of like elements (e.g., standards) and position together the ones that are similar. Because it is a judgmental process, not all people will agree on every alignment. It is here that we can use standards to provide strength and credibility to locally defined values. For example, social justice can be aligned with diversity.
>
> *Guiding Question: "Does the standard I am reading have a lot in common with my local values or conceptual framework?"*

Table 4.1. Aligning National and Local Dispositional Indicators

Base Standard	INTASC Principle	Institution/District
Continuous Improvement	*Principle #9:* The teacher is *a reflective practitioner* who continually evaluates the defects of his or her choices and actions on others (students, parents, and other professionals in the learning community) and who actively *seeks out* opportunities to grow professionally. • The teacher values critical thinking and *self-directed* learning as habits of mind. • The teacher is *committed to reflection*, assessment, and learning as an ongoing process. • The teacher is *willing* to give and receive help. • The teacher is *committed* to seeking out, developing, and continually refining practices that address the individual needs of students. • The teacher *recognizes* his or her professional responsibility for engaging in and supporting appropriate professional practices for self and colleagues.	*Committed* to self-assessment and *reflection* (UAFS) Candidates are *curious* and follow their curiosities in order to remain continually *engaged* in learning. (MSUN) Candidates demonstrate *self-direction* in their learning and practice. (MSUN)
Diversity	*Principle #3:* The teacher understands how students differ in their approaches to learning and creates instructional opportunities that are adapted to *diverse learners.* • The teacher *believes* that all children can learn at high levels and *persists* in helping all children achieve success.	Culturally *responsive and responsible*, knowledgeable and *appreciative* of the diversity among

(Continued)

(Continued)

Base Standard	INTASC Principle	Institution/District
	• The teacher *appreciates and values* human diversity, shows respect for students' varied talents and perspectives, and is committed to the pursuit of "individually configured excellence." • The teacher *respects* students as individuals with differing personal and family backgrounds and various skills, talents, and interests. • The teacher is *sensitive* to community and cultural norms. • The teacher makes students *feel* valued for their potential as people and helps them learn to value each other.	learners (UAFS) Candidates *see value* in community and the role of families in learning and developing. (MSUN)
Role of the Teacher	*Principle #10:* The teacher fosters relationships with school *colleagues, parents*, and agencies in the larger community to support students' learning and well-being. • The teacher *values and appreciates* the importance of all aspects of a child's experience. • The teacher *is concerned* about all aspects of a child's well-being (cognitive, emotional, social, and physical) and is alert to signs of difficulties. • The teacher is *willing* to consult with other adults regarding the education and well-being of his or her students. • The teacher *respects* the privacy of students and confidentiality of information. • The teacher is *willing* to work with other professionals to improve the overall learning environment for students.	Partners, educational *advocates*, and leaders at the school level and in the wider community (UAFS) Candidates accept the role of educational *leader*. (MSUN) **Baldridge Criteria: Leadership**—Examines how senior executives guide the organization and how the organization addresses its responsibilities to the public and *practices good citizenship*. (PCS)

Some would argue that organizing only around local standards is the way to go, and this fits well with the requirement for a conceptual framework. It can be a little challenging, though, if a decision about licensure is based on the institution's or district's own set of standards. For that reason, we recommend using state or national standards for certification decisions and personally relevant standards as the organizing force for other goals.

In Table 4.1, we have taken excerpts from two conceptual frameworks showcased on the NCATE Web site: the University of Arkansas at Fort Smith (UAFS) and Montana State University–Northern (MSUN). Note how they add depth and breadth to the other standards. (We have sampled statements only from these two universities; they do not represent the complete conceptual frameworks.) We have also included a few "Baldridge criteria" (Baldridge National Quality Program, 2006), used in our local Pinellas County Schools (PCS), Florida. We have done this for just three standards, to demonstrate, and the related dispositional words are boldfaced.

Once this initial alignment is prepared at the standard level, a similar process can be used for the indicators. Table 4.2 aligns INTASC and Wisconsin standards on planning. Here, it is clear that the state and INTASC dispositional

Content Domains

Content domains consist of each grouping of standards that have been aligned because they are similar and convey the same basic set of ideas. In the case of disposition assessment, they might include indicators from INTASC and indicators of locally defined values.

Guiding Question: "Does this set of standards and indicators hang together to form a logical body of content that can be assessed?"

Table 4.2. Sample Alignment of an INTASC and State Standard	
INTASC Principle #7 for Planning: *The teacher plans instruction based upon knowledge of subject matter, students, the community, and curriculum goals.*	**Wisconsin Standard #7 for Planning:** *The teacher plans instruction based upon knowledge of subject matter, students, the community, and curriculum goals.*
The teacher values both long-term and short-term planning.	The teacher values both long-term and short-term planning.
The teacher believes that plans must always be open to adjustment and revision based on student needs and changing circumstances.	The teacher believes that plans must always be open to adjustment and revision based on student needs and changing circumstances.
The teacher values planning as a collegial activity.	The teacher values planning as a collegial activity.

indicators are identical. This is not always the case, but it certainly helps to know if it is, since even minor wording changes can impact system development.

Worksheet #2.1 provides a form you can use to do the same kind of alignment in your state or district. We have provided two formats for you, one using our base standards and one open-ended, in which you can start with the INTASC Principles.

Why Bother?

Alignment obviously takes some time and thinking, and that is why many assessment designers would like to skip the alignment step. That is not a good idea. Not only will it save time in the long run to align standards in this way, but this is also another big step forward toward validity. Standards typically have indicators that flesh out the depth and breadth of the intent of each standard. When we combine those indicators into one long list, we have a rich set of behaviors from which to choose. In measurement terms, we have a domain from which we can sample. The domain defines the various dispositions a teacher needs to have "on the job." From a practical standpoint, a group of 50 faculty members attempting to do this in a large group session may find this to be overwhelming, aggravating, and frustrating. Try getting a few talented and knowledgeable folks, maybe even just one, to take on this task and share it with others for review.

> **Job Analysis**
>
> A job analysis requires that we identify all the important things a teacher is expected to value to be able to perform the job well.
>
> *Guiding Question: "What does a teacher have to believe to be important to work effectively in today's schools?"*

The alignment of indicators to form a content domain for assessment purposes is the beginning of what we will refer to as a *job analysis*, a cornerstone of validity. After all, if we are preparing teachers for a professional position, we need to make sure that we know what that job entails and then assess them on all the important aspects of that job. While we think of this more traditionally in terms of job-related skills, the same principles hold true for dispositions. The standards, in essence, help us define those aspects, so this is not as daunting a task as it sounds. Teachers need to convey content and to plan lessons. They also need to *want* to do so. While there is much hairsplitting in the field about the details, essentially, the 10 Principles written by INTASC identify those critical skills and dispositions.

AERA, APA, and NCME *Standards* (1999)
and DAATS Step 2A

Standard 1.6:

When the validation rests in part on the appropriateness of test content, the procedures followed in specifying and generating test content should be described and justified in reference to the construct the test is intended to represent. If the definition of the content sampled incorporates criteria such as importance, frequency, or criticality, these criteria should also be clearly explained and justified.

Discussion

Since the construct of teacher performance is articulated in multiple sets of standards that are, at least in part, redundant, the content domains into which they are compiled in this step become an explicit part of the assessment design process through this procedure.

NOTE: Emphases added for clarity.

DAATS STEP 2B: VISUALIZE THE TEACHER DEMONSTRATING THE AFFECTIVE TARGETS

Once we have identified the dispositions we are measuring at the indicator level, it is time to begin thinking about how we will know them when we see them. This is accomplished with a rather simple strategy. We suggest that you just close your eyes for a minute and visualize in your mind a good teacher working—doing what a specific standard says is important. What does he or she look like? What is happening in the classroom, hallway, faculty lounge, cafeteria, meeting room, or even at home? How did it get that way? Can you describe it in terms of a specific behavior? Ask yourself the important questions listed in Box 4.1.

Box 4.1.   Questions to Operationalize Dispositions

"What does each standard or indicator look like in practice, when applied by a good teacher?"

OR

"How can we see that the teacher has the dispositions called for in the standards or our own mission/conceptual framework?"

In our examples, what does an educational leader look like? What does he or she do in front of children or in working with stakeholders? Think about planning. What does willingness look like, and how do we collect evidence of it? Can we measure willingness by reviewing some specific examples of a teacher initiating contact with other teachers about a problem in the curriculum that is not well planned? For the standard on collaboration, would the teacher initiate contact with a family without being prompted to do so? Could we ask colleagues and families for their input on the receptiveness of the teacher to listen to their concerns?

With each idea generated, assessors begin to think about data collection strategies. In the above examples, we may be looking at self-report data, which are relatively easy to collect, and we may be looking at interviews or surveys of colleagues or parents. For each strategy considered, we need to think about costs and benefits until we reach a useful, but practical, approach.

We advise against trying to cram dispositions into a portfolio process being used for assessing teacher skills. Forcing the standards into a box that does not fit can lead to all sorts of problems. By visualizing the teacher demonstrating the value or attitude, a different and useful collection method or set of methods should become obvious. As the practical aspects of assessment are defined and examined, assessors typically find the need to reduce the elements in the domain to a manageable list. We will explore that more in DAATS Steps 2C and 2D.

The AERA, APA, and NCME *Standards* (1999) make it clear that the assessment tasks need to be based on a thorough job analysis. When you visualize the teacher performing the standards, you are doing precisely that. If you do it systematically, standard by standard, you will have met the requirement for a thorough job analysis. Box 4.2 gives an example of behaviors we might visualize for a teacher who is committed to teaching critical thinking skills.

Box 4.2.   Behavioral Indicators for a Teacher Who Values Teaching Critical Thinking (INTASC Principle #4)

- The teacher is asking students questions frequently, causing them to think about big issues. The teacher **appears comfortable and at ease** with this process, smiling and nodding when they respond as he or she had hoped.

- The teacher is assigning work for students to do in groups and interacting with each group in a rotation. The teacher does not withdraw to his or her desk, work exclusively with a single high-achieving group but **appears equally comfortable** encouraging each group.

- The teacher is **clearly excited** when a child expresses a new idea or important concept, congratulating the child or saying something very positive to the child.

- The teacher uses a **wealth** of information and **extra** resources to support learning.

Sometimes it is also useful to imagine a poor teacher who is doing the opposite of demonstrating the standard. Some examples are given in Box 4.3.

Box 4.3. Behavioral Indicators for a Teacher Who Does NOT Value Teaching Critical Thinking (INTASC Principle #4)

- The teacher avoids asking questions and works mostly from the book. When questions are presented, he or she **appears _uncomfortable and _not_ at ease_** with this process, grimacing, frowning, or fidgeting.

- The teacher avoids assigning work for students to do in groups and interacting with each group in a rotation. The teacher withdraws to his or her desk or works exclusively with a single high-achieving group and is clearly **_uncomfortable._**

- The teacher is **_expressionless, _nonreactive, or _uncomfortable_** when a child expresses a new idea or important concept, failing to congratulate or encourage the child.

- The teacher **adds _little or nothing_** to the curriculum provided by the district.

Worksheet #2.2 is designed to provide a place for you to record your visualization of the behaviors that define the dispositions. For "advanced visualizing," try to imagine a teacher with more, or less, of a disposition along a continuum—instead of just "good teacher" versus "bad teacher"!

Now that you can see the teacher performing the standard, it is time to translate that vision into assessments.

AERA, APA, NCME and *Standards* (1999)
and DAATS Step 2B

Standard 14.4:

When empirical evidence of predictor-criterion relationships is part of the pattern of evidence used to support test use, the criterion measure(s) used should reflect the criterion construct domain of interest to the organization. *All criteria should represent important work behaviors or work outputs, on the job or in job-relevant training, as indicated by an appropriate review of information about the job.*

Discussion

Using the visualization process, we help to ensure the job-relatedness aspect of the system—it is not what you do in your classes and workshops, but rather what teachers do in their own classrooms that counts!

NOTE: Emphases added for clarity.

DAATS STEP 2C: SELECT ASSESSMENT METHODS AT DIFFERENT LEVELS OF INFERENCE

The ideas that you generated as part of DAATS Step 2B originated in your vision of a teacher performing in a way that demonstrated a value. These are typically assessed using an observational process. In the examples provided in DAATS Step 2B, much can be learned through interviews, questionnaires, and focus groups as well. For example, one could ask both the teacher and the student questions about the materials used in class. Students could talk about teacher reactions to their questions, interactions with groups, and so on. There are many other ways to assess dispositions, as we indicated in Chapter 2.

It is now time to select a set of assessment methods, and we recommend at least three, at increasing *inference levels.* See Chapter 2 for more specific recommendations on each of the possible strategies. In this step, we start to plan on the basis of the indicators themselves. We will provide detailed suggestions on how to create these instruments in DAATS Step 3 (Chapter 5). We will return to our INTASC example on planning to do this.

As you think through the behaviors, you will find that many of them can be assessed using more than one method. It is not necessary to be compulsive about this. The goal is to select a variety of possibilities, aiming for a *balance* among methods that are *appropriate* methods for specific behaviors.

In our *critical thinking* example above, most of the behaviors can be measured using any method, but some dispositions are best measured with a specific method. In the *favoritism* behavior (second indicator), it would be difficult to assess this without the child's perspective. Other indicators, such as the first one on *questioning* children, might be better assessed using the methods other than the child's viewpoint, such as expert observation. At this point, your goal is to find a best method, if there is one, and to rule out methods that are not likely to succeed in yielding valid information.

It is also important to consider costs and benefits associated with each method and the items that become a part of it. In Box 4.4, we provide some thoughts on pros and cons of the most popular methods.

Box 4.4.   Scales, Questionnaires, and Observations—The Good, the Bad, and the Ugly

- *Scales:* We can cover a lot of ground with a belief scale that is machine scored. It is easy to administer, easy to score, and easy to interpret. Although the items may take more time to create, in the long run, it helps to put effort there for reasons of time and money, if nothing else. Respondents can second-guess what we want and provide a "socially acceptable" response, regardless of what they truly believe.

- *Questionnaires:* Every questionnaire item you write, like every essay item on a test, has to be read carefully and scored. That takes time. It is still possible for teachers to say what they know you want to hear, but questions requiring specific examples of actions reduce that risk. Issues of reliability creep in as raters shift in their judgment processes.

- *Observations:* Everybody's favorite! It is just so tempting to lump everything into that observation process. This leads us to waiting until it may be too late, burdening the observer with an overwhelming amount of detail to track, and often relying on adjuncts in a university setting to make the big decisions for full-time faculty. It also can lead to a "good show" put on by the teacher. Faking is possible (doing it once), and that is an important, oft-forgotten deficit.

That last statement in Box 4.4 reminds us of a sad anecdote. We remember a troubling conversation with one dean who was devastated by her own observation of a candidate. She thought he was wonderful in the classroom, attending to each child, including all minorities, clearly sensitive to diversity. Then, he sat informally in her office one day, talking about how one should just expect less from "those kids." Yes, observations can be very misleading, too!

HINT

Beware of faking disposition assessments!

It is more insidious and pervasive than cheating on tests and tasks.

Worksheets #2.3 through #2.5 should help you sort out these issues. Expect these charts to change over time as you design instruments. Unlike the blueprints in cognitive assessment, this is just a starting point. It is acceptable to cross out methods as instruments are developed. Once they are developed, one can then look back and make sure each indicator was assessed somewhere, and assessed adequately; cost factors were not excessive; and faking was minimized.

In our example on planning under DAATS Step 2D, we will use a belief scale, a teacher questionnaire, an observation, an event report, a K–12 focus group, and an observation.

AERA, APAF, NCME and *Standards* (1999)
and DAATS Step 2C

Standard 1.6:

When the validation rests in part on the appropriateness of test content, the procedures followed in *specifying and generating test content should be described and justified in reference to the construct* the test is intended to represent. If the definition of the content sampled incorporates criteria such as *importance, frequency, or criticality*, these criteria should also be clearly explained and justified.

Discussion

Again, the process of brainstorming summative tasks based on the visualization process of DAATS Step 2B reinforces the job-relatedness aspect of the system.

NOTE: Emphases added for clarity.

DAATS STEP 2D: BUILD AN ASSESSMENT FRAMEWORK CORRELATING STANDARDS AND METHODS

All good assessment requires a sampling plan or blueprint or map. These plans are among several types of alignments, also called *assessment frameworks*. Frameworks of various types help us to be sure that we have covered everything we need, without having either too much or too little. They also help us know what kinds of items to write when and where and at what inference level. Architects make blueprints before they start putting down bricks. That way, they are sure that there will be enough doors and windows and they will be in the right places. If you have ever looked at a blueprint, you will notice that there are many parts to it: electrical, structural, inside, outside, and so forth. It is the same thing with frameworks—multiple views of the same thing. Assessment designers need to start with a plan, too, or they will end up with what we like to call "just a bunch of stuff"—too much of some stuff and not enough of other stuff.

> **Frameworks**
>
> Frameworks are two-way grids that help one conceptualize a balanced and appropriate set of assessments.
>
> *Guiding Question: "What do I have in my system that helps me chart out my stuff in an organized way so I can check to see whether I have everything I need, where I need it?"*

The beginning of the sampling plan is the vision of the teacher demonstrating appropriate dispositions, as discussed in DAATS Step 2B. It is now time to think about how to create the measures for this. Is it something that we must observe, or is it something that we can ask teachers to self-report? Is it something we need to have children tell us, or a combination of all of these? How many times do we need to check on an individual indicator before we have confidence that we have assessed what we want? The answers to these questions will change over time as the process is completed. For a start, though, let us think through the three INTASC dispositional indicators for planning and see how they can fit into a blueprint based on our selected methods. Here are the indicators again, with our numbers on them:

7.1: The teacher values both long-term and short-term planning.

7.2: The teacher believes that plans must always be open to adjustment and revision based on student needs and changing circumstances.

7.3: The teacher values planning as a collegial activity.

We start by thinking about each method and each indicator and making a yes/no decision about including it on each instrument type in a table such as the one illustrated in Table 4.3. We also leave ourselves a place to keep notes in case we think of some other method while we're moving through this task.

Table 4.3.	Allocation of Indicators to Instrument Types				
Indicator	*Scale*	*Questionnaire*	*Focus Group*	*Event Report*	*Observation*
7.1	Yes	Yes			
7.2	Yes	Yes	Yes		Yes
7.3	Yes	Yes		Yes*	

NOTE: Let's think about adding an interview of the principal or colleagues about collegial planning for Indicator 7.3.

Here is our rationale for the above selections:

- Almost any indicator can be converted to an "agree/disagree" statement or a questionnaire item of some sort. The trick will be to avoid overly simplistic statements, such as "I think planning is important." We will model this in the next chapter under DAATS Step 3 (Chapter 5).

- Children will provide our best evidence of the willingness of the teacher to adjust. We may observe adjustments during a lesson, but this is a critical indicator that may not be a part of the teacher's routine when we are not watching. So, kids count! Of course, we can also observe this indicator, but it is not likely that the teacher will do something really offensive warranting an event report.

- Children are not likely to know whether the teacher acts collegially, but colleagues can report to us if the teacher does something offensive. Hence the event report is a likely source of information for the teacher with a problem in this indicator. An interview with the principal or other colleagues would be better, and we might choose to add such an instrument later, so a note is added.

Worksheet #2.3 is provided to help you think through this process. In Table 4.4, we provide more examples of what K–12 students may or may not be able to judge. It is important to keep these distinctions in mind as methods are selected:

Table 4.4. Sample Analysis of Judgment Capacities of Assessors

K–12 Students Can Judge	K–12 Students Cannot Judge
Commitment to short-term planning and willingness to adapt instruction based on circumstances	Commitment to long-term planning over a grading period, semester, or year
Interest in meeting individual children's needs	Willingness to work with colleagues in planning

Once you have made the yes/no decisions, indicator by indicator, you can convert them to a larger table that helps to provide an overview of what is covered where. This will help with the instrument design process in DAATS Step 3, not to mention DAATS Step 5, where we consider validity. Yes, it is your first validity study, and we are only in DAATS Step 2! A sample for INTASC 7 is shown in Table 4.5, with Worksheet #2.4 provided for your work.

Table 4.5. Content Validity Study of Indicators

	Scale	Questionnaire	Focus Group	Event Report	Observation
INTASC 1					
INTASC 2					
Etc.					
INTASC 7	7.1, 7.2, 7.3	7.1, 7.2, 7.3	7.2	7.3	7.2
Etc.					

There is no need to be obsessive about completing the charts. Not every cell needs to have assessments in it, and single assessments can appear in multiple rows and columns. These are just planning tools that help ensure the appropriateness, balance, and feasibility of the complete disposition assessment system. The goal here is to think about which indicators can and cannot be measured by certain techniques. Also, remember to go back to those notes to see whether different methods should be used for some principles.

Worksheet #2.5 provides some opportunities to practice this planning technique. While we have used the INTASC Principles and this set of assessment methods to create the form, you can use whatever indicators and methods you choose.

AERA, APA, and NCME *Standards* (1999)
and DAATS Step 2D

Standard 3.1:

Tests and testing programs should be developed on a *sound scientific basis*. Test developers and publishers should compile and document *adequate evidence bearing on test development*.

Standard 3.11:

Test developers should document the extent to which the content domain of a test represents the defined domain and test specifications.

Standard 13.3:

When a test is used as an indicator of achievement in an instructional domain or with respect to specified curriculum standards, *evidence of the extent to which the test samples the range of knowledge and elicits the processes* reflected in the target domain should be provided. Both tested and target domains should be described in sufficient detail so their relationship can be evaluated. The analyses should *make explicit those aspects of the target domain that the test represents as well as those aspects that it fails to represent.*

Standard 14.8:

Evidence of validity based on test content requires a thorough and explicit definition of the content domain of interest. For selection, classification, and promotion, the characterization of the domain should be based on a *job analysis*.

Standard 14.14:

The *content domain to be covered by a credentialing test should be defined clearly and justified* in terms of the importance of the content for credential-worthy performance in an occupation or profession. A rationale should be provided to support a claim that the knowledge or

(Continued)

(Continued)

skills being assessed are required for credential-worthy performance in an occupation and are consistent with the purpose for which the licensing or certification program was instituted.

Discussion

We have just listed four standards from three different chapters that all say essentially the same thing: Build frameworks or blueprints or specifications to show how you are covering the standards that define the job of teaching in your tasks. We easily could have listed four more! Judging from the sheer repetition in the AERA, APA, and NCME *Standards,* the importance of this step should be evident.

NOTE: Emphases added for clarity.

V̈ WRAP-UP

In this chapter, we have outlined a series of steps to take you through the planning process in a way that will maximize your opportunities to make valid decisions about teacher dispositions. Step 2 of the DAATS model is designed to help you develop a valid sampling plan so that you avoid a hodgepodge of assessments that do not give you the answers you need about teachers' beliefs.

We organized the standards into assessment domains to avoid the redundancy and frustration inherent in the multiple sets of standards and to maximize their benefit in designing assessment tasks. We visualized the teacher demonstrating appropriate dispositions in order to begin the design process. We began to think about how to ensure that the overall disposition assessment system is balanced in a variety of ways, covering not only the standards, but doing so in a way that touches on all the dispositions we need to address. We used a blueprint process to do this, keeping an eye on the use of varied inference levels to increase confidence in the resulting decisions. We began a formal process of gathering evidence of validity.

Story Starters

Starter #1:

Professor/Teacher Paneinthebutt stomps into your office and says,

"There are just too many standards, and we are wasting too much time on this stuff. Obviously, all of our teachers like to plan lessons or they wouldn't be teachers. We don't need to beat a dead horse to death. I have never seen a teacher who doesn't use lesson plans. And they all ask questions, too, so what's the big fuss? I tell all my teachers to make sure they recognize each child at least once during a lesson, so I know they are committed to diversity. And they all read a newspaper article about a teacher who was arrested for sexually abusing a child, so they know not to try it. I don't see any value in all of this hogwash. Like I said before, I have tenure, and you can't make me."

You say . . .

Starter #2:

On the surface, Mr. Kidzartuph seems like he will be a great teacher. He has high test scores, dresses professionally, and is always on time. He's really a quick study! But he just can't shift gears when things aren't working in the classroom, and he gets annoyed when kids ask him questions that cause him to lose focus. I heard him make a racist remark in the hall the other day. What do I do?

DAATS STEP 2—WORKSHEET #2.1

Organizing for Alignment (Version 1)

Explanation:

Align the national standards with the standards of your choice.

INTASC Principles	_____ Standards
Principle #1: The teacher understands the central concepts, tools of inquiry, and structures of the discipline(s) he or she teaches and can create learning experiences that make these aspects of **subject matter** meaningful for students.	
Principle 2: The teacher understands how children **learn and develop** and can provide learning opportunities that support their intellectual, social, and personal development.	
Principle #3: The teacher understands how students differ in their approaches to learning and creates instructional opportunities that are adapted to **diverse learners.**	
Principle #4: The teacher understands and uses a variety of instructional strategies to encourage students' development of **critical thinking**, problem solving, and performance skills.	
Principle #5: The teachers uses an understanding of individual and group motivation and behavior to create a **learning environment** that encourages positive social interaction, active engagement in learning, and self-motivation.	
Principle #6: The teacher uses knowledge of effective verbal, nonverbal, and media **communication** techniques to foster active inquiry, collaboration, and supportive interaction in the classroom.	
Principle #7: The teacher **plans** instruction based upon knowledge of subject matter, students, the community, and curriculum goals.	
Principle #8: The teacher understands and uses formal and informal **assessment** strategies to evaluate and ensure the continuous intellectual, social, and physical development of the learner.	
Principle #9: The teacher is **a reflective practitioner** who continually evaluates the defects of his or her choices and actions on others (students, parents, and other professionals in the learning community) and who actively seeks out opportunities to grow professionally.	
Principle #10: The teacher fosters relationships with school **colleagues, parents**, and agencies in the larger community to support students' learning and well-being.	

DAATS STEP 2—WORKSHEET #2.1

Organizing for Alignment (Version 2)

Explanation:

Align the national standards with the standards of your choice. Select some keywords to help you think about what the state and national standards have in common.

Base Standard	_____ Standards	INTASC Principle
Assessment		*Principle #8:* The teacher understands and uses formal and informal *assessment* strategies to evaluate and ensure the continuous intellectual, social, and physical development of the learner.
Communication		*Principle #6:* The teacher uses knowledge of effective verbal, nonverbal, and media *communication* techniques to foster active inquiry, collaboration, and supportive interaction in the classroom.
Continuous Improvement		*Principle #9:* The teacher is *a reflective practitioner* who continually evaluates the defects of his or her choices and actions on others (students, parents, and other professionals in the learning community) and who actively seeks out opportunities to grow professionally.
Critical and Creative Thinking		*Principle #4:* The teacher understands and uses a variety of instructional strategies to encourage students' development of *critical thinking*, problem solving, and performance skills.
Diversity		*Principle #3:* The teacher understands how students differ in their approaches to learning and creates instructional opportunities that are adapted to *diverse learners*.
Human Development and Learning		*Principle 2:* The teacher understands how children *learn and develop* and can provide learning opportunities that support their intellectual, social, and personal development.
Knowledge of Subject Matter		*Principle #1:* The teacher understands the central concepts, tools of inquiry, and structures of the discipline(s) he or she teaches and can create learning experiences that make these aspects of *subject matter* meaningful for students.
Learning Environment		*Principle #5:* The teachers uses an understanding of individual and group motivation and behavior to create a *learning environment* that encourages positive social interaction, active engagement in learning, and self-motivation.
Planning		*Principle #7:* The teacher *plans* instruction based upon knowledge of subject matter, students, the community, and curriculum goals.
Role of the Teacher		*Principle #10:* The teacher fosters relationships with school *colleagues, parents*, and agencies in the larger community to support students' learning and well-being.

DAATS WORKSHEETS

DAATS STEP 2—WORKSHEET #2.2

Visualizing the Dispositional Statements

Explanation:

List the behaviors you think demonstrate that a teacher has the values you are looking for, based on a specific standard. Then, list the behaviors that show the value is missing.

Standard or Principle: _____

List the indicators you can assess for this standard or principle. Use the model for critical thinking in this chapter. Underscore the words that show this is a disposition and not just a skill.

1: *The teacher* _____

2: *The teacher* _____

3: *The teacher* _____

4: *The teacher* _____

5: *The teacher* _____

DAATS WORKSHEETS

DAATS STEP 2—WORKSHEET #2.3

Selecting Assessment Methods for INTASC Indicators

Explanation:

Write the word *yes*, or place a check mark, in each cell where you think you might create an item for the indicator. If you think of another method for one of the indicators, note it next to the indicator number.

Indicator	Scale	Questionnaire	Focus Group	Event Report	Observation
1.1					
1.2					
1.3					
1.4					
2.1					
2.2					
3.1					
3.2					
3.3					
3.4					
3.5					
4.1					
4.2					
5.1					
5.2					
5.3					
5.4					
5.5					
6.1					
6.2					
6.3					
6.4					
7.1					
7.2					
7.3					
8.1					
8.2					
9.1					
9.2					
9.3					
9.4					
9.5					
10.1					
10.2					

DAATS WORKSHEETS

DAATS STEP 2—WORKSHEET #2.4

Assessment Methods for INTASC Indicators: Blueprint

Explanation:

Fill in the INTASC indicators for each INTASC Principle to be measured by the assessment method, transferring your work from Worksheet #2.3.

Indicator	Scale	Questionnaire	Focus Group	Event Report	Observation
INTASC 1					
INTASC 2					
INTASC 3					
INTASC 4					
INTASC 5					
INTASC 6					
INTASC 7					
INTASC 8					
INTASC 9					
INTASC 10					

DAATS STEP 2—WORKSHEET #2.5

Cost-Benefit and Coverage Analysis of Assessment Methods

Explanation:

Place a *yes* or a *no* in response to each question in each cell. Replicate this worksheet for all standards sets, including any locally defined standards, indicators, or outcomes.

Indicator	At Least One Item on Each Instrument for This Principle?	At Least One Item for Each Indicator Principle?	Minimal Cost for This Principle?	Maximum Benefit of each Instrument for This Principle?	Faking Minimized?
INTASC 1					
INTASC 2					
INTASC 3					
INTASC 4					
INTASC 5					
INTASC 6					
INTASC 7					
INTASC 8					
INTASC 9					
INTASC 10					

DAATS WORKSHEETS

Where We Have Been So Far

By now, it should be pretty obvious that we are planning for validity, that little puppy that never leaves our side. We have focused our assessment thinking by clearly articulating the purpose(s), use(s), and content of the system in DAATS Step 1—all within our own local value system and operational context. Using our decisions about content, particularly about standards, we visualized the teacher performing on the job exhibiting the values, beliefs, and attitudes expected—a job analysis. We combined the standards of interest (national and our own plus any others identified as important) to form assessment domains from which we could sample. We identified potential methods for obtaining information on the indicators, seeking to ensure a balanced and appropriate set of instruments that covered the standards and indicators adequately. Our goal was just enough—not too much and not too little—because the job of writing up and conducting the assessments is a very time-consuming one.

We now have our marching orders—a "blueprint"—just like architects who are going to build a building. It is now time to move on to DAATS Step 3: developing the instruments to do the job.

5

DAATS Step 3

Instrument Development

If we shall take the good we find, asking no questions, we shall have heaping measures.
—Ralph Waldo Emerson

ince the disposition assessment system is only as good as the sum of its parts, each instrument needs to be carefully and thoughtfully designed. In this chapter, we will provide some advice on how to write scale items, questionnaire items, focus group items, observational items, and thematic apperception test items. We will help you learn how to write items that lead to variability—an important key to measuring. This will entail showing some ways to write items that are easy and some that are difficult, allowing you to tell the difference between teachers who are highly consistent with the INTASC Principles and teachers who are not so consistent. We will provide both hints and examples for everything we present.

> **DAATS Step 3: Create instruments aligned with standards and consistent with the sampling plan.**

In this step, you will complete just two substeps:

DAATS Step 3A: Draft items and directions for each instrument.

DAATS Step 3B: Review items for applicability to values, domain coverage, and job relevance.

Before Moving On . . .

1. How do you feel about spending some time assessing teacher dispositions? Is it worth it?

2. Given a choice, which would you pick: (1) a machine-created score that provided quick and useful information that was potentially misleading information or (2) reading answers and/or talking to teachers and students, which provided better information but took more time? Why?

3. Are all of the INTASC Principles (dispositions statements) equally important? Are there some you could skip in good conscience? Which ones, and why?

4. How do you feel about using stakeholders or experts to make sure you have done a good job in designing your work?

DAATS STEP 3A: DRAFT ITEMS AND DIRECTIONS FOR EACH INSTRUMENT

Item

The statement or question posed.

Guiding Question: "What's the question?"

Instrument

The paper designed to elicit responses. This could be a survey, a questionnaire, or a test.

Guiding Question: "What is the device that is designed and created to scientifically measure the construct?"

There is a wide variety in the types of items and instruments you can develop to measure affect or dispositions. In DAATS Step 3A, we will look at scales; questionnaires, interviews, and focus groups; observed performance; and thematic apperception tests (which we will call "situation reflection assessments"). Let's begin with scales.

Thurstone Agreement Scales

As a quick reminder, Box 5.1 provides the description and example we provided of Thurstone Agreement Scales in Chapter 2. We now introduce the term "dichotomous response" as a descriptor of these scales—two choices only. These items require the respondent to "agree" or "disagree," and **there is no room for gray!**

Box 5.1. Description and Example of a Thurstone Agreement Scale

Description of Thurstone Scale:

A set of statements is provided to respondents. They must agree or disagree with the statements, which typically number at least 20 to 45. Statements provide for a range in the attribute being measured.

Sample Thurstone Items:

- All children can learn.

- If I give it my best, **most** children can learn when given enough help.

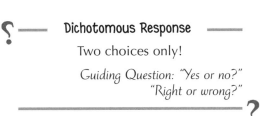

The hardest part about writing an agreement scale is to provide a balance of items both (1) across the indicators and standards to be measured and (2) across levels of difficulty that demonstrate different amounts of commitment to the disposition. If everyone answers every item correctly, we have not learned very much about the teachers we are assessing. The same is true if everyone gets everything wrong. The key to good assessment is to have a range of scores that reflects the underlying construct—some variability—so that we can tell judgmentally and empirically whether we are really measuring what we intended to measure. If those teachers who seem to be high in dispositions get good scores and those who seem to be low in dispositions get low scores, we have confidence that we are on the right track. But if they all get the same scores, we are going nowhere. We know in our hearts (and brains) that all teachers are not created equal—emotionally! We must consider the difficulty of items that make up our measures in order to have validity.

Dichotomous Response

Two choices only!

Guiding Question: "Yes or no?"
"Right or wrong?"

In Figure 5.1, we compare an imaginary person named "Lee" (the vertical line) against four types of instruments to show what happens when we do not have the variability we need to measure dispositions.

Figure 5.1. Sample Item Distributions for Varying Levels of Difficulty

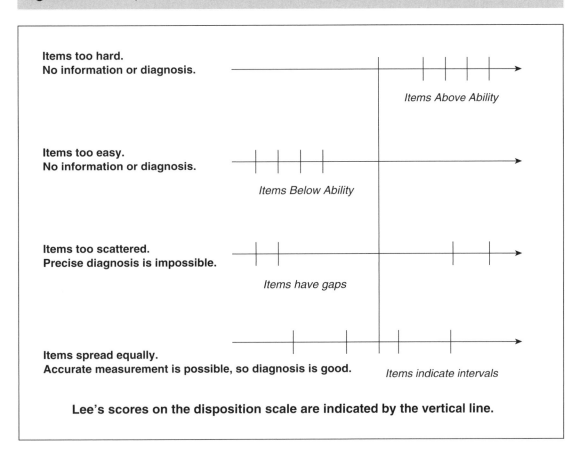

Items too hard.
No information or diagnosis.

Items Above Ability

Items too easy.
No information or diagnosis.

Items Below Ability

Items too scattered.
Precise diagnosis is impossible.

Items have gaps

Items spread equally.
Accurate measurement is possible, so diagnosis is good.

Items indicate intervals

Lee's scores on the disposition scale are indicated by the vertical line.

As you read Figure 5.1, note the following:

- In the first line, Lee is faced with items that are all too hard and gets them all wrong. We have not found anything good about Lee.
- In the second row, Lee gets the items all right, and we have no room for diagnosis and improvement. Lee is perfect!
- In the third row, we do not have enough items in the middle, so we can't tell precisely how good or bad Lee's dispositions are. Again, there's not too much we can do for Lee!
- In the fourth row, we have a good spread of items, so we know the most about Lee. We know just where her dispositions started to be inconsistent with the INTASC Principles, so we can step in and help!

In the sections that follow, we will provide a little more detail on what we mean by "easy," "difficult," and "middle-range" items.

Easy Items

It is relatively easy to write a series of "agree/disagree" statements (items) that most people will answer "correctly." So, we recommend that you start with these items. An example of an easy item is given in Box 5.2.

Box 5.2. Example of an Easy Survey Item

Item: "All children can learn." (Correct answer is "agree")

Explanation: Everybody should answer correctly, and we begin to wonder about those who disagree.

The first example we provided was "All children can learn." This statement has become a kind of mantra in the education profession. No Child Left Behind legislation, combined with accreditation requirements and our own humanistic values as teachers, makes this one what appears to be a "no-brainer." Or at least, so we hope. We operate under the assumption that all teacher candidates and all teachers are drilled into believing this and virtually all will respond "agree" because they know that is the expected response, even if they do not really believe it (which may be sad but true).

Dispositional Baseline

This is the bottom line for dispositions. If teachers are below the baseline, they probably should not be teachers.

Guiding Question: "How poor can the values be before we deny a license?"

There is little true or deep commitment to each child in this statement—"can" and "do" represent very different levels of expectation. So, this is an important type of item to ask to determine whether teachers are at the "dispositional baseline." If teachers do not believe that all children CAN learn, then certainly they will give up and not attempt to help each child actually learn. There will always be those children in the classroom for whom the teacher has no hope.

If you want to bump this item up a notch, looking for a deeper level of commitment, change "can" to "will" and watch what happens. The percent correct should go down.

For those teachers who disagree, we must take their answers very seriously. These are the teachers we want to help improve, and they are also the teachers whom we want to watch carefully. We will certainly want to follow up and find out why they disagreed. If we use good item analysis strategies, we will know whether this answer was inconsistent with their other answers or whether it is one of several dangerous indicators of a "below-baseline" teacher. We will address diagnostic strategies for item analysis in Step 4. For now, let's focus on a definition of "dispositional baseline." The "dispositional baseline" is a term we have coined to mean the bottom line for dispositions. If teachers are below the baseline, they probably have beliefs inconsistent with our standards for teachers.

> **Item Analysis**
>
> An analysis of each item to see whether it is functioning as expected: consistently with other items, difficult or easy.
>
> *Guiding Question: "Is this item good?"*

So, what we call "easy" items like this one (ones where we expect most everyone to provide the anticipated response), are important to use for diagnostic purposes at the individual level. We can counsel students who believe otherwise and look for other indicators of dispositional issues in those candidates or teachers. If we find that there are a lot of teachers who answer incorrectly on an easy item like this, then we have some serious concerns at the programmatic level. Are we giving them the wrong message somewhere in our programs or schools? Do we need to redesign some coursework, counsel a faculty member or administrator, or develop some professional development opportunities for the district? Or did we just write a bad item or misjudge how easy it was? These are questions answered through an analysis of our programs and an analysis of the items.

> **REMINDER**
>
> Never assume that your teachers know or believe something. Always measure it! You may be surprised. You may need to fix something you thought was not broken.

When we think about items like this simple one, we are reminded of that old adage about the word "assume"— you know the one—what it makes out of you and me. In our field test results of our instruments, we were rather surprised to find that 23% of our 801 teacher candidates answered "disagree." Most of them were in one institution, which now has some very useful program improvement information to address. They were, of course, pretty shocked at the result. So, assumption is, indeed, a dangerous thing! Easy items, or what we perceive to be easy items, are a must on any assessment!

Difficult Items

Writing the difficult items, ones for which we do not expect everyone to answer as anticipated, is much more challenging. This is where imagination and creativity are important. Our first example, "All children can learn" is at one extreme end. We expect it to be very easy and everyone to believe this. We do not assume they will all get it right, so we ask the question. Now, we need to think about the other extreme. We need to find those teachers who are extraordinarily committed to a value. The highly committed teachers should be the only ones to answer correctly. These are the teachers who would go to the ends of the earth to ensure that each child learns. They are the Mother Theresas and Mahatma Ghandis of teaching. One way to do this is to substitute "will" for "can" in our first example. Box 5.3 provides another alternative, a bit more sophisticated.

> **Box 5.3. Example of a Difficult Item**
>
> *Item:* "If I give it my best, most children will learn when given enough help." (Correct answer is "disagree")
>
> *Explanation:* Only the truest believers will answer correctly, refusing to accept the word "most." For them, *all* children *will* learn.

What does the idea of "truest believers" mean for our item? You were probably surprised to learn here that the correct answer is "disagree." We would expect the extreme believer to take issue with the word "most," because it implies that there are still some children who will not learn. The extremely committed teacher will wrestle with that item, struggling with the word "most," and finally disagree. In measurement terms, we call this internal struggle "dissonance." The item is intended to make the teacher a bit uncomfortable, digging deeply into heart and soul to make a decision. Here, we expect many incorrect answers, not because the teachers who answer "agree" are likely to be bad teachers, but because this type of question sorts out the most committed from the acceptably committed. The typical teacher will "slide" past the word "most."

REMINDER

In affective measurement, wrong answers are helpful and necessary. They show us the teachers who are so committed that they may burn out and quit.

This can be a very difficult concept for assessors to grasp. We are writing items here that we expect teachers to get wrong. Wow! That is a mouthful, isn't it? Humanistic item writers and advocates of mastery learning will struggle with this approach because they want every teacher to get every item correct. This is the difference between building a scale that shows differences in teacher values and a scale that just confirms that we are doing what we think we are doing in teacher training and supervision. If your purpose is to measure how good a job you are doing with teachers and/or to find and celebrate the truly committed, then the extreme items will be necessary. It is also necessary to provide a contrast to those teacher candidates whom we suggest move to the accounting department, where they can work with numbers and pieces of paper all day!

When we looked at the Bloom and Krathwohl affective taxonomy examples for planning, remember that we noted that the best planner (characterization) may become so frustrated by the lack of time to plan that he or she burns out and leaves the profession. Extremes—both high and low—are bad in measuring dispositions. In cognitive assessments, a perfect score is great; in affective assessments, it may not be!

Middle-Range Items

The middle-range items will be answered correctly by good teachers, so such items get us above the "dispositional baseline" and help us locate all those teachers who are just fine. We can aim for a normal distribution and have most items in this range. We provide some examples of these items in Box 5.4.

> **Box 5.4. Examples of Items With Middle-Range Difficulty**
>
> *Example 1:* "If I give it my best, all children can learn when given enough help." (Correct answer is "agree")
>
> *Example 2:* "Based on each child's needs, I individualize instruction so that every child receives the help and resources he or she needs to succeed in my classroom." (Correct answer is "agree")
>
> *Example 3:* "The teacher's day is very long, so it is often too time-consuming to tailor instruction to individual children. (Correct answer is "disagree")
>
> *Explanation:* The majority of teachers should answer any of these items correctly, and the majority of items on the scale should be written at this level of difficulty. Note the use of reverse-coded item in the third example, where the correct answer is "disagree."

For the first item, we have eliminated the dissonant word "most," and we have added a level of commitment that exceeds that needed for the easy item. Here, the teacher has to try to work with all children, but there is nothing that says he or she will succeed or not succeed in any single case. The teacher is obligated, and the children have the opportunity.

The second item is similar. Teachers will need to think about what they will actually do in the classroom that is based on their values. Will they individualize or not? They can fake this answer, so it is not as useful as a questionnaire item or an observation, but if they do believe that they should individualize instruction for each child, aiming for achievement, they will agree with this statement. This does not commit them to every child's success—only their efforts to help each child succeed. Failure for a child or two is still possible.

The third example is built on the same ideas as the second example, but it models a way to rewrite a statement in such a way that the correct response is "disagree" without using negative words like "not," which tend to confuse the respondent. This is a very important survey-item-writing technique. If the correct answer is always "agree," respondents move way too quickly through an instrument and just agree with everything. You get a much better measure of their true beliefs if you create a mix of items.

There are a few general rules you can follow in writing statements for belief scales. We have spent a lot of time discussing the concepts of dissonance and difficulty above. In Box 5.5, we provide a few hints intended to get you started or to use in the review of scales you may find that others have written. Included are Thurstone (1927a, 1927b, 1928) and Likert (1932), but the same general guidelines apply to rating scales and semantic differential scales.

REMINDER

In affective measurement, average is great! We expect teachers to be average—not too weak and not too strong!

A MENTAL HURDLE

The difficult part of writing affective items is accepting that it is okay for many teachers to get some items wrong. Extremes (very high and very low scores) are not good. In fact, any item that everyone gets right or everyone gets wrong is not really useful as a measure. Some measurement techniques actually drop such items.

Box 5.5. Hints for Writing Agreement Scale Items

1. Aim for at least two or three items for each Principle and/or indicator (INTASC dispositional indicators and locally defined indicators) measured. A total of 50 is a good number to have from a reliability standpoint.

2. Write items in pairs or triads and then mix the order in the final instrument. Balance items by these criteria:
   - Difficulty—Create some that are easy, some medium, and some very difficult items.
   - Response—Create approximately equal numbers of items with which teachers should agree and disagree.

3. Limit the number of statements where teachers can "fake" the response or give a socially correct answer but include a few to ensure they are not below your baseline. These tend to be the very easy items.

4. Avoid unnecessary complexity that borders on confusion:
   - Negative words (e.g., not, never, don't), because they are very confusing—double negatives introduce unnecessary complexity.
   - Multiple concepts in a single item—unless they are clearly related and result in the same response, "agree" or "disagree."

5. Use the language of the standards where feasible.

6. Consider using a sheet that can be scanned for machine scoring.

7. Report results in raw scores and standard scores.

8. Conduct an item analysis to make sure the items are useful for decision making.

Worksheet #3.1 provides a format for you to create your own scale items and to ensure that you balance them by difficulty and correct response. You will also align them with standards.

❢ ——— **Directions** ———

Statements that tell someone precisely how to work or respond. These should be written for both the teacher and the person asking questions.

Guiding question: "How do I do it: step by step, please?"

——————————————— **?**

Finally, directions should always be provided to respondents. These directions should include the following points:

- The reason for the instrument
- The intended use of information
- The length of time respondents will need to complete the instrument
- A call for honesty of response
- A statement about confidentiality if the responses are confidential
- The manner in which teachers should respond (check, bubble, etc.) and the source of items

A sample is shown in Box 5.6.

Box 5.6. Sample Directions for Survey Instrument

This survey is designed to measure your consistency with national standards for teachers—specifically the dispositions indicators of the INTASC Principles. Your responses will be used to help you identify any beliefs that are contrary to national (or local) expectations. Your responses will also be pooled with the responses of other teachers so that we can improve our preparation (or staff development) programs. The survey should take you about 10 minutes to complete.

Please answer honestly! You are likely to find some items more difficult than others. Read carefully and answer from your heart! Then, indicate your agreement or disagreement with each of the statements by bubbling a "1" for "agree" and a "2" for "disagree." Don't forget to bubble in your name at the top.

Questionnaires, Interviews, and Focus Groups

As a quick reminder, the descriptions and examples we provided for questionnaires, interviews, and focus groups in Chapter 2 are shown in Table 5.1, renumbered for this chapter.

Table 5.1.	Examples of Questionnaire, Interview, and Focus Group Items	
Format	*Explanation of Technique*	*Example*
Questionnaires	Respondents are asked a predetermined set of questions, the responses to which often require intense analysis, training, examples of responses, and rubrics. The questions are designed to elicit a high level of specificity to help ensure that the "correct" response is not given with a yes/no answer. The assumption here is that if a teacher can describe in some detail an action taken, he or she is probably telling the truth and values the disposition enough to have it be a part of his or her work life.	Describe the last time you talked to a colleague about a problem with a student. What did the colleague recommend? What did you do? Did it work? Would you go back to that colleague again for advice? Note: If teachers don't value the advice of colleagues, they don't seek it. Sometimes they will even state that directly.
Interviews	The same type of questions used in a questionnaire can be administered orally. The advantage is that the teacher can't check with others and fake a response as easily. The disadvantage, of course, is time. Interviews take longer.	Same questions and same assumption as for the questionnaire.
Focus Groups	Questions are written for children to answer in a small group, and several can answer at the same time. These questions elicit data about how children perceive the teacher as a window onto the teacher's beliefs. Yes/no answers are acceptable in some instances.	Does your teacher listen to everyone in the class? Does he or she become impatient when you do not understand?

Note the following item-writing strategies:

- *Questionnaires and Interviews:* The series of questions in the string require a very specific response. Both allow assessors to make judgments about how seriously the teacher takes the notion of working with colleagues, as operationally defined by seeking advice. The teacher is asked not only about the types of advice sought but also to make some evaluative decisions about the quality of the input received. Teachers who do not value this relationship are likely to ask very simplistic questions of colleagues. The description of a specific instance will help the assessor determine whether the teacher uses the input from colleagues wisely or just asks for routine information, such as when or where study hall is. Did the teacher pose an appropriate question to the colleague that has an impact on K–12 learning, for example? The judgment question about the quality of advice sought and received helps provide information on the valuing of the experience. If the colleague was asked an important question and the teacher made a reasonable judgment about the helpfulness of the response, we infer that the teacher is placing value on the potential relationship. Sometimes, teachers simply say that they do not need help. There, the decision is pretty clear-cut. Collegiality in this instance is not valued. The questionnaire is an instrument that the teacher completes alone, whereas the interview is completed using a protocol and recording form with the teacher.

  ?— **Recording Form or Protocol** —

  The structured form and process used to gather data.

  Guiding Question: "How can I organize my work so it is neat and looks the same for every interview or focus group and provides consistent information?"

- *Focus Groups:* Note in this example that the questions are child focused. We ask the students what the teacher does and how he or she reacts to children in the classroom. These are the kinds of questions children can answer. If the child indicates a lack of patience on the part of the teacher, then we have data on negative dispositions. The visualization of the teacher "performing" the value is particularly helpful in writing focus group questions. Seeing the teacher in one's mind will most likely have children in the mental picture reacting to the teacher positively or negatively.

The items or questions for these three types of instruments are much easier to write than the items for belief scales. While the focus in the scales was on increasing levels of difficulty and dissonance, here the focus is on specificity of response and differentiating skill from disposition. As with competency assessment, we visualize the good (and bad) teacher exhibiting the disposition (or exhibiting its absence). Remember that one of the principles we cited in Chapter 2 was about specificity. If you believe in or value something, then you will do it and you can describe what you did with some level of detail—and even enthusiasm—and children will respond accordingly. The teacher who believes in working with colleagues will work with colleagues and can describe an interaction and how it impacted his or her teaching. The teacher who is committed to children's learning will be patient with them, and they will feel that level of patience.

A MENTAL HURDLE

One of the hardest parts of writing affective questions is separating skill from disposition. You have to address mistakes in skill application under competency and give credit for wanting to do the right thing here. Heart counts. Not brain.

The more difficult part of writing questions for interviews, questionnaires, and focus groups is to sort out skills from values.

They are, of course, related. Here we are using skills only as they apply to what the teacher *wants* to do. Keep your eye on heart and soul, not mind. It is possible for a skill to be applied incorrectly but applied with enthusiasm. Part of the struggle with validity is to make sure we make the right decisions in the right places. Skill-based errors need to be factored into the competency assessment process, not the disposition assessment process. Here, it is about making a conscious choice to do something that counts—not whether the action is completed correctly. That, like dissonance, can be a bitter pill to swallow.

That may not make a lot of sense without a concrete example. Let's take assessment as the example. Those who are assessment literate know that we need to use a variety of strategies for different assessment purposes. We use formative assessments to provide feedback without grades, and we use summative assessments to make decisions with grades about what children learned. Informal assessments are useful as formative measures and should occur all of the time. Teachers might watch children's reactions to a concept. At a formative level, practice tests and other written and oral assessments are useful to help the teacher redirect instruction. Box 5.7 shows a misguided response from the skill perspective but not the affective perspective.

Box 5.7. Good Affect, Bad Skill

I assess my students all of the time. I know that I cannot be a good teacher unless I monitor what my students are learning every day. I always watch them to see if they look like they are understanding what I say, and I give them points for attendance and paying attention in class. I look at every activity they complete to see if they are catching on and give them lots of points if they just try. I also give them lots of homework and grade their work for points. I grade these activities so I have enough assessment data in my gradebook because I know I need multiple measures, and this gives me lots of information to work with. When I am done with the unit, I always use the test in the teacher's guide because I know the publisher does a good job of writing tests, so I never change them. It is important to me to be confident about their scores. I look at every child's test to see what he or she did not understand, and I work with each child to help him or her get better. I am really pleased when I can make a difference with an individual child based on my assessment results, and I send thank-you notes to all of the parents who help their children learn.

In the above example, this teacher shows good affect and bad skills. He or she clearly believes wholeheartedly in assessment. This teacher should be less reliant on the publisher's tests and should not grade practice activities and homework. He or she understands the value of multiple measures but does not use alternative assessment at all or individualize assessment strategies for different children or learning targets. While supportive of helpful parents, this teacher has no strategies to communicate with families whose children are working alone. If we were scoring this teacher, we would certainly want to redirect him or her in terms of skill (mind), but the affect rating (heart and soul) would be high. This teacher is a "keeper" who needs help.

There are a few general rules you can follow in writing questions. We have spent a lot of time discussing specificity and differentiating between skill and affect in making the decisions about an individual teacher. Box 5.8 lists a few hints intended to get you started or to use in the review of questionnaires you may find that others have written.

Box 5.8. Suggestions for Items in the Question Format

1. Write items in clusters that will facilitate response and elicit detail.

2. Create pointed questions that require a high level of specificity in the response. Consider asking for examples of what the teacher did or rationales that explain why the teacher did something the children may have observed or felt. This will help reduce faking and socially correct responses.

3. Avoid yes/no questions. If you use them, always follow up with a request for explanation (e.g., "Please explain" or "Why"?).

4. Difficulty is less of a concern, but some dispositions will be more rare than others. Target your expectations based on your intuitions about difficulty.

5. Create a model response to ensure the question can be answered.

6. Avoid unnecessary complexity in wording.

7. Use the language of the standards where feasible, especially in teacher questionnaires/ interviews.

8. For interviews with teachers or K–12 students:
   - Use a recording form (protocol) for interviews and K–12 focus groups so the interviewer has a place to write down the answers.
   - Include directions for the interviewer to standardize the process.
   - Include sample prompts for the interviewer in case he or she needs to probe for a response, particularly from children.
   - Create two kinds of questions for children: "around the table," where all may respond, and "toss-outs," where you expect one child to respond.
   - For K–12 focus groups, include variations of the questions for different age groups and developmental levels.
   - Remind children to focus their answers on what the teacher actually does, not what they like or expect.

9. Use a rubric for scoring with preferably three points on the scale (e.g., "target," "marginal," "unacceptable"), and identify exemplars at each level of proficiency to ensure consistency.
   - Look for specificity or elaboration as the difference between the high and middle scores.
   - Look for the expression of negative ideas as the rationale for an unacceptable response. In many cases, the middle score is based on reading between the lines.

10. Report results in raw scores unless item response theory is used and items can be combined in a meaningful way to present a scaled score. (More in the next chapters on this)

11. Conduct an item analysis to make sure the items are useful for decision making. (More in the next chapters on this)

Finally, directions should always be provided to respondents. These directions should include the following points:

- The reason for the instrument
- The intended use of information
- The length of time respondents will need to complete the instrument
- A call for honesty of response
- A statement about confidentiality if the responses are confidential
- The manner in which teachers should respond

Directions should specify source of items, reason for instrument, use of information, length of time, honesty of response, and the manner in which teachers should respond (typed, handwritten). Samples are shown in Box 5.9 and 5.10.

Box 5.9.   Sample Directions for Respondents to Questionnaires

This questionnaire is designed to measure your consistency with national standards for teachers—specifically the dispositions indicators of the INTASC Principles. Your responses will be used to help you identify any beliefs that are contrary to national (or local) expectations. Your responses will also be pooled with the responses of other teachers so that we can improve our preparation (or staff development) programs. The questionnaire should take you about 30 minutes to complete.

Please answer honestly! Read each question carefully and answer from your heart! Be as specific as you can. You may answer in handwritten or typed form. If you need additional space, feel free to use the back of the questionnaire or additional sheets of paper.

Box 5.10.   Sample Directions for Respondents to Interviews

This interview is designed to measure your consistency with national standards for teachers—specifically the dispositions indicators of the INTASC Principles. Your responses will be used to help you identify any beliefs that are contrary to national (or local) expectations. Your responses will also be pooled with the responses of other teachers so that we can improve our preparation (or staff development) programs. The interview should take you about 30 minutes to complete.

Please answer each of the questions frankly and in detail. Answer from your heart and provide as many examples as you can. Expect for us to spend about 30 minutes together.

In the special case of interviews, we need to add directions for the interviewers—not just the interviewees. Box 5.11 provides an example of interviewer directions.

Box 5.11.   Sample Directions for Interviewers

Prepare for the interview by reading the questions and the INTASC Principles so that you know what beliefs you are looking for. At the interview, explain to the interviewee that the items are designed to measure their consistency with national standards for teachers—specifically the dispositions indicators of the INTASC Principles. Tell them that their responses will be used to help the two of you to identify any beliefs that are contrary to national (or local) expectations, so it is important that they respond honestly, answering from their hearts. They should expect to spend about 30 minutes with you. As you proceed through the interview, read the questions provided and use follow-ups to elicit more detail. Try to get as specific a response as possible, seeking to determine whether they are answering honestly or making things up as they go.

Do not correct them until a later date if they say things that show a lack of knowledge or skill. Record whatever they say either in writing or on a tape recorder. If they ask how they did, tell them the report will be scored and you (or someone else) will get back to them within a specified time period to talk about the results. Assure them that there is a good scoring process and that a rubric with examples will be used to make the decisions.

Worksheet #3.2 provides a format for you to write your questions for any of these types of instruments. You will also align them with standards.

Observed Performance

As a quick reminder, the descriptions and examples we provided for observed performances in Chapter 2 are provided in Table 5.2, renumbered for this chapter.

Table 5.2. Examples of Observations, Behavior Checklists, and Event Reports		
Observations	One or more performances can be evaluated looking for specific affective characteristics that are rated or counted, typically counted.	Frequency count (tally) of teacher recognition of majority and minority children.
Behavioral Checklists	Items may be the same as the types on the observation instrument, but an overall impression of frequency is provided.	3 = frequently 2 = occasionally 1 = rarely Recognition of minority children.
Disposition Event Report	This report is completed on an ad hoc basis when a person in authority (professor, mentor, principal) observes (or learns of) an action on the part of the teacher that is inappropriate. The report is used only for serious incidents, needs to be documented carefully, and should include follow-up between the author and the teacher to attempt to remediate the problem. Disposition event reports could also be used to describe extremely positive events, but this is rare.	Racist remark, physical contact with a child, cheating, written reflection that indicates all students are "dumb" or certain students are incapable of learning, continuous late arrival for class, continuous inappropriate dress.

Tally

Counting and making little sticks on a paper to keep track. Typically, there are four vertical sticks and then a horizontal stick crossing through them so we can count by five.

Guiding Question:
"How many times did you see it?"

Observations bring a new set of advantages and disadvantages to the disposition assessment process. Faking and socially acceptable responses are less likely here, but there is rarely a written record of what was observed. Videotaping provides an opportunity to maintain the record. An even more complex problem, though, is that the information collected during observations requires more judgment to interpret, making this a high-inference assessment. We realize that some of you have been thinking, "What about reliability?" To this we say, "Validity first!" Regardless, skill-based interference is strongest in observations, and we will talk in greater detail about validity and reliability in DAATS Step 5.

There is a very clear distinction between the first two types of observation presented here (the traditional teacher observation and the behavior checklist) and the third (the disposition event report). One or both of the first two should be conducted as a matter of routine for each teacher, whereas the second is used only in special circumstances, which are typically negative.

In deciding whether to use traditional observations and/or behavior checklists, the institution or district will need to consider the availability of personnel, as well as their roles with the teacher candidates, to determine which strategies are feasible. The observation provides a snapshot of teacher dispositions, which may be taken two or three times, whereas the behavior checklist provides for an overall impression, based on repeated observations of the teacher. Hints are provided separately for the disposition event report. The behavior checklist is also a useful instrument for addressing some professional issues.

Figures 5.2 through 5.5 provide examples of extracts from observation forms. The first three are directed at INTASC Principle #3 on diversity and the fourth on professionalism (INTASC Principle #10):

Figure 5.2. Example of an Affective Behavior Checklist for Diversity (Partial)

Valuing of Diversity in the Classroom

Name of Teacher: _____

Name of Observer: _____

Date: _____   Location: _____

Instructions: Check "yes" for all behaviors that are observed regularly.

_____ yes _____ no   Treats students equally, with pleasant demeanor.

_____ yes _____ no   Treats all students with respect.

_____ yes _____ no   Addresses different learning styles enthusiastically.

_____ yes _____ no   Instructs all students with patience and understanding.

_____ yes _____ no   Provides an open climate.

Figure 5.3. Example of an Affective Rating Scale for Diversity (Partial)

Valuing of Diversity in the Classroom

Name of Teacher: _____

Name of Observer: _____

Date: _____   Location: _____

Instructions: At the conclusion of your observation, rate each behavior on this scale:
F = frequently; O = occasionally; R = rarely; NO = not observed

Treats students equally, with pleasant demeanor.	_____ F	_____ O	_____ R	_____ NO
Treats all students with respect.	_____ F	_____ O	_____ R	_____ NO
Addresses different learning styles enthusiastically.	_____ F	_____ O	_____ R	_____ NO
Instructs all students with patience and understanding.	_____ F	_____ O	_____ R	_____ NO
Provides an open climate.	_____ F	_____ O	_____ R	_____ NO

Figure 5.4. Example of a Tally Sheet for an Affective Observation of Diversity (Partial)

Valuing of Diversity in the Classroom

Name of Teacher: _____

Name of Observer: _____

Date: _____   Location: _____

Instructions: During the observation, write a tally mark each time a behavior is observed.

Effective Attitude	# of Effective Observations	# of Ineffective Observations	Ineffective Attitude
Is **responsive** and has a pleasant demeanor toward a child from protected population, LEP, or low SES.			**Ignores, frowns, or fails** to respond to child from protected population, LEP, or low SES.
Speaks with **respect** to child from protected population, LEP, or low SES.			Speaks with **disrespect** or shows **impatience** to child from protected population, LEP, or low SES.
Modifies instruction for different *learning styles* willingly.			Uses **same** strategies for all learning styles or shows annoyance when needing to adapt.
Welcomes opinions representing diverse views.			**Berates opinions** representing diverse views.
Seeks **consensus** among students.			Is comfortable allowing single-group or student *domination*.

Figure 5.5. Example of an Affective Behavior Checklist for Professionalism (Partial)

Professionalism in the Classroom

Name of Teacher: _____

Name of Observer: _____

Date: _____   Location: _____

Instructions: Check "yes" for all behaviors that are observed regularly.

_____ yes   _____ no   Dresses appropriately for school culture.

_____ yes   _____ no   Dresses appropriately for school events.

_____ yes   _____ no   Arrives on time or earlier for work.

_____ yes   _____ no   Leaves on time or later after work.

The examples in Figures 5.2 through 5.5 provide some samples of the formats that can be used to measure teacher affect through observation. Box 5.12 provides some suggestions on how to develop such instruments.

Box 5.12.   Suggestions for Teacher Observations and Behavior Checklists

1. For observations in general, items should be organized on the basis of the order in which you expect behaviors to occur. So, if you are going to evaluate the teacher's beginning of the class, that should be the first item on the list. This may be less important in measuring affect than in measuring skill, but it is typically the first piece of advice for a live performance.

2. Difficulty is less of a concern in observational measures, but some dispositions will be more rare than others by virtue of the frequency of their occurrence. It makes adding up scores impossible.

3. Use items that reflect affect or good attitudes about teaching. You are looking for indicators that the teacher feels good about the skills being demonstrated, about teaching in general, or about children. Look for a word or words in what you write that shows the feelings.

4. Assess only the values that are clear to see: how the teacher feels about children in general as well as children of different backgrounds and needs, changes of focus, professional demeanor, level of comfort with the subject areas, student rights and emotional needs, democratic values, and so on.

5. Avoid unnecessary complexity in wording. Keep items very short so you do not spend a lot of time finding the item you want to score. Highlight keywords wherever possible, especially when tallying behaviors.

6. Use the language of the standards where feasible, especially in teacher questionnaires/interviews.

(Continued)

(Continued)

7. Prepare the form so that you can record as you go.

8. Include directions for the interviewer to standardize the process.

9. The points on the scale need to be clearly differentiated.

10. Use a rubric for scoring with preferably 4 points on the scale (e.g., "frequently," "occasionally," "rarely," and "not observed"). Count behaviors wherever possible and use tally marks. Frequencies can then be converted to the proficiency scale. Allow for the possibility of "not observed."

11. Make sure that negatives and positives are properly separated. "Credit" should not be given for bad behaviors (e.g., persists on same topic when children do not understand, ignores minority children), unless you are observing specifically for both effectivity and ineffectivity. In a scale or a checklist, restate in terms of an effective behavior (e.g., readily shifts focus as needed; interacts equally with minority children) or use the word "avoids."

12. Report results in raw scores unless item response theory is used and items can be combined in a meaningful way to present a scaled score. (More in subsequent chapters)

13. Conduct an item analysis to make sure the items are useful for decision making. (More in subsequent chapters)

No specific examples of directions are provided for the observations, since they are typically governed by local rules. A minimal set of instructions is provided on the top of each figure. Typically, more detailed ones will be required by the district. Be sure to be consistent across all candidates in terms of time spent and reporting back, to avoid legal complaints.

Worksheets #3.2 through #3.5 provide formats for writing each of the three techniques demonstrated in this section.

Thematic Apperception Tests or Situation Reflection Assessment

As a quick reminder, here are the descriptions and examples we provided for thematic apperception tests in Chapter 2, now renumbered as Box 5.13.

Box 5.13. Example of Situation Reflection Assessment

Explanation of Technique	*Example of Technique*
Teachers are shown a picture and asked to say what they see. The interviewer records their reactions, searching for evidence of teaching values in their responses.	Teacher is shown a picture of a young woman dressed in a very short skirt. The prompt is: "Tell me about this teacher." Most teachers would discuss the clothing, but if not, an additional prompt might be necessary. A teacher with appropriate values would question the attire; a teacher with inappropriate values would admire it or dismiss it as okay.

A more specific example is shown in Figure 5.6.

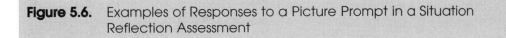

Figure 5.6.　Examples of Responses to a Picture Prompt in a Situation Reflection Assessment

---

Prompt: What is this teacher doing?

Response #1: "A teacher should never dress like this, but I suppose she is thinking about her last lesson."

Our judgment: Best answer

Response #2: "A teacher should never dress like that."

Our judgment: Good answer

Response #3: "She is thinking about her next lesson."

Our judgment: Not okay!! This teacher ignores the obvious inappropriate dress.

Response #4: "This is a really cute teacher. I like her sense of fashion." She is going to teach children who are too young to look up her skirt, so it is great to dress this way!"

Our judgment: We need to have a long talk with this teacher, who may need to go to fashion school.

Thematic apperception tests are typically used by highly trained clinical psychologists. In our application, we are comfortable using them in a less formalized way. We are not seeking to make important diagnoses of neuroses or other clinical issues. Instead, we are looking for some glaring instances of misplaced values that can be corrected. The teacher who thinks that the style of dress described in Figure 5.6 is acceptable for a classroom needs our help. We don't have to be licensed psychologists to know that. We do need to be careful about using this technique in ways for which we are not trained and for decisions that would not be valid. It is useful only for finding the serious outliers. Suggestions on how to implement this technique are provided in Box 5.14.

Item Response Theory

A measurement method that maximizes the information obtained about each item so that decisions can be made at the item level, not just the instrument level.

Guiding Question: "How good is each item and each score?"

Box 5.14. Suggestions for Situation Reflection Assessment

1. Pick provocative, gender-balanced (some male, some female) cards and questions based on themes. Use pictures that can be interpreted for affect or good attitudes about teaching. The obvious exception here is if you are looking for a gender-loaded response, as in the example illustrated in Figure 5.6.

2. Use prompts like "Tell me more" or "Why do you say that?"

3. Use a recording form and include locations (pointing) and verbalizations.

4. Include directions for the interviewer to standardize the process.

5. Use a rubric for scoring with preferably 3 points on the scale (e.g., "target," "marginal," "unacceptable") and identify exemplars at each level of proficiency to ensure consistency.

6. Discuss results with the teacher.

7. Report results in raw scores unless item response theory is used and items can be combined in a meaningful way to present a scaled score. (More in subsequent chapters)

8. Conduct an item analysis to make sure the items are useful for decision making. (More in subsequent chapters)

Here are some possible directions for a situation reflection in Box 5.15.

Box 5.15. Sample Directions for Interviewers

Prepare for the interview by looking at the pictures and reviewing the INTASC Principles so that you know what beliefs you are looking for. At the interview, explain to the interviewee that the items are designed to measure their consistency with national standards for teachers—specifically the dispositions indicators of the INTASC Principles. Tell them that their responses will be used to help the two of you to identify any beliefs that are contrary to national (or local) expectations, so it is important that they respond honestly, answering from their hearts. They should expect to spend about 15 minutes with you. As you proceed through the interview, read the questions provided and use follow-ups to elicit more detail. Try to get as specific a response as possible, seeking to determine whether they are answering honestly or making things up as they go.

Do not correct them if they say things that show a lack of knowledge or skill or a skill-based value that you find suspect. Record whatever they say either in writing or on a tape recorder. If they ask how they did, tell them the report will be scored and you (or someone else) will get back to them within a specified time period to talk about the results. Assure them that there is a good scoring process and that a rubric with examples will be used to make the decisions.

AERA, APA, and NCME *Standards* (1999)
Influencing DAATS Step 3A

Standard 3.20:

The *instructions presented to test takers should contain sufficient detail* so that test takers can respond to a task in the manner that the test developer intended. When appropriate, sample material, practice or sample questions, criteria for scoring, and a representative item identified with each major area on the test's classification or domain should be provided to test takers prior to the administration of the test or be included in the testing material as a part of the standard administration instructions.

Standard 3.22:

Procedures for scoring and, if relevant, *scoring criteria* should be presented by the test developer *in sufficient detail and clarity as to maximize the accuracy of scoring.* Instructions for using rating scales or for deriving scores obtained by coding, scaling, or classifying constructed responses should be clear. This is especially critical if tests can be scored locally.

Discussion

It is clear from the above Standards that it is important to maximize the accuracy of decisions by creating clear and detailed instructions and scoring rubrics. We will discuss rubric creation in DAATS Step 4.

NOTE: Emphases added for clarity.

DAATS STEP 3B: REVIEW ITEMS FOR APPLICABILITY TO VALUES, DOMAIN COVERAGE, JOB RELEVANCE

In this step, you will review each item and each instrument to make sure you followed the item-writing hints and good coverage of the standards. Each item should reflect a skill-based value that is necessary for good teaching. This is an important step to make sure you stay on track from a validity perspective. Using the suggestions from DAATS Step 3A, we provide some review worksheets for you in Worksheets #3.6 through #3.9.

If you have not already involved some stakeholders in the process, now is the time to do so. A critical measure of the quality of your instruments is the extent to which they are related to the real job of teaching, as perceived by stakeholders. This is a great opportunity for colleges and school districts to interact and share their unique perspectives and talents.

The worksheets attached to this chapter give you a comprehensive approach to reviewing each instrument. Once you have completed a review of your individual instruments, it is time to go back and check your coverage of the standards and indicators one more time. Things have a way of shifting and changing during the item-writing process even for those who have attempted to meticulously implement their blueprints from Step 2. An example is given in Table 5.3, and Worksheet #3.10 provides a format for ensuring coverage.

Table 5.3. Sample Review of Indicator Coverage

Principle #1: The teacher understands the central concepts, tools of inquiry, and structures of the discipline(s) he or she teaches and can create learning experiences that make these aspects of subject matter meaningful for students.

#	Indicator	Scale	Questionnaire	Focus Group
1.1	The teacher realizes that subject matter knowledge is not a fixed body of facts but is complex and ever evolving. He or she seeks to keep abreast of new ideas and understandings in the field.	17	1	
1.2	The teacher appreciates multiple perspectives and conveys to learners how knowledge is developed from the vantage point of the knower.	9 42 49		1c 2a
1.3	The teacher has enthusiasm for the discipline(s) he or she teaches and sees connections to everyday life.	10 16	1	3a 4b
1.4	The teacher is committed to continuous learning and engages in professional discourse about subject matter knowledge and children's learning of the discipline.	16	1 2	

With these data in hand, there are questions you can ask yourself to decide whether you have good coverage. They are as follows:

✓ Are all the critical aspects of the standard assessed adequately in the instruments?

✓ Will these instruments all together help me to distinguish among teachers who have the dispositions I want to see, or not?

✓ For any indicators not represented, are they important to me in my visualization of a teacher with the right standards-based dispositions, or am I comfortable that they can be omitted from my system? If I need to add something to address them, where should I add it?

✓ Have I overloaded any of the indicators? If so, is it a really important indicator, therefore needing a higher proportion of items to assess it adequately, or should I delete something?

When you provide your instruments to stakeholders for review, you can ask them whether each item meets the criteria of criticality and authenticity. This process doubles as your first validity study and will be discussed in more detail in DAATS Step 5. For now, know that the most important criterion against which to measurement your assessment systems—both cognitive and affective—is job-relatedness. For colleges of education, critical stakeholders might be district personnel. For districts, critical stakeholders might be college personnel or parents or even children. A sample validity study is shown in Table 5.4.

Table 5.4. Sample Stakeholder Validity Study on Job-Relatedness

Rate each of the items on a scale of 1–5, with 5 being high on the extent to which the dispositional statement is critically important for a teacher and an authentic reflection of what teachers should value.

#	Item	Criticality					Authenticity				
1.	I usually think about children's home life and environment so that I can tell if something is wrong. (agree)	5	4	3	2	1	5	4	3	2	1
2.	It is more important that I know and teach my subject well than it is to adapt to the age and grade of students in my class. (disagree)	5	4	3	2	1	5	4	3	2	1
3.	I believe good teachers learn about the students' backgrounds and community in order to understand their motivations. (agree)	5	4	3	2	1	5	4	3	2	1

Worksheet #3.11 will help you create your first stakeholder review form.

AERA, APA, and NCME *Standards* (1999)
Influencing DAATS Step 3B

Standard 13.5:

When test results substantially contribute to making decisions about student promotion or graduation, there should be *evidence that the test adequately covers only the specific or generalized content and skills* that students have had an opportunity to learn.

Standard 14.14:

The *content domain to be covered by a credentialing test should be defined clearly and justified* in terms of the importance of the content for credential-worthy performance in an occupation or profession. A rationale should be provided to support a claim that the knowledge of skills being assessed are required for credential-worthy performance in an occupation and are consistent with the purpose for which the licensing or certification program was instituted.

Discussion

This first validity study helps to provide evidence that the instruments elicit all of the important aspects *of the content standards and are*, therefore, clearly defined and justified.

NOTE: Emphases added for clarity.

V WRAP-UP

Educators are finding some difficulty in designing traditional tests and alternative assessments for knowledge- and skill-based tasks. Unfortunately, some affective instruments are even a bit tougher to create. However, with practice, item writing becomes easier. For the faint of heart (or those in a hurry), it can be helpful to call on measurement faculty or staff in the organization or even retain an outside consultant with some prior experience in creating affective measures. In-house staff may be in the testing office or in the department of measurement and research or educational psychology. They may even be in the psychology department of arts and sciences.

In this chapter, we provided some specific hints about how to develop such items, so that users in low-stakes environments can work on their own or have some guidelines to review the work of those who write items for them. This chapter, though, was not intended to be an "everything you ever wanted to know" or "definitive how-to" treatise on the subject of writing affective measures. It is just an introductory piece.

Since most affective measurement for teachers is relatively low stakes, there is more room for trial and error, and what we have written here may be all the user needs. Field tests and careful analysis of the results, so that items can be revised, are a must for any assessment and should be expected. We will head in that direction in the next chapter.

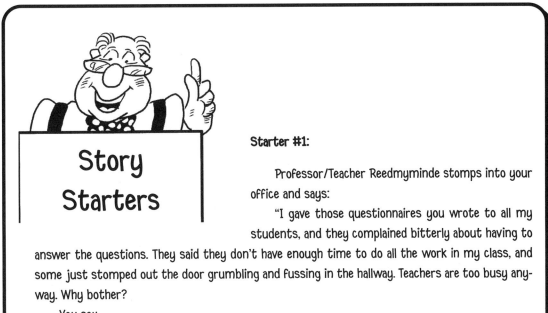

Story Starters

Starter #1:

Professor/Teacher Reedmyminde stomps into your office and says:

"I gave those questionnaires you wrote to all my students, and they complained bitterly about having to answer the questions. They said they don't have enough time to do all the work in my class, and some just stomped out the door grumbling and fussing in the hallway. Teachers are too busy anyway. Why bother?

You say . . .

Starter #2:

Mr. Hartintheriteplace really likes the idea of affective assessment. He is a good test writer and wants to take a stab at writing the instruments. Should I let him?

DAATS STEP 3—WORKSHEET #3.1

Creating Scales

Explanation:

Use this worksheet to write items for scales. Write a statement, indicate whether you think the correct response is "agree" or "disagree" ("a" or "d"), and then rate the level of difficulty as "easy," "medium," or "hard" (E, M or H). **Tabulate** the numbers and see whether you have a balanced set of items. When you are finished, renumber the items so that there is a mix of response and difficulty on the survey. Don't forget to decide what type of instrument you want—Thurstone, Likert, and so on.

Scale Type: _____ Thurstone _____ Rating

_____ Likert _____ Semantic Differential

#	*New #[1]*	*Item Draft*	*Standards Assessed*	*Response*[2]	*Difficulty Level*[3]:
1				A D	E M H
2				A D	E M H
3				A D	E M H
4				A D	E M H
5				A D	E M H
Etc.				A D	E M H

NOTES:

1. The "new number" is the number you assign to mix the items by standard and answer.

2. Circle the correct response: "A" for "Agree" or "D" for "Disagree."

3. Circle the anticipated difficulty level: "E" for "Easy," "M" for "Middle," or "H" for "Hard."

DAATS WORKSHEETS

DAATS STEP 3—WORKSHEET #3.2

Creating Questionnaires, Interviews, or K–12 Focus Group Protocols

Explanation:

Use this worksheet to write items for questionnaires, interviews, or K–12 focus groups. Align the items with the standards or indicators being addressed.

#	*Item Draft*	*Standards Assessed*
1		
2		
3		
4		
5		
Etc.		

DAATS WORKSHEETS

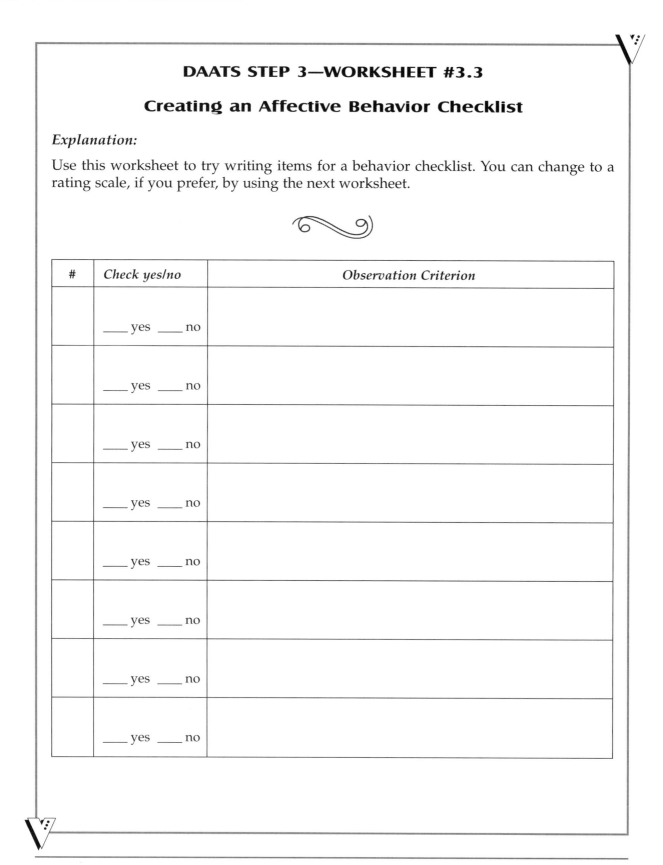

DAATS STEP 3—WORKSHEET #3.3

Creating an Affective Behavior Checklist

Explanation:

Use this worksheet to try writing items for a behavior checklist. You can change to a rating scale, if you prefer, by using the next worksheet.

#	*Check yes/no*	*Observation Criterion*
	____ yes ____ no	
	____ yes ____ no	
	____ yes ____ no	
	____ yes ____ no	
	____ yes ____ no	
	____ yes ____ no	
	____ yes ____ no	
	____ yes ____ no	

DAATS STEP 3—WORKSHEET #3.4

Creating an Affective Behavior Rating Scale

Explanation:

Use this worksheet to try writing items for a behavior rating scale. You can change to a checklist by using the previous worksheet. In your scale, think about providing three ratings plus a "not observed." Ratings might be like ours or some other indication of frequency. "Frequently," "sometimes," and "rarely" were the scale points we used.

#	*Observation Criterion*	*Rating*

DAATS WORKSHEETS

DAATS STEP 3—WORKSHEET #3.5

Creating a Tally Sheet for Affective Observation

Explanation:

Use this worksheet to try writing items for a behavior checklist for counting observations of effective and ineffective behaviors. Think in pairs of opposites.

Effective Attitude	*# of Effective Observations*	*# of Ineffective Observations*	*Ineffective Attitude*

NOTE: Don't forget to highlight your affective words.

DAATS STEP 3—WORKSHEET #3.6

Checklist for Reviewing Scale Drafts

Explanation:

Use this checklist to review your work on any scale you created. If you are unable to check a criterion, go back and fix the instrument.

_____ 1. There are at least two or three items for each Standard and/or indicator.

_____ 2. There are a total about 50 items or a sound reason for having a lot more or a lot less.

_____ 3. Items for each Standard are in pairs or triads.

_____ 4. Items are mixed in the final instrument by difficulty level and correct response.

_____ 5. The number of statements that can be "faked" is limited (i.e., not many easy items).

_____ 6. Items are clearly written and not confusing.

_____ 7. Negative words (e.g. "not,"" never") have been avoided.

_____ 8. The item includes a single concept unless both concepts yield the same response.

_____ 9. The language of the Standards was used where feasible.

_____ 10. The instrument can be scored by machine if many teachers will be assessed.

_____ 11. The language of each item is clear.

_____ 12. The language of each item is free from bias.

DAATS WORKSHEETS

DAATS STEP 3—WORKSHEET #3.7

Review Sheets for Questionnaires and Interviews

Explanation:

Use this checklist to review your work on questionnaires and interviews. If you are unable to circle a "yes" response, go back and fix the instrument.

___ Yes   ___ No   Are the directions clear?

___ Yes   ___ No   Is the recording form easy to use?

#	Clarity		Affective		Standards		Specificity		Judgmental	
1	Yes	No	Yes	No	Yes	No	Yes	No	Yes	No
2	Yes	No	Yes	No	Yes	No	Yes	No	Yes	No
3	Yes	No	Yes	No	Yes	No	Yes	No	Yes	No
4	Yes	No	Yes	No	Yes	No	Yes	No	Yes	No
5	Yes	No	Yes	No	Yes	No	Yes	No	Yes	No
6	Yes	No	Yes	No	Yes	No	Yes	No	Yes	No
7	Yes	No	Yes	No	Yes	No	Yes	No	Yes	No
8	Yes	No	Yes	No	Yes	No	Yes	No	Yes	No
9	Yes	No	Yes	No	Yes	No	Yes	No	Yes	No
10	Yes	No	Yes	No	Yes	No	Yes	No	Yes	No

Description of Items:

- *Clarity* of language in items
- *Affective* versus skill-based focus
- Use of *standards*-based terms in the item
- Is there a level of *specificity* that will make faking and socially responsible answers likely?
- Is there a *judgment* made that helps ensure that the teacher is committed to the value assessed?

DAATS STEP 3—WORKSHEET #3.8

Review Sheets for K–12 Focus Group Protocols

Explanation:

Use this checklist to review your work on K–12 focus group protocols. If you are unable to circle a "yes" response, go back and fix the instrument.

___ Yes   ___ No   Are the directions clear?

___ Yes   ___ No   Is the recording form easy to use?

#	Clarity		Affective		Standards		Language		Vision		Clusters		Prompts and Toss-Outs	
1	Yes	No	Yes	No	Yes	No	Yes	No	Yes	No	Yes	No	Yes	No
2	Yes	No	Yes	No	Yes	No	Yes	No	Yes	No	Yes	No	Yes	No
3	Yes	No	Yes	No	Yes	No	Yes	No	Yes	No	Yes	No	Yes	No
4	Yes	No	Yes	No	Yes	No	Yes	No	Yes	No	Yes	No	Yes	No
5	Yes	No	Yes	No	Yes	No	Yes	No	Yes	No	Yes	No	Yes	No
6	Yes	No	Yes	No	Yes	No	Yes	No	Yes	No	Yes	No	Yes	No
7	Yes	No	Yes	No	Yes	No	Yes	No	Yes	No	Yes	No	Yes	No
8	Yes	No	Yes	No	Yes	No	Yes	No	Yes	No	Yes	No	Yes	No
9	Yes	No	Yes	No	Yes	No	Yes	No	Yes	No	Yes	No	Yes	No
10	Yes	No	Yes	No	Yes	No	Yes	No	Yes	No	Yes	No	Yes	No

Description of Items:

- *Clarity* of language in items
- *Affective* versus skill-based focus
- Use of *standards*-based terms in the item
- Is the *language* appropriate for a child?
- Does the question reflect a *vision* of the teacher working effectively with children?
- Are the *clusters* meaningful for children (i.e., placed in their context)?
- Are there *prompts* and *toss-outs* for the interviewer?

DAATS WORKSHEETS

DAATS STEP 3—WORKSHEET #3.9

Checklist for Reviewing Observations and Behavior Checklists

Explanation:

Use this checklist to review your work on observations and behavior checklists. If you are unable to check a criterion, go back and fix the instrument.

_____ 1. Items are organized in a logical order.

_____ 2. The points on the scale are clearly differentiated.

_____ 3. An opportunity for "not observed" is provided.

_____ 4. Items reflect affect or good attitudes about teaching.

_____ 5. Only values that are clearly observable are assessed.

_____ 6. Wording is understandable and as simple as possible.

_____ 7. Keywords are highlighted as needed, especially when tallying behaviors.

_____ 8. The language of the standards is used where feasible.

_____ 9. The form is easy to use.

_____ 10. Directions for the assessor are included.

_____ 11. If both negatives and positives are used, they are clearly separated.

_____ 12. The use of negative words, such as "not" or "never," are avoided.

DAATS STEP 3—WORKSHEET #3.10

Coverage Check

Explanation:

Use this checklist to make sure you have good coverage of the indicators. This is a validity check. Then, do the self-check at the bottom and adjust your instruments, as needed.

For each Standard, write the item numbers from the instruments in the appropriate cells.

Standard #1:

Indicator #	Instrument 1	Instrument 2	Instrument 3

Self-Check:

_____ All the critical aspects of the standard are assessed in one or more instruments.

_____ This combination of items will help me to distinguish between teachers who have the dispositions and those who don't.

_____ For any indicators not represented, I feel comfortable that they can be omitted from my system.

_____ I have not overloaded any of the indicators or any of the instruments.

DAATS STEP 3—WORKSHEET #3.11

Rating Form for Stakeholder Review

Explanation:

Use this format to create a stakeholder review form for district or college personnel or other stakeholders to ensure that the questions you have asked are job related. If the mean score falls below a 3 on any item, it is time to revise.

Rate each of the items on a scale of _____, with _____ being high on the extent to which the dispositional statement is critically important for a teacher and an authentic reflection of what teachers should value.

#	Item	Criticality	Authenticity
1			
2			
3			
4			
5			
6			
7			
8			
9			
10			

Where We Have Been So Far

To this point, we have drilled the need to build a set of disposition assessment instruments that are standards based and provide for increasing levels of inference (and confidence) in the decisions reached about teachers as individuals and about program successes and failures. We created the instruments to do so and ensured that they were aligned with standards and met the criteria of authenticity and criticality from stakeholders' perspectives. We ensured that the tasks provided adequate and appropriate coverage of the standards. We included directions to ensure that teachers and their assessors knew what to do to ensure consistent data across individuals, and we mentioned the need for scoring rubrics—yet to be developed. Now, we turn to those rubrics and how we use them to make decisions that are both useful and safeguard the rights of our teachers.

6

DAATS Step 4

Decision Making and Data Management

It is a capital mistake to theorize before one has data. Insensibly one begins to twist facts to suit theories, instead of theories to suit facts.

—Sir Arthur Conan Doyle

The best assessment instruments in the world are of little use if the results remain known by only an individual person. This is one of the greatest challenges currently being faced by teacher preparation programs seeking NCATE reaccreditation. Because faculties tend to teach and assess within the confines of their own classrooms, sharing of information is typically elusive, and the NCATE Board of Examiners teams are finding many weaknesses about data aggregation in Standard 2.

If we take the view, however, that decision making needs to be shared, all decision makers need access to a common core of data from which they can make their decisions. When we talk about decisions here, we are speaking not only about the decisions about an individual teacher's dispositions on an

> **DAATS Step 4: Design and implement data aggregation, tracking, and management systems.**

individual assessment but also about that teacher's dispositions across all measures over time. Only when we build a data aggregation system can we hope to obtain data that will be useful for decision making about teacher graduation, growth, credentialing, and program improvement. As we approach DAATS Step 4 in this process, that dual focus—individual teacher and overall program—needs to be kept clearly in mind.

In Step 4 of the DAATS model, we begin thinking about what we will do with the data once we get it. There are three substeps of the model:

DAATS Step 4A: Develop scoring rubrics.

DAATS Step 4B: Determine how data will be combined and used.

DAATS Step 4C: Develop implementation procedures and materials.

Before Moving On . . .

1. Are the assessments you are planning to decide about teacher dispositions aligned with individual teacher standards such that you can make decisions that are standards based? If not, why not? Do you want to go back and revisit?

2. Have you thought about how the data from one instrument builds on the data from the others? Will the sum total of instruments help you make decisions about consistency with the INTASC dispositions indicators at the standards level, for example, values planning?

3. Are you still comfortable with the way you visualized the teacher with dispositions needed to help children learn? If not, what will you do with teachers who are not ready to move on?

4. Are you committed to due process? Have you reviewed your procedures recently? If not, review your graduation/promotion procedures right now. What do you say about dispositions?

DAATS STEP 4A: DEVELOP SCORING RUBRICS

Developing scoring rubrics is one of the most important parts of the assessment design process. Two different strategies are needed: one for dichotomous response items, such as the belief scale, where there is a correct and an incorrect answer, and one for rating scales that provide partial credit, like the questionnaires and observations that are not tallied. We address both in this next section.

Dichotomous Response Scoring Keys

For dichotomous response instruments, like the belief scale, an answer key is clearly needed to show which items should have "agree" as the correct response and which items should have "disagree" as the correct response. Supplementing this answer key can be an explanation of why the expected response is "agree" or "disagree" and what the expected difficulty of the item is. This should help in explaining the results. We provided an informal example of this for our sample items in Step 3 of the DAATS model. We will formalize that for a few of the items in Table 6.1.

——— Scoring Key ———

The answers.

Guiding Question:
"May I have a cheat sheet, please?"

Creating this key can be time-consuming and may be more work than assessors want to do. It is really not critical unless the instrument is high stakes and there are many teachers who will be assessed using it. In the end, it can save lots of time in answering questions about "Why is that a 'disagree' answer?" Worksheet #4.1 provides a place for you to work on recording your rationales for each correct response.

	Correct Response	Difficulty Level	
Item			*Explanation*
All children can learn.	Agree	Easy	Because of NCLB legislation and accreditation standards, all teachers should have this fundamental belief. We should expect 100% of the answers to be correct. Counseling is in order if the answer is incorrect. This is a "dispositional baseline" item.
Based on each child's needs, I individualize instruction so that every child receives the help and resources he or she needs to succeed in my classroom.	Agree	Moderate Difficulty	We expect the majority of teachers (at least half) to support the need for individualized instruction. This item falls short of all children succeeding, so even the "true believers" can agree.
If I give it my best, *most* children will learn when given enough help.	Disagree	Difficult	This is an item with which we expect most teachers to agree, but "agree" is the incorrect answer. While they are committed to helping all children, they are satisfied if the majority succeed and do not feel they should be blamed for a failure or two. The "true believers"—teachers who are extremely committed to the concept of all children actually learning (not just able to learn)—will disagree because of the words "most" and "will," which make room for an occasional failure.

Table 6.1.   Sample Dichotomous Scoring Key and Explanation

Rating Scale Rubrics

As in the task-based system we have proposed for measuring competence, we recommend a 3-point scale such as the following:

- Target or exemplary
- Acceptable or satisfactory
- Unacceptable or needs improvement

Three levels of proficiency tend to provide for a middle ground that many raters want to use. The limit of three levels also helps to provide for rater consistency when judgments across four or more categories are difficult to make. Even with just 3 rating points, it is often difficult to distinguish between the higher two points. An excellent statistical example of determining the number of rating scale categories can be found in Chapter 8 of *Making Measures,* by Wright and Stone (2004).

Because values can be more difficult to recognize than skills and, in fact, are often confounded with skills, it is useful to define both the general rating points as well as their application for each instrument and each item. In Table 6.2, we provide our example of a rubric for the 3 general rating points.

In the rubric in Table 6.2, the middle category is the one that is the most unusual. In skill-based assessments, we would rarely allow a "probably" decision to result in an "acceptable" rating. Here, though, the process is much more complex, and the stakes lower. It is very hard to know what is really in a person's heart, so we err on the side of leniency. If we include multiple measures of increasing levels of inference in the overall system, most real problems will surface somewhere—probably in the results from observations or talking with children.

Table 6.2. Example of Generic Rubric for All Ratings in All Scaled Dispositions Instruments

Target	Acceptable	Unacceptable
Target responses allow the rater to infer that the candidate tends to act in ways that indicate a belief in the Principle being measured. There is clarity, enthusiasm, and/or commitment in the responses. The candidate (or the students) convinces you that he or she really means what is written or said, often with words like "anxious," "excited," "really," or "always." Questionnaire responses show effort and detail; focus group results show consistency and confirmation from one member to the next. This candidate is a go-getter, and it shows in what he or she says or what students say. The rater finishes reading this answer with a resounding "Yes!" If the rater were hiring a teacher, this candidate would be actively recruited.	*Acceptable* responses leave the rater relatively confident that the candidate acts in ways that show a belief in the Principle being measured, but the rater is less convinced and confident about it than in a target response. Something is missing, but it is not serious enough to say the answer is unacceptable. There is nothing obviously wrong about the beliefs in the answer, although the skills may be off-base. In such cases, values are not interfering with the skills; training or experience is. Or the rater may be less convinced because of what was not said, rather than what was said. In this case, the candidate or the focus group members may just be having trouble thinking of examples or understanding the questions. Another possibility is that the candidate (or the students) is just saying what they think should be said, but this concern is not serious enough to state that the tendency is just not there, or worse, the opposite tendency is there. The rater finishes reading this answer with a "probably" conclusion. If the rater were hiring and all other assessments of the interviewee were positive, the rater would extend an offer.	*Unacceptable* responses are used when the rater infers that this candidate is not likely to act in ways supportive of the Principle being measured. The rater is convinced that this candidate does not have his or her heart in the attitude or value being measured. In the questionnaire, answers are very vague, having little relation to the question, talk about what somebody else did, or express beliefs contrary to the Principle (e.g., I do not like working with colleagues, or I do not give rewards, or I am the boss in the classroom). This candidate does not even know what the "correct" or "socially responsible" answer is, so he or she cannot fake it. Focus group members provide clear, consistent, and convincing evidence that the candidate's actions are contrary to the Principle. The rater finishes this response with a resounding "No." Further analysis of this candidate's beliefs, particularly with regard to this Principle, is in order. If the rater were hiring and there were other indications of a potential problem, skill based or dispositional, this candidate's application would be low on the list.

As noted above, it is also important to provide detailed specific rubrics for each item to be rated, because of the high level of inference required in these instruments. Anchor examples help to support the rubric and bring consistency to the process. Figure 6.1 provides an example of this process, taken from the rubric for the first Teacher Questionnaire item. (Multiple examples of target, acceptable, and unacceptable responses are provided in the actual rubric, but only one example of each is provided in this book.)

— Anchor Examples —

These are model responses selected as examples of each level in the scoring process. They are used to develop rubrics, train raters, and serve as reminders during the scoring process.

Guiding Question: "What does a response at the _____ level look like?"

Figure 6.1. Example of Specific Rubric and Anchor Examples for a Specific Question

---

Question #1: How have you kept abreast of current developments in your field? For example, did you attend any workshops, subscribe to any journals, read or buy a new book? If so, describe in one to two sentences something you learned and the source.

> **INTASC Principle:** 1.1—The teacher realizes that subject matter knowledge is not a fixed body of facts, but is complex and ever evolving. S/he seeks to keep abreast of new ideas and understandings in the field.

Example of Specific Rubric for Question #1

Target	Acceptable	Unacceptable
The candidate shows evidence of being engaged, disciplined, and committed to learning on his or her own about the field. He or she has identified one or more specific sources of learning beyond the campus classroom experience (required workshops, readings, etc.). The discussion of learning is specific enough to indicate that the candidate has, in fact, assimilated the information and made use of it. The candidate may indicate a future course or expectation of continued growth. The candidate expresses respect and/or responsibility for keeping abreast of new ideas and understandings in the field.	The candidate is probably engaged, disciplined, and committed to learning on his or her own about the field. The candidate has generally identified one or more sources of extracurricular workshops or readings and mentions briefly something learned in very general terms (e.g., "I learned a lot about teaching or new instructional strategies or about science"). The candidate might list items purchased or provide a list of intended subscriptions, memberships, or purchases, but he or she does not explicitly state an intention to follow through and read or attend. The fact that something is listed allows the assessor to infer intent (and source) to follow through unless the response concludes with something negative (e.g., "I just don't have time to read/attend"). If the candidate does not list what was learned, more than one extracurricular source of content knowledge needs to be identified.	The candidate has provided no evidence of being engaged, disciplined, and committed to learning on his or her own about the field through typical professional development activities. This may occur in one of two ways: (1) The candidate does not identify any learning opportunities beyond the program requirements. Any workshops or readings identified are part of the curriculum and, therefore, not extracurricular. This candidate only meets requirements and is not likely to go beyond them in the K–12 classroom either/or (2) the candidate states specifically that he or she does not need to engage in continued learning and will learn when asked to or forced to by staff development or recertification.

Question #1: How have you kept abreast of current developments in your field? For example, did you attend any workshops, subscribe to any journals, read or buy a new book? If so, describe in one to two sentences something you learned and the source.

> **INTASC Principle:** 1.1—The teacher realizes that subject matter knowledge is not a fixed body of facts, but is complex and ever evolving. S/he seeks to keep abreast of new ideas and understandings in the field.

Anchor Examples for Question #1

Target:

I feel like in general I try to stay on top of current developments in education. I am constantly discussing and reviewing articles and watching CNN for the latest news on different legislations. During the 50th anniversary

Figure 6.1. (Continued)

---

of *Brown vs. Board of Education,* there was a great special about the "resegregation" of schools. **On a more practical classroom application level, I regularly attend staff development meetings.** This spring, I finished participating in the "Framework for Understanding Poverty" seminars. Throughout the year, I have read professional books, including Miller's *Reading With Meaning.* I also attended the IRA reading conference and brought back many new ideas for integrating arts and music into the classroom, **which I used immediately with great success.**

Acceptable:

I have had the opportunity to attend several workshops. **I attended a session on phonemic awareness that I feel will be very beneficial for me next year**. I also receive monthly publications through Kappa Delta Pi.

Unacceptable:

Unfortunately, I have not kept up with any of the current development in my field of education. I have been unable to attend any workshops, but I do plan eventually to subscribe to journals and read and buy new books. I have not had much personal time. I have been given numerous magazines and books that I could use for my own good and also bring into the classroom for different reasons and **entertainment value for the students.**

Worksheet #4.2 provides a workspace for you to develop your rubric design.

AERA, APA, and NCME *Standards* (1999)
and DAATS Step 4A

Standard 3.14:

The *criteria used for scoring test takers' performance on extended-response items should be documented.* This documentation is especially important for performance assessments, such as scorable portfolios and essays, where the criteria for scoring may not be obvious to the user.

Standard 3.22:

Procedures for scoring and, if relevant, *scoring criteria* should be presented by the test developer *in sufficient detail and clarity as to maximize the accuracy of scoring.* Instructions for using rating scales or for deriving scores obtained by coding, scaling, or classifying constructed responses should be clear. This is especially critical if tests can be scored locally.

Standard 5.9:

When test scoring involves human judgment, *scoring rubrics should specify criteria for scoring.* Adherence to established scoring criteria should be monitored and checked regularly. Monitoring procedures should be documented.

Discussion

It is clear from the above Standards that it is important to maximize the accuracy of decisions by creating clear and detailed scoring rubrics.

NOTE: Emphases added for clarity.

DAATS STEP 4B: DETERMINE HOW DATA WILL BE COMBINED AND USED

Need for Shared Data

If we are to overcome the tendency of assessors to store the data they collected for their own personal use, we need to have some form of tracking system that allows us to store and retrieve data for shared administrative and faculty use. This is far less complex for disposition assessments than it is for performance- or competency-based assessments.

Perhaps the most obvious example is the faculty member or administrator who sees a serious problem and has no means to know whether others have seen a similar problem. At the university level, this problem becomes particularly difficult for internship supervisors, who often do not know which dispositional aspects have been seen as positive or negative by their predecessors in the program. It can also be the case for the principal who just hired a teacher from another school. A system for sharing data is, therefore, vital in making a summative decision about a teacher's readiness to enter the profession or stay in it.

Data Storage

For competency- or performance-based assessment systems, there currently appear to be three trends for data storage, two of which are applicable to disposition assessment: teacher/student folders and electronic databases. The course grade option is not appropriate here, since most disposition assessment will be non-graded and may occur outside of traditional coursework. In fact, a combination of the folders and databases may be the best option for this type of assessment. We will briefly explain the strengths and weaknesses of both.

> **Data Aggregation**
>
> Data are compiled in ways to make different decisions for individual teachers and programs. Percents and frequencies are most common, but sophisticated analyses using item response theory are also possible.
>
> *Guiding Question: "How can I combine data to make a decision about a teacher or program or a unit?"*

Student or Teacher Folders

In this approach, the administration, possibly the student advising office or the human resources office, keeps a folder on each candidate or teacher, with records showing disposition assessment results. Since there are relatively few assessments, this is certainly a viable option. Data aggregation across teachers for program improvement or staff development purposes, however, is very difficult if everything remains in an individual folder. So, this could be a serious drawback unless there are very few teachers (20 or less) in the program, school, or district. In programs of this size, it does not pay to set up an electronic system.

We recommend that the folder include the following information for each instrument in the dispositions assessment system:

- Instrument name
- Date administered or created
- Score or results
- Counseling (if any)
  - Personnel
  - Date
  - Action plan

- Follow-up, if any
- Comments
- Signatures

Electronic Data Management System

The electronic storage system has become pretty much mandatory in NCATE-accredited universities, and it is certainly advisable in large districts as well. It is the best way to aggregate data for decision-making purposes, which are described next. Once there are more than 20 teachers in a system, it becomes very time-consuming to aggregate data by hand. There are many options available for how an electronic database can be set up, and that is beyond the scope of this book. In dispositions assessment, we are not recommending a common rubric format across tasks, as we do in the competency assessment process. All that is really needed here is a way of tracking scores of teachers on each scored instrument. A database or spreadsheet software package may be best suited for this.

? —— Management or Tracking System ——

The management or tracking system is the process used to keep track of scores in the system so that reports can be generated for decision making. It may be kept by hand or on a computer.

Guiding Question: "What procedures and materials do I need to have in place to store and retrieve data?"

?

Data Aggregation

Before we begin to aggregate data, it is important to develop a reporting procedure for the results of a single teacher on a single instrument. These important data will then be entered into a computer for aggregating across teachers. Table 6.3 provides an example of how we can report data on a single person on a single instrument.

Table 6.3. Sample Score Report for an Individual Assessment for an Individual Teacher

Joannie's Feedback for Questionnaire

Criteria	*Target*	*Acceptable*	*Unacceptable*
Q1: Currency and enthusiasm in subject area (INTASC 1)	X		
Q2: Work with colleagues (INTASC 10)	X		
Q3: Learning environment and rewards (INTASC 5)		X	
Q4: Learning environment and cooperative learning (INTASC 5)			X
Etc.			

Interpretation: Joannie is enthusiastic about her discipline and works well with colleagues. She should receive some guidance on creating an effective learning environment and working better with children since her problems in those areas could have a negative impact on student learning.

Entering data into a database or statistical file is the next step in the process. Data may be hand entered or exported from another system, such as an e-portfolio package. It really helps to develop a numbering system for the instruments and items from the beginning, so this is possible later on. For example, instruments could be numbered D1, D2, D3, and so on, and items within them numbered 01, 02, 03, and so on. So, D204 would be the fourth item in Disposition Instrument #2. As the database is designed, consideration should be given to how the data will be exported and reported, remembering that a single row of data for an individual teacher is the best way to go. Typically, this would include demographics first, followed by each score on each criterion on each task in the same order. A data row might be hand entered or exported, as shown in Box 6.1.

Box 6.1. Example of Data Coding and Entry for Statistical Analysis

Variables:

SSN, gender, ethnicity, certification area, item scores (e.g., D101, D102, etc.)

Sample data:

999999999 1 1 03 333223333111333

Decoding:

999999999 is the SSN, 1 is female, 1 is Caucasian, 03 is Biology, and 333223333111333 are the scores.

Once data are entered into a database or spreadsheet, excellent information for decision making is available. As programmers or assessors set up reports, the general output format in Table 6.4 (for a 3-point scale) is useful for review of the results of a group. Note numbers or any descriptive words can be used instead of target, acceptable, and unacceptable, and you can also count the number and percent of agree/disagree or correct/incorrect responses on a dichotomous scale with one less column. Creating tables like Table 6.4 will provide the information needed for rudimentary decision making about programs, and it will satisfy accreditation requirements. At a minimal analysis level, it can be helpful to count the number of ratings at each proficiency level to get an overall picture of the dispositional position of the teachers. Using this general format of numbers and percents, here are some examples of the type of reports that can be generated and the table numbers in which we present examples and data interpretations:

1. Results for an individual teacher for all instruments (Table 6.5)

2. Results for all teachers for all instruments (Table 6.6)

3. Results for an individual teacher candidate for all standards (Table 6.7)

4. Results for a group of teachers on an individual assessment (Table 6.8)

Many of the e-portfolio software packages currently on the market will prepare reports similar to the one in Table 6.4 and calculate means and standard deviations on the scores. This is useful for a first level of analysis and may be where many colleges and districts want to stop. These will show trends and patterns across criteria and programs, although users need to be aware of the statistical problems

Table 6.4. General Format for Reporting the Results of a Group

Criteria	Target		Acceptable		Unacceptable	
	#	%	#	%	#	%
D201*						
D202*						
D203*						
D204*						
Etc.						

NOTE: *Keywords or the actual items could be used instead of the code numbers.

Table 6.5. Example #1: Results for an Individual Teacher for All Instruments

John's Results on All Instruments

$N = 50$

Criteria	Target or Correct		Acceptable		Unacceptable or Incorrect	
	#	%	#	%	#	%
Belief Scale	40	80	n/a	n/a	10	20
Questionnaire	4	50	4	50	0	0
Focus Group	3	30	7	70	0	0
Observation	15	75	5	25	0	0
Disposition Event Report					none	

Interpretation: John has the dispositions needed to teach, since there are no unacceptable ratings or event reports. The number of incorrect responses on the belief scale is acceptable, although they should be examined to look for standards-based trends between the incorrect answers and the acceptable ratings on the other instruments. Most ratings are in the target range, although there are a relatively high number of acceptable ratings. The balance of "target" to "acceptable" between children's perceptions of him and the observation is reversed, indicating a need for further review of the data and possible counseling.

Table 6.6. Example #2: Results for All Teachers for All Instruments

Pinota County's School District

$N = 1,000$

Criteria	Target or Correct		Acceptable		Unacceptable or Incorrect	
	#	%	#	%	#	%
Belief Scale	650	65	n/a	n/a	350	35
Questionnaire	700	70	250	25	50	5
Focus Group	600	60	350	35	50	5
Observation	850	85	150	15	0	0
Disposition Event Report					5	

Interpretation: Overall, the teachers in the district have the dispositions needed to teach, and this is supported strongly by the data. Results from all instruments are strong. The number of incorrect responses on the belief scale is as expected, although, as usual, they should be examined to look for standards-based trends between the incorrect answers and the acceptable and unacceptable ratings on the other instruments. The vast majority of ratings are in the target range; other ratings should be examined for possible staff development implications. Observations yield significantly higher results than other methods—particularly the focus groups. A work group should be formed to determine the reason for this discrepancy. Follow-up on the five event reports should be verified.

Table 6.7. Example #3: Results for an Individual Teacher Candidate for All Standards

John's Results on All Instruments

Criteria	Demonstrated		Partially Demonstrated		Not Demonstrated	
	#	%	#	%	#	%
INTASC 1	3	100	0	0	0	0
INTASC 2	2	50	2	50	0	0
INTASC 3	4	100	0	0	0	0
INTASC 4	3	67	1	33	0	0
Etc.						

Interpretation: John is a good teacher and has demonstrated the dispositions necessary for effective teaching. He is committed to growth in the discipline and believes in working with diverse groups of children. His most immediate need for discussion or staff development services (or for assistance during internship) is in the area of learning and development, with a secondary need in the importance of teaching critical thinking and problem solving.

Table 6.8. Example #4: Results for a Group of Teachers on an Individual Assessment

Secondary Teachers' Results on the Belief Scale

$N = 50$

Criteria	Correct		Incorrect	
	#	%	#	%
I usually think about children's home life and environment so that I can tell if something isn't right.	10	20	40	80
If students complete all the lessons I teach and do all the assigned work, they will learn what they need to know.	25	50	25	50
I believe good teachers learn about the students' backgrounds and community so they can understand their students' motivations.	15	30	35	70
It is most important that I know and teach my subject well, regardless of the age and grade of students in my class.	20	40	30	60
Students need to learn to think, and that is a goal that I have that is built into all my lessons.	40	80	10	20

Interpretation: Secondary teachers in this program are more committed to teaching critical thinking than to developmental and personal needs of children. Data on elementary teachers (not shown) indicate that this is not a problem for those teachers.

Recommendation: Mentoring or other strategies to improve secondary teachers' relationships with families should be considered, along with more work on human development.

associated with calculating means and standard deviations from ordinal-level data. Programming these kinds of analyses can also be handled relatively easily at a local level through standard spreadsheet software packages such as Microsoft Excel.

We are comfortable with just reporting frequencies and percents unless you want to go to a more sophisticated level of analysis that is useful for other purposes, such as research-based decision making and improvement. In Step 5 of the DAATS model, we will discuss the judgmental and empirical analyses necessary for ensuring credibility (validity, reliability, and fairness) of decisions, but here we note in passing a statistical technique that helps make data for the individual teacher more meaningful and useful while providing the credibility data for the groups. We are talking about an item analysis technique called item response theory (IRT), which can radically improve the utility of the data for decision making (Baker & Kim, 2004). In our case, we have chosen a particular method of IRT called the "Rasch model" (Smith & Smith, 2004). Your assessment person may chose a different method, as in other aspects of the DAATS model. We prefer this method because our experience with it has demonstrated effective results with a minimal level of complexity. See Chapter 8 for details on this procedure.

> **HINT!**
>
> **KISS—Keep it statistically simple!!!**

In this chapter, we leave you with a teaser on Rasch as we have used it, to give you a sense of the power of the Rasch model for individual diagnostics. We tell you two stories of teacher candidates Antoinette and Ruby, both of whom needed a little counseling to become great teachers. IRT helped us focus on their problems and get us where we wanted to go with them.

Antoinette was 1 of about 300 teacher candidates in the first pilot study of our belief scale. She was ranked 13th in the group, with a percent score of 88%, because she answered almost all questions correctly. There were a few items that the computer said she answered incorrectly unexpectedly, and we saw a pattern in them. Box 6.2 shows the items Antoinette should have gotten right, based on the model's probabilistic prediction.

Box 6.2. What Antoinette Should NOT Have Missed!

1. I usually think about children's home life and environment so that I can tell if something isn't right. (She answered "Disagree")

27. If we could give every student a plan and teacher committed to him or her personally, they would achieve more than many students do today. (She answered "Disagree")

37. I customize all my lessons for the type of student and community so that students can identify with the topic. (She answered "Disagree")

41. Students who can't think are basically dumb, so I don't think giving kids time to "brainstorm" is anything except a waste of time. (She answered "Agree")

Antoinette needed some help with the utility of thinking about children's home life, individualizing instruction, and teaching critical thinking. If we had looked only at her 88% score, we might never have noticed this pattern.

Like Antoinette, Ruby had a score that did not make sense mathematically. In Box 6.3, we tell the story of Ruby.

Box 6.3. The Story of Ruby

Ruby had a good score on our belief scale—about 60 at a time when our range was between 40 and 73.

In Ruby's case, we saw a problem in something called a "fit" statistic, produced in the Rasch model at the person and item level. This statistic tells us whether or not the score is reliable for an individual person, not just the whole group of people taking the "test." As it turned out, Ruby was answering easy items incorrectly and hard items correctly. It was all backwards. If it had not been for this statistic, we would not have noticed Ruby's score as unusual. So, we talked to Ruby.

Ruby's father and her husband had told her for many years that she was essentially worthless, stupid, and not capable of being a teacher. She was filled with anxiety and low self-esteem, and that was reflected in her score. We encouraged her and helped her to start to let go of her past, sharing our confidence in her as a future teacher. We were the first to ever tell her she was good. A shy person, she had never shared her fears with any other faculty. And no one noticed.

We like to think we saved a teacher because we had some very powerful data.

DAATS STEP 4C: DEVELOP IMPLEMENTATION PROCEDURES AND MATERIALS

As in any instructional or assessment system, it is important to determine how to use the data and then to develop information materials for candidates and faculty explaining the instruments and their use. We see dispositional data very differently from competency data. In most assessment systems, either traditional or alternative preparation programs, a certification-based decision is required that ensures competency. With the difficulties inherent in affective measurement, it is less likely that users will be amenable to denying certification, except in extreme cases. It is important, however, to have credible data on all teachers in order to support those decisions, especially when the teachers with poor dispositions have high scores on performance-based tasks and GPAs. The validity, reliability, and fairness data gathered as part of Step 5 of the DAATS model should help to make such decisions legally defensible when they are necessary.

Preponderance of the Evidence Versus Cut Scores

Institutions and districts should determine how results will be combined to make the decisions predicted in DAATS Step 1 (use). Because dispositions pose so many measurement issues, a word of caution is appropriate at this point. Typically, a single bad result should not generate terminating a candidate or a teacher from a program or school—unless, of course, it is inexcusable or illegal. An obvious example is a teacher having sex with a student or toting a gun to school. They need to be extreme!

In using these kinds of measures, faculty and administrators are best advised to look at the preponderance of the evidence. If there are several event reports, a low score on the Thurstone scale, problems in the observation of performance, or bizarre answers on the questionnaire, then it is probably time to suggest the teacher change majors or jobs. A single questionable result, however, can be very useful in redirecting the candidate and helping him or her change a negative attitude.

Scores can be combined on all instruments (with the exception of the disposition event report) using IRT, as noted above, or one can look at individual scores at the criterion level or instrument level to find areas for improvement. The decision will be based on your preferences for continued study of the results and your overall propensity for research.

The data management and aggregation system should be designed to support these decisions, providing clear evidence that those who are certified have different scores than those who are not. In ability-based decisions, cut scores are appropriate, but because of the nature of affective assessment, we do not recommend the use of cut scores here on these instruments. There is no hard-and-fast rule about how to make the yes/no decision, but we provide an example in Table 6.9 for John, where we rework our previous example #3 in Table 6.5. His results are changed for the worse, and he should not be a teacher.

Table 6.9. Example #3: Reworked Results for an Individual Teacher for All Instruments

John's Results on All Instruments

Criteria	Target or Correct #	Target or Correct %	Acceptable #	Acceptable %	Unacceptable or Incorrect #	Unacceptable or Incorrect %
Belief Scale	25	50	n/a	n/a	25	50
Questionnaire	0	0	5	50	5	50
Focus Group	0	0	3	30	7	70
Observation	10	50	5	25	5	25
Disposition Event Report					5	

Interpretation: John does not have the dispositions needed to teach, since there are multiple "unacceptable" scores and more incorrect responses on the belief scale than the school average. The mean raw score for the school is 40, as opposed to John's score of 25. The discussions by children in the focus group are disturbing, and the results have been recorded and shared with him. Because of the low ratings on the questionnaire, results were confirmed by two other trained raters. A second observation was conducted, with the results also confirmed. The disposition event reports are excessive; most teachers have none; no teachers in the school have more than two. John's results are in the bottom 2% of the school. The following major problems have been documented: _____.

Units may be able to establish a percent that works. In the example we provided, we set a cut point of the bottom 5% of the population. The validity and reliability data collected as part of DAATS Step 5 should support that decision. If challenged, one would argue that he did much worse than his colleagues in a standards-based process, in an era of accountability, on instruments that are valid, reliable, and fair.

Advising and Due Process

Once a decision is made about how the data will be used for making difficult decisions and for providing support to teachers, the institution, school, or district needs to create advising/counseling structures and due process procedures for teachers exhibiting dispositional problems. Written explanations and procedures need to be in place stating the unit's policies and procedures and the opportunities teachers have to appeal any adverse decisions or reports entered into their files. Sample statements for universities and school districts are shown in Boxes 6.4 and 6.5.

Box 6.4.   Sample University Advising and Due Process Policy

_____ University requires that all teacher candidates demonstrate the dispositions required of effective teachers in order to maximize the opportunities for all children to learn. University faculty will monitor and assess the dispositions of teacher candidates through a variety of assessment methods, which are provided to students during orientation. Faculty are required to advise candidates of any identified deficiencies in dispositions and to provide counseling and opportunities to remediate. When ____ or more pieces of evidence of dispositional deficits are identified, a faculty committee is convened to determine whether the teacher candidate will be allowed to graduate from an approved teacher certification program leading to licensure in the state of _____. Teacher candidates in the bottom 5% of the unit may be dismissed. In rare instances, a violation of law or the code of ethical conduct in the State of _____ can lead to an immediate decision to deny graduation.

Approved: _____   _____

University General Counsel   Date

Box 6.5.   Sample School Board Counseling and Due Process Policy

_____ County Schools requires that all teachers demonstrate the dispositions required of effective teachers in order to maximize the opportunities for all children to learn. District administrators monitor and assess the dispositions of teachers through a variety of assessment methods, which are provided to teachers during their initial employment orientation. Supervisors are required to advise teachers of any identified deficiencies in dispositions and to provide counseling and opportunities to remediate. When ____ or more pieces of evidence of dispositional deficits are identified, a district personnel committee is convened to determine whether the teacher will be terminated or nonrenewed. Teachers in the bottom 5% of the district may be dismissed. In rare instances, a violation of law or the code of ethical conduct in the State of _____ can lead to an immediate dismissal.

Approved: _____   _____

University General Counsel   Date

Teachers need to know what is expected of them. This should be first discussed at the time of admission or hire, with feedback provided regularly. Advisors or human resource personnel should provide updates to teachers on their progress during the appropriate phases of program completion or career development. Any disposition event reports created should be discussed with the teacher within two or three working days of the incident, with all efforts to remediate recorded and filed. A disposition event report should contain the following information (also see Worksheet #4.5):

- Name of teacher or candidate
- Date of the incident
- Description of the incident
- Author of report

- Date of counseling session
- Summary of counseling session
- Action plan, including a schedule for second meeting, if any
- Results noted or follow-up required

All policies and procedures should be in writing and made available to the teachers when they begin their programs or jobs. Included in these materials should be a statement of their rights and responsibilities, appeals processes, and other issues related to due process. Universities and districts should also consider having the teachers sign a form, approved by legal counsel, which explains the institution's or district's expectations with regard to program completion and removal from the program.

Scoring Procedures

Faculty and administrators often need guidance in how to score analytic instruments. It can help to outline a set of steps for them, such as the instructions in Box 6.6.

Box 6.6. Sample Instructions to Raters

Before rating the questionnaires, read through the scoring rubric in its entirety, including both general descriptions of the scale and then the individual rubrics for each question. Analyze the anchor example to get an overall sense of how the scoring process is intended to work and how we differentiate between points on the scale. Then begin scoring. It helps to follow this sequence:

1. Work on one question at a time for all candidates. It could be any question from the set.

2. Start by reading the question and the INTASC Principle(s) being measured.

3. Read the scoring guidelines and examples for that item one more time.

4. Score each candidate.

5. Go back and rescore candidates if you think your scoring shifted during the process.

6. Go to the next question and repeat Steps 1 through 5.

7. Remember that some questions may be harder than others. It is okay for some questions to have high ratings and some to have low ratings on any individual questionnaire.

It can also help to lay out expectations to prevent ceiling effects. In our work, we have found that faculty members tend to be humanistic; they always want to say that the rating is target—even if it is not. It can be helpful to demonstrate for raters that some questions may be more difficult than others. For example, a question about taking initiatives to keep current in the field is likely to have less "target" ratings than one that deals with positive

Maintenance System

The maintenance system is the set of procedures and plans used to keep the system going and to make updates and changes as needed.

Guiding Question: "How will I know what needs to be changed, when, and by whom?"

reinforcements in the classroom, since faculty tend to teach reinforcement strategies and teacher candidates are more prone to use and value them than to seek out new knowledge on their own. We have suggested a strategy for indicating the level of difficulty for scaled items; a similar strategy could be used for open-ended responses, such as the questionnaire.

Implementation

Once the system is determined and moving along in the implementation stage, a plan to manage it needs to be developed. Included in this plan should be an assignment of responsibilities and a timeline, as well as a formal maintenance plan. The following are some elements of the plan to be developed (Worksheet #4.6 provides a format):

- *Oversight:* Responsibilities for oversight of the instruments should be delegated to a small group of faculty or district administrators, with representation from certification areas, generalists (e.g., foundations faculty or human resource personnel), and at least one measurement specialist or educational psychologist. This committee should be charged with ensuring that the assessments are working as intended and revised as needed. Revisions should not be made by individual faculty or administrative personnel without some level of central coordination to ensure that the intent of the assessments, as it relates to validity and reliability issues, is not hurt.

- *Training:* All individuals who are responsible for assessing need to understand the assessments and the scoring rubrics. Discussions on how to use each score point, with examples provided at each level, need to be provided and practiced to improve reliability. These sessions can be short, but they must be conducted. Decisions need to be made about who will assess: mentor teachers, university supervisors, faculty, building administrators, district personnel, or some combination of these. Training should be provided to all assessors, with rubrics explained and samples provided. Much of this will need to be developed over time, as assessors and assessment designers identify examples of acceptable and unacceptable responses.

- *Maintenance:* It is just so easy to start a system and hope it will run by itself and need no changes. Formal review times need to be built into the system so that problems can be discussed and fixed. This could be just once a year, but it needs to be organized and accomplished.

- *Programmatic Improvement:* Since much of the need for performance-based certification is the result of the public outcry for increased accountability, it is important to document improvements as they are made. This will serve as a public statement that the institution or district is committed to the same level of continuous improvement that it expects its teachers to value. Running records of improvement are a useful strategy and can be built into the management system database, linked to individual tasks. Other records can be kept of improvements to program maintenance issues.

AERA, APA, NCME and *Standards* (1999)
and DAATS Step 4D

Standard 3.23:

The *process for selecting, training, and qualifying scorers should be documented by the test developer.* The training materials, such as the scoring rubrics and examples of test takers' responses that illustrate the levels on the score scale, and the procedures for training scorers should result in a degree of agreement among scorers that allows for the scores to be interpreted as originally intended by the test developer. Scorer reliability and potential drift over time in raters' scoring standards should be evaluated and reported by the person(s) responsible for conducting the training session.

Standard 5.10:

When test score information is released to students, parents, legal representatives, teachers, clients, or the media, those responsible for testing programs should provide appropriate interpretations. *The interpretations should describe in simple language what the test covers, what scores mean, the precision of the scores, common misinterpretations of test scores, and how scores will be used.*

Standard 5.16:

Organizations that maintain test scores on individuals in data files or in an individual's records should develop a *clear set of policy guidelines on the duration of retention of an individual's records, and on the availability, and use over time, of such data.*

Standard 8.2:

Where appropriate, test takers should be *provided, in advance, as much information about the test, the testing process, the intended use, test scoring criteria, testing policy, and confidentiality protection* as is consistent with obtaining valid responses.

Standard 8.6:

Test data maintained in data files should be adequately protected from improper disclosure. Use of facsimile transmission, computer networks, data banks, and other electronic data processing or transmittal systems should be restricted to situations in which *confidentiality can be reasonably assured.*

Standard 8.9:

When test scores are used to make decisions about a test taker or to make recommendations to at test taker or a third party, the *test taker or the legal representative is entitled to obtain a copy of any report of test scores or test interpretation,* unless that right has been waived or is prohibited by law or court order.

(Continued)

(Continued)

Standard 8.13:

In educational testing programs and in licensing and certification applications, test takers are entitled to *fair consideration and reasonable process, as appropriate to the particular circumstances, in resolving disputes* about testing. Test takers are entitled to be informed of any available means of recourse.

Standard 14.16:

Rules and procedures used to combine scores on multiple assessments to determine the overall outcome of a credentialing test should be *reported to test takers, preferably before the test is administered.*

Discussion

Each of the above standards has been embedded in this step to ensure candidates or teachers have every chance to succeed and institutions and districts are reasonably well protected in the event of legal challenges. We have not provided specific examples of each requirement in these *Standards* in our discussion. In this step of the model, we suggest that our readers look closely at the above *Standards* and use them as a planning tool to check their existing policies, such as giving proper notice to teachers about the use of scores, records retention, confidentiality, and other common policies used in schools.

NOTE: Emphases added for clarity.

▽ WRAP-UP

In this chapter, we have reviewed implementation and maintenance procedures for disposition assessments; however, the advice provided in this chapter fits most assessment systems for the most part. We looked at the development of scoring rubrics and a process for aggregating data so that decisions can be made at the individual and programmatic levels. We recognized that data kept by an individual faculty member or administrator are not useful for the unit as a whole. As professionals, for the good of the children, we need to share what we know. That can be a painful process that involves strong feelings about accountability, individual rights, and academic freedom, but, in the end, the needs of the child must prevail.

To protect the individual teacher or teacher candidate, we looked at procedures for informing and advising, due process, and scoring procedures. Although we did not speak directly about the rationale for the scoring procedures, it was based on improving the reliability, and hence the validity, of the decisions we will make. That provides a transition for us to the next chapter on measurement properties of validity, reliability, and absence of bias.

Story Starters

Starter #1:

Mrs. Kidsaretutuff has completed every workshop you offered, and the trainers filed their checksheets with you. They did not offer anything related to collegiality per se, but teachers are complaining that she is aloof and won't plan with them or discuss remediation needs of individual children. You had a workshop in which lessons were planned and included collaborative work and feedback, and the trainer says she did okay on that one—about average for the group. Now what do you do?

Starter #2:

Mr. Wecandoitall, chief sales rep for Portfolios United (PU) Corporation, tells you their software does everything you need to make standards-based decisions about teacher dispositions. You ask him whether you can retrieve separate decisions for each standard assessed in a single task. He tells you that you don't need to do that for NCATE or your state; the PU system is better because it will give you statistics.

You say . . .

DAATS STEP 4—WORKSHEET #4.1

Explanation of Dichotomous Scoring Decisions

Explanation:

For each item on the "agree/disagree" scale, note the correct response, the level of difficulty, and an explanation of why the response is "agree" or "disagree."

Item	Correct Response	Difficulty Level	Explanation of Response
	A D	E M D	
	A D	E M D	
	A D	E M D	
	A D	E M D	
	A D	E M D	
	A D	E M D	
	A D	E M D	
	A D	E M D	
	A D	E M D	

*A = Agree; D = Disagree

**E = Easy; M = Moderately Difficult; D = Difficult

NOTE: This form could be modified for questionnaires by eliminating the second column.

DAATS STEP 4—WORKSHEET #4.2

Rubric Design

Explanation:

Describe in general terms the points on your scale. Make sure the differences between points are about equal and clearly articulated. You can use more than 3 points on the scale, or you can describe "acceptable" and "unacceptable" (just 2 points). Then, start writing specific rubrics, with examples for each scored item. Check for consistency between "General" and "Specific."

General Description of Points on the Scale:

High (_____)	Middle (_____)	Low (_____)

Specific Rubrics and Anchor Examples for Each Item:

High (_____)	Middle (_____)	Low (_____)
Rubric:	Rubric:	Rubric:
Example with key words boldfaced:	Example with key words boldfaced:	Example with key words boldfaced:

DAATS WORKSHEETS

DAATS STEP 4—WORKSHEET #4.3

Sample Format for Candidate/Teacher Tracking Form

Explanation:

Decide what information you need to track for each instrument in your process.

Teacher's Name: _____

Teacher's ID: _____

Instrument #1

Instrument Name: _____

Date Administered: _____

Score/Results: _____

Counseling (if any): _____

_____

Personnel: _____

Date: _____

Action Plan: _____

_____

Follow-up, if any: _____

_____

Comments: _____

_____

_____   _____
Teacher's signature and date   Counselor's signature and date

DAATS STEP 4—WORKSHEET #4.4

Format for Data Aggregation

Explanation:

Use this form as a template for as many instruments and reports as possible.

Criteria	Level 3 (high)		Level 2 (medium)		Level 1 (low)	
	#	%	#	%	#	%

DAATS WORKSHEETS

DAATS STEP 4—WORKSHEET #4.5

Sample Disposition Event Report

Explanation:

Review this form as a model for a disposition event report and change it based on your needs.

Name of teacher or candidate: _____

Date of the incident: _____

Description of the incident: _____

_____

_____

Author of report: _____

Date of counseling session: _____

Summary of counseling session: _____

_____

_____

Action plan, including a schedule for second meeting, if any: _____

_____

_____

Results noted or follow-up required: _____

_____

_____

Signatures required at time of creation and during any meetings involving this report.

_____	_____
Report author and date	Teacher/Candidate and date
_____	_____
Report author and date	Teacher/Candidate and date
_____	_____
Report author and date	Teacher/Candidate and date

DAATS STEP 4—WORKSHEET #4.6
Management Plan

Oversight

Person(s) Responsible	Committee Charge	Meeting Schedule	Revisions Procedures
Measurement Professional			

Training

Persons to Be Trained	Schedule	Plan and Materials

Maintenance

Date	Item to Be Reviewed	Personnel Responsible

Programmatic Improvement Log

Date	Problem to Be Addressed	Improvement Made

DAATS WORKSHEETS

Where We Have Been So Far

Throughout this book, beginning with DAATS Step 1, we have been applying the theories and standards that guide the process of gathering evidence of psychometric integrity or credibility. We have learned that the most important of these is the latest set of standards published in 1999 by a joint committee of the American Educational Research Association (AERA), the American Psychological Association (APA), and the National Council of Measurement in Education (NCME), called the *Standards for Educational and Psychological Testing*. They establish the requirements for determining psychometric integrity and are the foundation for this chapter and much of what we have done in the previous four steps of the DAATS model. So, the good news here is that we have been building a process, which has most of what we needed from the *Standards* already built in, and we have documented that by including selected AERA, APA, and NCME Standards at the end of each substep. This will be helpful to colleges and districts or states that want to demonstrate that their assessment system has been designed with psychometric integrity in mind. The procedures we have recommended and the psychometric standards we have applied are similar to, but a little less extensive than, those we used in our CAATS model for competencies.

Many, many years ago, one of us went on a class field trip to Washington, DC, from New Jersey. The teacher was plagued for five hours with teenagers asking how much farther it was. He answered consistently (that would be reliably), "We're almost exactly halfway there." Although the answer was not accurate (that would be validity), it is where we are now in this journey of standards-based disposition assessment. We are more than halfway there. Just one more step to go, and that step will require some fine-tuning or revisiting and a few more pieces of the puzzle, as we continue to apply the *Standards for Educational and Psychological Testing* to ensure the credibility of the data we produce and use for decisions about teacher dispositions.

7

DAATS Step 5

Credible Data

The block of granite which was an obstacle in the pathway of the weak, became a stepping-stone in the pathway of the strong.

—Thomas Carlyle

hile federal and state legislators and NCATE accreditation agents say that they require evidence of credibility, technically known as "psychometric integrity," this is an issue that college faculty, school administrators, and state department of education personnel say, like Scarlett O'Hara, they will "think about tomorrow." If they do acknowledge the need to ensure any aspect of psychometrics, it tends to be a study of rater agreement, with little or no attention to validity or fairness other than possibly some due process procedures (which are a different matter altogether!). That seems to be the case with competency-based assessment. With dispositions assessment, the situation is worse. Validity, reliability, and fairness rarely even enter the picture. Hence legal and other challenges are beginning to surface, and we will discuss a few of those in our concluding chapter.

> **DAATS Step 5: Ensure credibility and utility of data.**

In this chapter, we will think about what it takes to achieve more credible information about the validity, reliability, and fairness of disposition-based decisions so that we have data that are both credible and useful. Prior to delving into the details, we will provide some background information on what psychometric integrity is and why it is important. We will then move on to Step 5 of the DAATS model and its two substeps. As we progress through this chapter, readers should find that if they paid close attention to the processes outlined in DAATS Steps 1 through 4, they have already completed much of what they need to do for solid psychometrics, and we will carefully document those successes in Step 5.

In DAATS Step 5A, we will depart somewhat from our previous format of including the AERA, APA, and NCME Standards (1999) at the end of the substep. Here, we will propose a planning process within a planning process. We have been planning an assessment system and now move on to the plan for credibility of data that is embedded in the overall process in DAATS Step 5A. That plan will have eight elements, and we will align our AERA, APA, and NCME Standards with each of the eight elements.

There are two substeps of DAATS Step 5:

DAATS Step 5A: Create a plan to provide evidence of validity, reliability, fairness, and utility.

DAATS Step 5B: Implement the plan conscientiously.

Before Moving On . . .

1. Before reading this book, did you spend much time thinking about validity? How do you feel about it now? What about reliability? Which do you think is more important? Why?

2. Have you detected informally or formally any differences in decisions among protected populations? If so, what is causing this, and what have you done about it?

WHAT IS PSYCHOMETRIC INTEGRITY, AND WHY DO WE HAVE TO WORRY ABOUT IT?

When we make an important decision in any aspect of life, we want to have confidence that we are making the right decision. That is what psychometric integrity is really all about. "Psychometric" simply means we are trying to measure some function that involves thinking or feeling, and integrity means that we are doing it honestly.

Psychometric

Psychometric is a big word that refers to the measurement of aspects of people such as knowledge, skills, abilities, or personality.

Guiding Question: "What do the data tell me about validity, reliability, and fairness in this test?"

There are three cornerstones to psychometric integrity—validity, reliability, and fairness—with fairness being a more recent addition to the long-standing issues of validity and reliability. We also add to that the notion of utility. Why collect great data if they are not going to be useful for decision making? So, if our measurement process does not help us to identify the really good and the really bad, what good is our measurement process other than to allow us to pat ourselves on the back about the great job we did and hide our heads in the sand when the bad teachers are found out? Kids and parents can tell; and legislators, who are often parents, too, try to force the issue. That is precisely what is happening in the competency assessment world with those inter-rater reliability coefficients of 1.0, based on all raters saying all teachers are great.

If we think of validity as truthfulness (being accurate so that we can be honest about what we are measuring) and reliability as trustworthiness (doing it consistently), then the terms may be a little less intimidating. Fairness simply means that no one group is treated favorably or unfavorably because of the measurement process and that all people's rights are conscientiously observed. So, perhaps if we look at psychometric integrity as just plain doing what's right, we can better see that this is an ethical issue and moral imperative that we face as education professionals. If we do it wrong, someone gets hurt, and that someone could be the children in the schools or the teacher who wants to teach them. At a gut level, this is motherhood and apple pie.

Unfortunately, integrity often has a price. To do the right thing, we often have to make difficult decisions that take careful thought. Such is the case with psychometric integrity. There is substantial analytical work involved in ensuring that no one is hurt by design. Typically, when faced with a difficult decision, the analytic thinker gathers evidence to support the decision-making process, and this is precisely how we make decisions about the truthfulness and trustworthiness of data in the world of social science measurement.

> **Psychometric Integrity**
>
> Psychometric integrity, like other forms of integrity, is about doing what is right—in this case when we assess teachers. It is all about making sure people (children and teachers) don't get hurt by design.
>
> *Guiding Question: "Will I be able to sleep at night if I make these decisions?"*

> **Utility**
>
> "Utility of data" refers to usefulness. There's no point in collecting a bunch of stuff to fill a filing cabinet if you have no expectation of using it.
>
> *Guiding Question: "Will the data I collect give me useful information so I can have better teachers and programs?"*

By this time, it should come as no surprise that the DAATS model has a heavy focus on planning, and, as might be expected, we advocate for a plan to ensure credibility so that the process is systematically designed and implemented.

CAVEAT

In this DAATS step, we will provide some alternatives for those who become seriously interested in assessing dispositions and ensuring the integrity of their decisions. The suggestions here are a reduced version of what we suggested in the CAATS competency assessment process; however, depending on the stakes associated with your decisions, you may decide to reduce them even further. We have created for you the ultimate system; it is your choice how far to take it. It will, of course, depend on your beliefs about the importance of dispositions.

STEP 5A: CREATE A PLAN TO PROVIDE EVIDENCE OF VALIDITY, RELIABILITY, FAIRNESS, AND UTILITY

Elements of a Plan

It is *not* typically necessary to have a formal written psychometric plan unless this is a high-stakes process in a large-scale program (large school district or state), but we

Credibility

Believability.

Guiding Question: "Is there any evidence that this stuff is right?"

are providing some elements of the planning process that can help. As usual, we are using worksheets. We are also providing a set of examples to help illustrate the statistics we are proposing. Embedded in a couple of them are some opportunities to practice the techniques with a calculator or an online statistics link, because they are very simple to do and provide good evidence of the credibility of your assessments.

We also remind our readers at this point that much of what we have seen in the AERA, APA, and NCME *Standards* points to the need to keep records of how we put together and monitor our assessments. This is not unlike what NCATE requires in the accreditation context.

Based on our review of the AERA, APA, and NCME *Standards,* we recommend the inclusion of eight elements in the planning process for credibility and utility. Most of them are already complete if you have been following the DAATS model, although we use some fancier names here. We discuss each in some detail, providing examples from our previous work and referencing you back to what you have already done in the worksheets from previous steps. We note, where necessary, the work that remains to be completed. Here we present yet another blueprint, this time for psychometrics. Since most of the elements of this plan have already been developed, we will not repeat the APA, AERA, and NCME *Standards* until we get to new elements.

Box 7.1 lists the eight elements of the planning process for credibility and utility of cognitive (and dispositional) data (Lang & Wilkerson, 2006).

Box 7.1. Elements of a Psychometric Plan—A Plan for Credibility and Utility

1. Purpose and Use

2. Construct Measured

3. Interpretation and Reporting of Scores

4. Assessment Specifications and Content Map

5. Assessor/Rater Selection and Training Procedures

6. Analysis Methodology

7. External Review Personnel and Methodology

8. Evidence of Validity, Reliability, and Fairness

Element 1: Purpose and Use

Purpose drives every aspect of the design and implementation process. We spent much time in DAATS Step 1 talking about that. The AERA, APA, and NCME *Standards* make the decision about purpose easy in our context. As part of an assessment system that leads to a credentialing decision, the purpose is essentially predefined by the *Standards* as protection of the public. The *Standards* tell us the following: "Credentialing also serves to protect the profession by excluding persons who are deemed to be not qualified to do the work of the occupation" (p. 156). We repeat here, in Box 7.2, the purpose statement suggested in DAATS Step 1, since it meets the need for this part of the psychometric plan.

Box 7.2.   Sample Statement of Purpose #1

To protect the public from unqualified practitioners by determining whether the teachers assessed have demonstrated the essential dispositions, as defined in the standards of _____. These dispositions are necessary for safe and appropriate practice and certification in the State of _____.

We have identified some other potential purposes—diagnosis and remediation of individual teacher and program needs being among the most important. Additional statements of purpose would need to be written for those purposes. Strictly speaking, we would collect additional evidence of validity for each purpose, but this is not necessary in assessment systems of this nature. We also talked about use in DAATS Step 1, noting that assessment results could be used for both low-stakes (e.g., advising) and high-stakes (e.g., firing or not certifying) decisions. We adapt some of the uses we noted in DAATS Step 1 for this part of the psychometric plan with an example provided in Box 7.3.

Box 7.3.   Sample Statement of Use

Aggregated data are used to determine, in part, whether teachers are eligible to graduate and/or to receive the state certificate or license (or to continue employment in the district). Scores are also used for advising and remediation of individual teachers and locating potential program improvement areas.

At this point, you may want to review your work on Worksheet #1.2 for DAATS Step 1.

Element 2: Construct Measured

The AERA, APA, and NCME *Standards* help us define the construct in this assessment system. For competencies, it was simply stated as "teacher performance." Here, we state it formally and publicly as "teacher dispositions" in Box 7.4. The important thing about a construct is that it be unique or different and able to be operationally defined. As we look at gathering evidence of validity, one strategy we will consider is correlating teacher scores on performance-based tasks with disposition assessments. The relationship will probably be weak, since these are two different constructs, and that will serve as evidence of divergent validity. We illustrate that under Element 8 and in the examples at the end of this chapter.

Box 7.4.   Sample Statement of the Construct

Teacher Dispositions

Element 3: Interpretation and Reporting of Scores

Useless data need not be collected. Knowing how we will use the data has a significant influence on what data we collect, as well as when and how we collect them. The AERA, APA, and NCME *Standards* remind us on page 1 that the most important thing we do to help ensure that we are making valid decisions is to determine how we will interpret the scores or data we obtain. If the interpretation is wrong, we are in trouble. Examples of bad interpretations would be to say that (1) a teacher has the necessary dispositions when he or she actually may harm children (a false positive) or (2) a teacher is harmful when he or she actually will be just fine (a false negative). Part of what we need to do is to think about how to minimize these bad decisions and the direction in which we want to err when we do err. As humans, we certainly will do that.

Interpretation provides meaning to a score. It is how we differentiate between good and bad, in either a quantitative or qualitative scale, or how we make an important decision based on the data. It determines what we will call "acceptable" and "unacceptable." The interpretation in this system is of acceptability for beginning practice. In DAATS Step 4, we talked about developing scoring rubrics and data aggregation. These aspects of system implementation help us focus on how to interpret scores in valid and reliable ways that reduce error. The public interpretation statement is modeled in Box 7.5.

Box 7.5.   Sample Statement About Interpretation of Scores

Teachers are determined to have the dispositions necessary to teach if there is a distinct pattern of dispositional consistency with unit or district standards across measures and if there is no record of extreme inconsistency, even in one instance, deemed to be serious enough for removal from the program or position. Measures in the bottom 5% of scores for the unit are considered too risky to be allowed to enter (stay in) the profession.

In DAATS Step 4, we also talked about advising and due process procedures that provide the framework for reporting scores. These can be repeated in this element of the psychometric plan. Score reporting must ensure that scores are maintained, reported, and secured. We established procedures for managing these aspects in DAATS Step 4, and in Box 7.6, we provide a public statement for our psychometric plan.

Box 7.6.   Sample Statement on Score Reporting

Reports of scores will be given to teachers on an ongoing basis as instruments are completed. Reports and scores will be stored in a database that can be accessed by university or school system administrators, faculty or mentor teachers, and assessors. Security provisions restrict access to those personnel directly responsible for the evaluation and performance of an individual teacher.

So, once again, the news is positive. Review your work on Worksheets #4.1 and #4.4 in DAATS Step 4 for this element. Three down, five to go.

Element 4: Assessment Specifications and Content Map

Assessment specifications and content maps provide us with a blueprint or a plan for assessment design. The AERA, APA, and NCME *Standards* provide guidance on how these should be organized, including the content, format, and scoring procedures. Readers should feel comfortable with these specifications, since they summarize much of what was already developed in the earlier steps of the model. Here, they merely establish that there was a plan, which you can now incorporate in all of your reports!

If you decide to write this up as a formal plan, Worksheet #5.1 for this step is provided for that purpose, with a sample provided below. We believe this is an often-overlooked step. In fact, most assessment planners simply make lists of existing measures or arbitrarily decide that three to five assessments seem about enough. Boxes 7.7 through 7.9 provide the components typically needed in assessment specifications: content, format, and scoring procedures.

Box 7.7. Sample Assessment Specifications—Content

- Instruments are measures composed of items that can be demonstrated both judgmentally and empirically to measure associated INTASC Principles. In accordance with the AERA, APA, and NCME *Standards,* they will be developed on the basis of a job analysis and will be limited to those beliefs deemed to be critical for teacher performance and student success.

- The set of instruments will be organized around the 10 INTASC Principles. The assessment system will ensure that most indicators from the Principles are measured at least one time. Locally defined standards and other state and national standards identified by the assessment designers will be integrated into the instruments, as appropriate.

- Instruments will use a variety of formats, including scales, questionnaires/interviews, focus groups, observations, and thematic apperception tests, as appropriate to the disposition being measured.

- Instruments will also have a focus on impact on K–12 learning wherever possible.

- Competencies represent a different construct and are measured using a different process.

- A content map will be developed to ensure adequate construct representation for each Principle.

Box 7.8. Sample Assessment Specifications—Format

- Each instrument will be developed and formatted in accordance with the literature on that methodology.
- All instruments will be accompanied by directions to examinees and examiners, as appropriate.
- The scale will use three decision points: either "target," "acceptable," and "unacceptable" or "frequently," "sometimes," and "rarely." Rubrics and anchor examples will be developed. "Not observed" will be an option only for frequency ratings.

> **Box 7.9. Sample Assessment Specifications—Scoring Procedures (Criterion Referenced)**
>
> - Composite scores/Decision rule: The affirmative credentialing decision (graduation leading to certification) is made if there is a pattern of consistency with the standards. One extreme inconsistency of a serious nature may be cause for denial of graduation and the license.
> - College faculty or district personnel are the assessors. Assessors provide feedback on items that are rated as unacceptable.
> - Scores will be entered into the electronic database and shared with teachers.
> - Examples and training will be provided to support accurate decision making.

In the above specifications, the content was determined in DAATS Step 1, the formats in DAATS Step 2, the need for rubrics in DAATS Step 3, and all of the scoring procedures in DAATS Step 4. The *content map* is typically a chart or matrix that shows how items come together in two dimensions. The coverage check in DAATS Step 3A and Worksheet #3.10 can serve this purpose. Here, we just insert that work as a public statement about the process.

Element 5: Assessor/Rater Selection and Training Procedures

Procedures need to be established for assessor or rater selection and training, and we settled on these procedures in DAATS Step 4C. Training should be provided to all assessors with rubrics explained and samples provided. The selection and provision of sample results is one of the most useful things one can do to ensure reliability, as we will discuss in more detail under Element 8. Much of this will need to be developed over time as assessors and assessment designers identify examples of acceptable and unacceptable work. A sample public statement about assessors is provided in Box 7.10.

> **Box 7.10. Sample Statement of Assessor/Rater Selection and Training Procedures**
>
> Training sessions will be provided in conjunction with faculty meetings. Training will be four hours in duration and will include explanations of the rubrics, examples of acceptable and unacceptable responses, and practice activities. Assessment decisions will be sampled, with feedback to assessors provided. Scheduled reviews, updates, and monitoring of assessors will occur every three years or when necessary.

Element 6: Analysis Methodology

You may decide to limit your analysis to descriptive statistics. This is the place to state that. If you opt to do more sophisticated statistical analysis of the results, this section is useful to explain a preference for classical test theory (CTT) or item response theory (IRT). This is beyond the scope of this book. An explanation of the IRT model we use is provided in Chapter 8. Readers are referred to more detailed discussion in the CAATS book (Wilkerson & Lang, 2007).

Element 7: External Review Personnel and Methodology

It is important that assessment designers not work in isolation and receive feedback from external reviewers. In DAATS Step 3, we encouraged the use of stakeholders in reviewing materials, so you may now wish to review the work you did on Worksheet #3.11. A sample public statement about external review is provided in Box 7.11.

Box 7.11.   Sample Statement of Instrument Review Personnel and Methodology

Ongoing review by practitioner experts in the districts (stakeholders) will be conducted to ensure practicality and utility. Practitioners will be used as expert panels to ensure the criticality of items and the quality of rubrics.

Methodological and theoretical review will be conducted by measurement experts and through peer-reviewed outlets.

Element 8: Evidence of Validity, Reliability, and Fairness (VRF)

The above design elements and much of the work already done in the DAATS model help to prepare the assessment developer at the institutional or district or even state levels to provide evidence of validity, reliability, and fairness (VRF). In this element, we review our previous work ("Psychometric Evidence Collected Already") and include a chart that shows how a number of the worksheets completed as part of the DAATS process have started the process of collecting evidence of validity, reliability, and fairness. We continue with the next steps ("Next Steps in Collecting Evidence of Validity, Reliability, and Fairness—VRF"), asking and answering three basic VRF questions and providing four examples of what the studies might look like. We end with a look toward the future ("Future Studies"), where more evidence of validity and additional research is on the horizon. That section includes another five examples of what the studies might look like if you move to the highest level of analysis. Not everyone will want to go the highest level, but the option is out there for those who chose to do so.

Validity

Validity is the extent to which assessment measures are truthful about what they say they measure or the degree to which evidence and theory support the interpretations and use of a test or assessment process.

Guiding Question: "Does this test really measure what it says it measures? Does the assessment system provide adequate coverage of the standards?"

Reliability

Reliability is the degree to which test scores are consistent over repeated applications of the process and are, therefore, dependable or trustworthy.

Guiding Question: "If a student took the same test again under the same conditions (or a similar version of the test), would he or she obtain the same score?"

REMINDER

As you read through this section, remember that we are providing you with lots of possibilities on how to gather evidence of VRF and conduct future research studies. Few, if any, institutions or districts will do them all! This is a menu with recipes. You can also add your own "daily specials."

Fairness

Fairness ensures that rights are protected and that people are not penalized because they are members of a protected group, because they don't have adequate opportunities to learn and succeed, because the criteria and tasks have language or contexts that are offensive to them, or because their rights to due process were violated.

Guiding Question: "Do all teachers have an equal opportunity to complete the tasks successfully, regardless of gender, ethnicity, or handicapping condition, and is there an appeals process in place?"

As in all of our work, we will provide you with some sample reports to demonstrate what you can do with the data once they are collected. These will be found at the end of the first and third subsections, since we look at previously collected information first and then combine the newly collected evidence into a second example report.

Psychometric Evidence Collected Already

In this section, we will identify the work you have already undertaken that can be used in a report of evidence of psychometric integrity. It is a good idea to have a formal report in case your decisions are ever challenged, even if you did not write a formal psychometric plan for the previous seven elements. The report is also useful for accreditation and other accountability purposes. In your report, you might want to attach the worksheets as documentation, describing the process you used to complete them in a brief narrative. References to meetings and minutes are always helpful, and meeting minutes should be kept in backup files.

Some of the worksheets you have already completed are direct evidence of your efforts at validity, reliability, and fairness considerations. In Box 7.12, we provide a sample of an institutional report that shows how you can use the worksheets to document your initial VRF evidence.

Box 7.12.   Sample Institutional Report on the Initial Credibility Studies

During the developmental phase of our assessment system, we completed a large number of worksheets (see Appendix) that helped us design a credible process. In this report, we summarize some of the psychometric aspects to which we were attending throughout our design process. We will refer to worksheets by the steps in the DAATS model we used and the worksheet within those steps. For example, #4.3 would be DAATS Step 4, Worksheet #3.

Validity: After defining our construct as teacher dispositions, we agreed upon the purpose, uses, and content of our process to ensure construct validity (#1.2). We further fleshed out our conceptual framework, including the propositions concerning what we believe and value about assessing teacher dispositions (#1.2). To ensure content validity, we conducted a coverage check (#3.10). We validated these through external reviews by stakeholders (#3.11), focusing on criticality and authenticity of the items. We developed procedures for aggregating data so that future studies can be conducted of improvement (one of our purposes) as well as monitoring the validity of our decisions for each teacher (#4.4). We planned for the collection of continuing evidence in the management plan (#4.6).

Reliability: The development of consistent and carefully constructed proficiency level descriptions (#4.2) allows for rater consistency. Similarly, the coverage report of indicators (#3.10) establishes an anticipatory set for judges that should bring consistency to the process.

Fairness: We have focused on providing information to teachers on decisions in a timely way and throughout programs, using a tracking form to keep all necessary persons informed (#4.3).

In the chart in Table 7.1, we align the worksheets you have already created (and discussed in your IR) with our three cornerstones of psychometric credibility: validity, reliability, and fairness. Start thinking about the kinds of "mini-studies" you could do to keep the worksheets current. Do not underestimate the importance of the judgmental process. Most people don't even think about it and miss many opportunities to showcase the credibility of their decisions!

		Table 7.1. Alignment of DAATS Worksheets With Psychometrics—Summary of Initial Credibility Studies		
Step	*Worksheet*	*Validity*	*Reliability*	*Fairness*
1	#1.2: Purpose, Use, Content	Construct		Decisions based on purpose (and not on anything else!)
	#1.3: Propositions	Conceptual Framework		
2	#2.1: Organizing for Alignment	Construct—domain specification		Decisions made based on professional, national, and state inputs
	#2.2: Visualizing the Dispositional Statements	Construct—job analysis		
3	#3.10: Coverage Check	Content—representative, relevant, and proportional	Rater consistency—anticipatory set	
	#3.11: Rating Form for Stakeholder Review	Content—representative, relevant, and proportional		Decisions based on authentic criteria
4	#4.3: Sample Format for Candidate/Teacher Tracking Form			Fair monitoring ensured
	#4.4: Format for Data Aggregation	Improvement as a purpose		Program weaknesses identified to improve opportunities to learn
	#4.6: Management Plan	Content validity through currency and updates	Checks for rater drift	Fair monitoring ensured

Next Steps in Collecting Evidence of Validity, Reliability, and Fairness

We now turn to your continuing collection of evidence of validity, reliability, and fairness. You already have a great head start, as the sample report above demonstrated, especially in the area of validity, and we will make those connections below as well. One useful approach to collecting such evidence is to ask and answer a question such as "Is my job analysis current and adequate?" A sample report on such an effort might look like the example in Box 7.13.

Box 7.13.   Sample Institutional Report on the Continuing Assessment Process Review

Two years after the implementation of our system, we conducted a follow-up job analysis to ensure that our original work remained current and adequate. We found that most items met that criterion. We removed the item on _____ and added an item on _____.

We surveyed principals to determine whether they found our teachers to have the necessary dispositions to teach. Of the 200 principals who responded, 180 (90%) said that they did. Several principals suggested the addition of more instruction in the area of critical thinking. We have added an additional component to _____.

Judgmental Evidence

Judgmental evidence relies on expert opinion rather than numbers.

Guiding Question: "What do the experts say?"

Empirical Evidence

Evidence based on numbers and scores that the assessment is credible.

Guiding Question: "What do the numbers tell us about credibility?"

We have developed the following series of additional questions and methodologies as a sample of the kinds of questions that could be asked to obtain credibility evidence. For these questions, it is useful to use a combination of two response strategies: one logical or judgmental (qualitative) and the other empirical (quantitative). We begin with three basic questions, shown in Box 7.14, and then expand to some more specific ones matched to the methodologies. With this level of expansion, we will show you examples at the end of the chapter to demonstrate how the processes work. Even though we cannot anticipate every situation you may encounter, the examples illustrate typical possibilities in your menu. Some of the data are manufactured for space and convenience, but some of the examples are real scores and analyses. We hope that most of our readers will complete most of the judgmental processes outlined, since they are usually easy to do. We also suspect that many programs or school districts will perform at least a few empirical analyses depending on their needs, choice of measurement model (classical or item response theories), and commitment to measuring dispositions.

Box 7.14.   Three Basic VRF Questions

Validity: Do the instruments provide adequate coverage of the standards?

Reliability: Are scorers consistent in their ratings?

Fairness: Do all teachers have an equal opportunity to demonstrate appropriate dispositions (consistent with INTASC)?

Tables 7.2 through 7.4 provide more specific questions and analysis techniques for each of the three cornerstones of credibility: validity, reliability, and fairness. In Table 7.2 on validity evidence, we have included both judgmental and empirical studies that can work with dispositional data. In our charts, we will refer you to many resources and examples in the worksheets and examples at the end of this chapter.

Table 7.2.   Questions and Methods for Collecting Validity Evidence

Psychometric Question	Judgmental Methods	Empirical Methods
1. Do the instruments provide adequate coverage of the standards? (content validity)	Content coverage check (DAATS Step 3, Worksheet #3.10)	*IRT method:* logistic ruler showing gaps in coverage, if any, concept map (Example #1)
2. Are the items an adequate representation of the job? Critical to job performance, authentic, and frequent? (content validity)	Stakeholder survey (DAATS Step 3, Worksheet #3.11)	*Classical method:* Content validity ratio (CVR, Example #2)
3. Are any teachers being denied diplomas or dropping out of the program or the profession who would be good teachers? (consequential)	Analysis of appropriateness of reasons for teacher failures (Worksheets #5.2 and #5.3)	*Classical method:* Disparate-impact analysis (Example #3)
4. Are program completers acquiring improved dispositions over time? (Note: This question applies only if continuous improvement is a stated purpose of the system.)	Analysis of improvement results (Worksheet #5.4)	*IRT method:* Increasing mean measures over time on a ruler

In a process such as this, the majority of validity evidence can be judgmental. The best news here is that you have already completed much of what you needed to do in earlier steps of the DAATS model. We add to the judgmental process reviews of the reasons for failure and the results of improvement efforts, if improvement was one of the purposes of the process. We consider all of these critical to complete. While we will not know in the rehire study (Worksheet #5.3) whether the teacher was ineligible for hire because of competencies or dispositions, we do know when there is a problem in a district. If the study is conducted by mail, a phone call follow-up can often allow for information about which problem predominated, especially if more than one teacher was let go.

On the empirical side, there is room for evidence in the early stages of the process, but it is not as critical as it is for reliability. Analyzing the difficulty of items in comparison to your expectations about them (concept map) is an easy product of the Rasch model. The methodology behind Example #1 will be explained further in Chapter 8; here you see the data (at the end of this chapter). The content validity ratio (CVR) is easy to calculate, and Example #2 will show you everything you need to know to do it.

Disparate impact is also easy to calculate with free software on line, so please refer to that example. Of all the empirical data, it may be the most important in terms of protecting your institution from legal claims. At a minimum, this study should be completed.

If you are serious about program improvement, both the improvement record and the Rasch data can help. A quick comparison of mean scores using the Rasch model is your best bet—if your teachers are learning more, the program is probably improving! The record of improvements may include improvements that have had no impact. Other validity studies are possible in the future, and we will deal with those in our last section of Element 8 ("Future Studies"). Let's now turn to reliability in Table 7.3.

Table 7.3. Questions and Methods for Collecting Reliability Evidence

Psychometric Question	Judgmental Methods	Empirical Methods
1. Are scorers consistent in their ratings (rater agreement)—conducted on a regular basis (e.g., every 3 years)?	Expert rescoring of instruments (Worksheet #5.5) Insertion of artificial cases (blind) analysis (described below)	*Classical Method:* Cohen's kappa (Example #4) OR *IRT method:* Rater effects and category probability analysis (see Chapter 8)
2. Are scores obtained on teachers sufficiently precise as to have confidence that they could be replicated under different or new conditions or administrations? (internal consistency and measurement error)		*IRT method:* Fit analysis of persons (see Chapter 8) OR *Classical method:* Cronbach's alpha and standard error (see explanation below)

Reliability is a tougher nut to crack judgmentally, so the empirical side of this chart overrides the judgmental one. In your early work in the DAATS model, you were able to establish a context in which reliability was likely to be present, but you were not able to actually examine it, as you were with content validity. In choosing your method of determining reliability, you might want to consider what is most important to your assessments: consensus of ratings, consistency over time, or fair correction of rater errors. ***You do not need to do all three; picking one would suffice.***

Consensus is likely best approached with a traditional Cohen's (1960) kappa statistic and rubric review. We have provided an example of the computation of Cohen's kappa (Example #4) so that you can do this easily, using free online software. This is a traditional check for inter-rater reliability. Expert rescoring allows you to compare ratings by different raters, and an example, with some opportunity to practice, is provided for you to use for that study. The computations are very simple. The blind review process in the table would allow you to select (or create) some anchor tasks that well represent each of the proficiency levels. You would give them to raters, along with new assessment tasks to score. If they score as you expected them to score, they are on track; if not, you have something to talk about. Here you would keep a record of whether or not they are consistent and advise them accordingly. If you want a modern discussion of methods to estimate inter-rater reliability, Stemler (2004) provides a readable overview and ends with a statement reflective of our view: "The appropriate approach to estimating inter-rater reliability will always depend upon the purpose at hand" ("Summary and Conclusions," ¶ 4).

We have done much in earlier steps to ensure that the construct is well-defined, so we are not likely to have other typical problems associated with reliability. Rater error (leniency or harshness) will be our biggest challenge. With regard to other forms of reliability evidence, clearly we are limited by the nature of the system. The test-retest approach to reliability would not work here because we cannot ask teachers to repeat their performances. Alternate or parallel forms are difficult to create because we have carefully selected and constructed our assessment instruments—all of which are critical to the job. That leaves us with internal consistency.

For those who want a reliability index (internal consistency), we note that one of the advantages of the Rasch model is that it automatically produces a traditional reliability coefficient that is similar to Cronbach's alpha but is called "separation reliability." We provide an example of how that works and what it looks like in Chapter 8. An even more important advantage of the Rasch model is that computer software called FACETS (Linacre, 1994) allows us to actually estimate the amount of rater error present and adjust for it with a minimal number of repeated ratings. This is a very intriguing possibility, but you would need some software training to perform the analysis. Again, see Chapter 8 for a few more details on this. Now, we turn to fairness in Table 7.4.

Inter-Rater Reliability

Inter-rater reliability is an index of consistency across raters calculated using correlations. Raters' scores should consistently go up or down across students. When one rater rates a student high, the other rater should rate him or her high. Low ratings should also be consistent across raters. If some raters score students high and the other raters score the same students as low, then the ratings are not consistent or reliable.

Guiding Question: "Are scorers consistent in their ratings?"

Table 7.4. Questions and Methods for Collecting Fairness Evidence		
Psychometric Question	*Judgmental Methods*	*Empirical Methods*
1. Do all teachers have an equal opportunity in the assessment process, regardless of gender, ethnicity, or handicapping condition? (nonbiased materials and processes)	Representative teachers and assessors' examination of items for offensiveness (Worksheet #5.6)	*IRT method:* Differential item and differential person fit analysis (Example #9) *OR* *Classical method:* Disparate-impact analysis (Example #3)
2. Are procedures in place to ensure that all teachers know the requirements and have adequate opportunity to remediate when there is a problem? (equal opportunity and nondiscriminatory practices)	Analysis of reasons for non-completion and remediation efforts and EO impact (Worksheet #5.7, which may be completed based on results of survey of non-completers)	*IRT Method:* Differential item and differential person functioning and fit analysis (Example #9) *OR* *Classical method:* Descriptive statistics on patterns by group

The question of fairness or absence of bias in an assessment is important in today's world. For the most part, judgmental studies provide adequate evidence, although we highly recommend some simple descriptive statistics for the second question—nothing more than numbers and percents. Our method suggested above to answer the first question is purely judgmental and common practice. It should be practical for most institutions or school districts looking for evidence. The second question is also reasonably easy to answer, and many reports include descriptive statistics divided by demographics.

There is only one issue that confronts the assessment systems today that is not addressed easily by judgmental and classical methods: the power to detect subtle bias in individual items or assessment tasks that add up to *disparate impact* despite the best intentions. There is likely no easy way to obtain this information without the use of advanced *differential item* and *differential person analysis* provided by the Rasch model (IRT). We are not going to detail the statistical models here, but would suggest that those interested consider the excellent illustration of techniques to detect item bias provided by Richard Smith (2004) for scored items and Elder, McNamara, and Congdon (2004) for performance items in the text *Introduction to Rasch Measurement.*

We have provided an example of DIF analysis with the Rasch model (Example #9) at the very end of this chapter as well. In our example, we focus on an unusual application of DIF: differences by program rather than differences by gender or

---

ᒍ—— **Differential Item Functioning (DIF)** ——

DIF is a statistical process that seeks to determine whether there are meaningful differences in the way subgroups perform, particularly groups that are classified as protected— women and minorities. It is okay for the performance to be different, as long as it is not because of problems in the construction or administration of the assessment itself.

Guiding Question: "Are minorities and women doing worse on the assessments because they are minorities and women?" ᒍ

ethnicity. We do this to illustrate the potential for varied uses of the same statistical procedure—information on bias as well as program improvement needs.

Future Studies

Over time, you may want to conduct some additional research studies for both evidence of validity and for general research purposes whether you use the Rasch model or not, and we will provide examples in this section of both classical and Rasch scores. If you have selected the Rasch model as your primary measurement model, many opportunities are available to you that might not be available with a classical approach. This is largely due to the fact that Rasch converts ordinal data (what you always have with rating scales!) into interval data. You may remember from your statistics training that some statistical computations are not supposed to be performed on ordinal data. You may also remember that most statistical tests, at least the parametric kind, require a normal distribution as one of their important assumptions.

Most performance assessment systems end up having a high degree of negative skew—otherwise known as "mastery learning." After all, that is our purpose in this system. We can try hard to convince raters not to use the high point on our rating scales, but often that simply is not a realistic expectation. Rasch does not presume a normal distribution and works with interval-level data. You may have noticed in our Cohen's kappa example at the end of this chapter that we had a bit of a problem with our raters in differentiating between "acceptable" and "exemplary." While we may try our darnedest to get past that, in all likelihood we will never succeed. So, you may see inadequate Cohen's kappas for eternity. With Rasch, you can simply make the correction and let it go.

The amount of research you can do with good data is virtually endless. We will suggest a few studies here to give you a flavor of "coming attractions." Some will add to your store of validity evidence. Others may add to your store of contributions to the knowledge base within your own system (evaluation) or generalizable (research) to the world at large, depending on how you design your studies and what other questions you ask. As in the previous section, we will use the question approach. We will suggest a possible or likely analysis and process. There are too many options to be complete and too many questions that can be asked, so please view these only as illustrations.

You will see from the outset that you can do much with descriptive statistics, graphs, and simple correlations. They are powerful and easy to produce, and you can easily do all of this yourself, just as you can do Cohen's kappa and the CVR yourself. You may also wish to progress to some more sophisticated techniques, such as regression analyses and significance tests, which may also be within your comfort zone. We are specifically not discussing SEM (structural equation models), HLM (hierarchical linear models), MANOVA (multivariate analysis of variance), discriminant analysis, canonical analysis, factor analysis, two- or three-parameter item response theory models, or all the "third-tier" statistics. These, like the Rasch model, may call for a statistician if you are not inclined to do much with statistics on your own.

Here are three questions to get our continuing analysis started. For each question, we provide a suggested design that includes your assessment scores (sometimes both raw scores and Rasch interval-level scores), other evidence, the type of analysis, and some brief comments (see Tables 7.5–7.7). We will also point out the uses of these questions in terms of validity and other research.

Question #1: Is there a relationship between assessment results and future external assessment(s) (e.g., hiring success, rehire rates, placement surveys, and/or principals' ratings of effectiveness)?

> This is an excellent source of ***predictive validity***. (See Example #6 and examples located at the end of the chapter.)

Table 7.5. Suggested Design for Research Question #1		
Your Assessment System Scores	*Other Unit Evidence or Outcomes*	*Type of Analysis*
Total raw score	Principal's mean satisfaction ratings	Spearman rho correlation coefficient
Total raw score	Hire/rehire status if available from your state or districts or dichotomous principal rating of satisfactory/unsatisfactory	Point-biserial correlation coefficient
Comments: While predictive validity is very desirable, do not be surprised if there is not as much relationship as you expected. The biggest challenge you face with predictive validity studies is that you do not have data on folks who failed the tasks but were certified and are teaching, so you only have half of the data you really need! You will also be faced with a preponderance of high scores: 4's and 5's. Following graduates for up to 5 years is useful.		

Question #2: Do assessments contribute *different* information about knowledge, skills, dispositions, and impact?

> This is an excellent source of ***discriminant or divergent validity***. (See Examples #5 and #7.) Divergent (also described by the corollary, convergent validity) and discriminant validity are two parts of construct validity. Essentially, things that should be related are related, and things that shouldn't are not (Trochim, 2000).

Table 7.6. Suggested Design for Research Question #2		
Your Assessment System Scores	*Other Unit Evidence or Outcomes*	*Type of Analysis*
Measures from the assessments produced by the Rasch model	Aggregations of related assessments that *should not* correlate	Pearson correlation matrix and SPLOM (scatterplot matrices) (Examples #5 and #7)
Comments: Dispositions scores should not correlate with Praxis or portfolio scores that tap the cognitive domain. Knowledge and skill task results should correlate substantially; knowledge and ethics results probably would not correlate; questionnaires and focus groups should correlate; questionnaires and unit plans might not. Taxonomies like KIDS or thematic folios would guide the aggregations.		

Question #3: How do teachers completing the elementary program compare with teachers completing the secondary program (or traditional versus alternative certification or 2 + 2 versus 4-year graduates or teachers from New Jersey versus teachers from South Carolina)?

This is an example of program *improvement data.* (See Example #8 for a *t*-test.)

Table 7.7. Suggested Design for Research Question #3		
Your Assessment System Scores	*Other Unit Evidence or Outcomes*	*Type of Analysis*
Rasch or IRT measures or standard scores by type of assessment	Results from pairs of programs with the same or linked assessments and items	Descriptive statistics, bar graphs, and *t*-tests to compare programs
Comments: A comparison across programs is a useful diagnostic tool to find and improve areas that vary based on content or background (Example #8).		

That brings us near the end. We note here that we have provided one more example at the end of the chapter to demonstrate differential item functioning (DIF). It is Example #9. In this example, we show how DIF can be used to identify programs or certification areas in which teachers are more or less consistent with the INTASC Principles. This can be useful information for finding success stories to share.

Before leaving the psychometric-planning process, it may be useful to have a vision for where these types of studies can take us and what kind of reports you should be able to write. A sample report is given in Box 7.15, based on fictitious data that show the type of conclusions you could reach if you addressed most or all of the questions we have identified under DAATS Step 5A, Element 8. Some of the data are taken from the worksheets and examples at the end of this chapter; other data are even more fictitious and written to aid in this example. In the following sample, we report on a number of validity studies in order to model a variety of techniques. We suspect that most users will conduct fewer studies.

REMINDER

This is a menu from which you can choose the studies you want to use. It is not a prescription for everything you HAVE to do or every way there is do it! It is a KISS starting point.

Box 7.15. Sample Institutional Report of Psychometric Studies—Validity

We conducted a wide range of validity studies. We used a combination of judgmental and empirical methodologies and classical and item response theories. Our conclusions follow:

- The assessment process provides adequate coverage of the INTASC indicators and our own values about teachers' dispositions and, therefore, has evidence of content validity. We created an alignment chart of indicators and instruments, and no indicators remained without at least one item. A logistic ruler showed that we had no gaps in coverage, either, and that items were ordered logically in terms of difficulty. For example, we expected Item 1 to be the most difficult and Items 4, 5, and 7 to be the easiest, and the measures calculated confirmed our expectations.

- The assessment system shows evidence of construct validity based on the results of a stakeholder survey during our developmental phase. We had responses from 75 principals and school system personnel who were asked to evaluate each item for criticality and authenticity. We dropped three items from the instruments based on this survey because their mean criticality ratings were less than 2.5. All other items ranged from 2.5 to 3.0, with 3 representing critical, 2 useful, and 1 not useful. We subsequently used the same scale with a panel of 10 expert judges and computed a Lawshe (1975) CVR for all items in the system. All items were in the .50 to .80 range, meeting the criterion of .50.

- The assessment instruments show evidence of divergent or discriminant validity; we correlated portfolio scores and Praxis scores with the scores from the belief scale, finding a Pearson's $r = .04$ and $.12$, respectively, demonstrating that we were measuring two different constructs. We used the Pearson correlation coefficient because of the Rasch scores, all of which were interval.

- The assessment instruments also show evidence of predictive validity; we correlated satisfaction ratings from principals and program completers for the 2005 year, finding a Spearman's rho correlation on these ordinal data of .83.

- The assessment process has evidence of convergent validity based on correlations of disposition instrument scores. We found that Pearson's product moment correlations were all positive and ranged from $r = .38$ to $r = .88$. As such, we concluded that instruments had relationships that were appropriate.

- Consistent with our program improvement purpose, we analyzed the mean ratings for all items and found that only three items fell below a mean rating of 2.0 on a 3-point scale. We initiated improvement efforts related to instruction for all three, and we will monitor results in analyses next year. We also used a Rasch analysis to determine that teachers' mean scores increased over a three-year period from 75 to 82. Finally, we performed a series of t-tests comparing results in various programs, finding only that there were significant differences between mathematics and science, with mathematics teachers having dispositions more consistent than those of science teachers with INTASC Principles by 4.8 points. We expect to explore reasons for this difference.

In the sample in Box 7.16, we report on three reliability studies in order to model a variety of techniques. We suspect that most users will conduct fewer studies.

Box 7.16. Sample Institutional Report of Psychometric Studies—Reliability

We conducted three reliability studies. We used a combination of judgmental and empirical methodologies and classical and item response theories. Two studies focused on scorer consistency and two on internal consistency. Our conclusions follow:

- The assessment system showed scorer consistency through a study of expert rescoring. In this study, we had three judges rescore the selected questionnaires and compared their ratings. While we found five differences between "acceptable" and "target" ratings for two judges, there were no discrepancies on the "unacceptable" rating. We also computed a Cohen's kappa, obtaining a .51 correlation coefficient, below our .70 expectation. We were pleased, however, to note that we had 100% agreement on the "unacceptable" ratings; hence we are comfortable that our baseline decisions are reliable. The difficulty is in separating "acceptable" and "exemplary" ratings. We will repeat both studies next year, and we are reviewing rubrics to determine areas of potential lack of clarity.

- The assessment system showed internal consistency through the Rasch approach. The reliability coefficient was .81, and we had no misfitting scores (MNSQ > 2.0) for any of our teachers.

In the report in Box 7.17, we report on three fairness studies, and we recommend the expert review and disparate impact analysis at a minimum.

Box 7.17. Sample Institutional Report of Psychometric Studies—Fairness

We conducted three fairness studies. We used a combination of judgmental and empirical methodologies and classical and item response theories. Our conclusions follow:

- Experts reviewed each item to ensure that there were no items that were potentially biased against protected populations. They looked specifically for cultural bias, finding none. We do have some Creole students, and we found through the differential item functioning (DIF) analysis (Rasch model) some statistically significant differences for our French-speaking population. We will review the translated items accordingly. The DIF analyses revealed no other gender or ethnic bias in the tasks.

- A disparate impact analysis, as referenced under validity, showed that minorities were having difficulty in demonstrating the expected dispositions, and we will explore the reasons for these problems in our study next year. These findings are inconsistent with the DIF analysis and may be attributable to factors other than the quality of the rubrics and rater judgments.

- We documented and reviewed remediation efforts for all members of protected populations who were struggling. There were only two minorities and one disabled person in this group, and we determined that all three had received extensive support but were unable to demonstrate the expected dispositions satisfactorily during the final observation with a level of quality consistent with other passing teachers.

AERA, APA, and NCME *Standards* (1999)
and DAATS Step 5A

ELEMENT 1

Standard 3.2

The *purpose(s) of the test*, definition of the domain, and the test specifications *should be stated clearly* so that judgments can be made about the appropriateness of the defined domain for the stated purpose(s) of the test and about the relation of items to the dimensions of the domain they are intended to represent.

Standard 13.1

When educational testing programs are mandated by school, district, state, or other authorities, the *ways in which test results are intended to be used should be clearly described.* It is the responsibility of those who mandate the use of tests to monitor their impact and to identify and minimize potential negative consequences. Consequences resulting from the uses of the test, both intended and unintended, should also be examined by the test user.

ELEMENT 2

Standard 14.14

The content domain to be covered by a credentialing test should be defined clearly and justified in terms of the *importance of the content for credential-worthy performance in an occupation or profession.* A rationale should be provided to support a claim that the knowledge or skills being assessed are required for credential-worthy performance in an occupation and are consistent with the purpose for which the licensing or certification program was instituted.

ELEMENT 3

Standard 14.17

The *level of performance required for passing a credentialing test* should *depend on the knowledge and skills necessary for acceptable performance in the occupation or profession* and should not be adjusted to regulate number or proportion of persons passing the test.

ELEMENT 4

Standard 3.3

The *test specifications should be documented, along with their rationale and the process by which they were developed.* The test specifications should define the *content of the test, the proposed number of items, the item formats*, the desired psychometric properties of the items, and the item and section arrangement. They should also specify the amount of time for testing, *directions to the test takers*, procedures to be used for test administration and *scoring*, and other relevant information.

ELEMENT 5

Standard 3.23

The process for *selecting, training, and qualifying scorers* should be documented by the test developer. The *training materials, such as the scoring rubrics and examples of test takers' responses that illustrate the levels on the score scale, and the procedures for training scorers* should result in a degree of agreement among scorers that allows for the scores to be interpreted as originally intended by the test developer. Scorer reliability and potential drift over time in raters' scoring standards should be evaluated and reported by the person(s) responsible for conducting the training session.

ELEMENT 6

Standard 3.9

When a test developer evaluates the psychometric properties of items, the *classical or item response theory (IRT) model used for evaluating the psychometric properties of items should be documented*. The sample used for estimating item properties should be described and should be of adequate size and diversity for the procedure. The process by which items are selected and the data used for item section, such as item difficulty, item discrimination, and/or item information, should also be documented. When IRT is used to estimate item parameters in test development, the item response model, estimation procedures, and evidence of model fit should be documented.

ELEMENT 7

Standard 3.5

When appropriate, *relevant experts external to the testing program should review the test specifications*. The purpose of the review, the process by which the review is conducted, and the results of the review should be documented. The qualifications, relevant experiences, and demographic characteristics of expert judges should also be documented.

ELEMENT 8: VALIDITY

Standard 3.6

The *type of items, the response formats, scoring procedures, and test administration procedures should be selected based on the purposes of the test, the domain to be measured*, and the intended test takers. To the extent possible, test content should be chosen to ensure that intended inferences from test scores are *equally valid for members of different groups* of test takers. The test review process should include *empirical analyses and, when appropriate, the use of expert judges* to review items and response formats. The qualifications, relevant experiences, and demographic characteristics of expert judges should also be documented.

Standard 13.2

In educational settings, when a test is designed or used to serve multiple purposes, evidence of the test's *technical quality should be provided for each purpose*.

(Continued)

(Continued)

ELEMENT 8: RELIABILITY

Standard 3.23

The process for selecting, training, and qualifying scorers should be documented by the test developer. The training materials, such as the scoring rubrics and examples of test takers' responses that illustrate the levels on the score scale, and the procedures for training scorers should result in a degree of agreement among scorers that allows for the scores to be interpreted as originally intended by the test developer. *Scorer reliability and potential drift over time* in raters' scoring standards *should be evaluated* and reported by the person(s) responsible for conducting the training session.

Standard 2.10

When subjective judgment enters into test scoring, evidence should be provided on both *inter-rater consistency in scoring and within-examinee consistency over repeated measurements*. A clear distinction should be made among reliability data based on (a) independent panels of raters scoring the same performance or procedures, (b) a single panel scoring successive performances or new products, and (c) independent panels scoring successive performances or new products.

Standard 2.15

When a test or combination of measures is used to make categorical decisions, *estimates should be provided of the percentage of examinees who would be classified in the same way* on two applications of the procedure, using the same form or alternate forms of the instrument.

Standard 14.15

Estimates of the reliability of test-based credentialing decisions should be provided.

ELEMENT 8: FAIRNESS

Standard 7.3

When credible research reports that *differential item functioning* exists across age, gender, racial/ethnic, cultural, disability, and/or linguistic groups in the population of test takers in the content domain measured by the test, test developers should *conduct appropriate studies* when feasible. Such research should seek to detect and eliminate aspects of test design, content, and format that might bias test scores for particular groups.

Standard 7.4

Test developers should strive to *identify and eliminate language, symbols, words, phrases, and content that are generally regarded as offensive* by members of racial, ethnic, gender, or other groups, except when judged to be necessary for adequate representation of the domain.

Standard 7.10

When the use of a test results in outcomes that affect the life chances or educational opportunities of examinees, evidence of mean test score differences between relevant subgroups of examinees should, where feasible, be examined for subgroups for which credible research reports mean differences for similar tests. Where mean differences are found, an investigation should be undertaken to *determine that such differences are not attributable to a source of construct underrepresentation or construct-irrelevant variance.* While initially the responsibility of the test developer, the test user bears responsibility for uses with groups other than those specified by the developer.

Standard 9.1

Testing practice should be designed to *reduce threats to the reliability and validity* of test score inferences that may arise *from language differences.*

NOTE: Emphases added for clarity.

STEP 5B: IMPLEMENT THE PLAN CONSCIENTIOUSLY

Like all good planning processes, it is important to think about who will do what, when, where, and how. It is advisable to develop a kind of action plan that helps keep the psychometrics on track. At least one measurement person should be involved from the start. While we do not need to see a dozen statisticians biting at the heels of teacher education faculty, it is a good idea to have one practical-minded measurement person to help with the nitty-gritty details and make sure you do not miss something that later could be embarrassing. In our above example, it would likely be a statistician who found the problem for Creole students. While the tail should not wag the dog, the dog should have a tail. Teamwork helps.

Make a sign to post over your door that says: "Keep it statistically simple. KISS." Point to it whenever you are confused by something being discussed. Even if you understand, point to it on occasion, just to keep everyone honest!

Box 7.18.   Double Secret Advice From an Anti–Tail Wagger

Have you seen the movie *Born Yesterday?* If not, rent it. Focus on the scene where Melanie Griffith memorizes a few standard phrases that dazzle the politicos at a Washington party. Then, memorize a few of the AERA, APA, and NCME *Standards* and sprinkle them into your conversations with measurement folks. Then tell them that you are going to use the Rasch model because you want to put the people back into the measurement process by using the fit statistic while reducing rater effect at the same time.

(Continued)

(Continued)

That may work even better than pointing to your KISS sign.

P.S. Don't let them see Chapter 8. Make them work harder. Refer them to Bond and Fox (2001) or M. Wilson (2005) if they don't know the model. It will be our little secret. The happy faces on the ruler might not work for everyone!

V᛫ WRAP-UP

In this chapter, we discussed the reasons why it is important to have data that are credible and useful, noting that there are standards for psychometrics just as there are standards for teacher competencies and dispositions. We used the AERA, APA, and NCME *Standards* (1999) as the basis for developing a plan for credibility and utility with eight elements in it: Purpose and Use; Construct Measured; Interpretation and Reporting of Scores; Assessment Specifications and Content Map; Assessor/Rater Selection and Training Procedures; Analysis Methodology; External Review Personnel and Methodology; and Evidence of Validity, Reliability, and Fairness.

We found that because we had done careful planning throughout the first four steps of the DAATS model, we were well on the way to ensuring credibility and utility of our data. Throughout this step, we reviewed our earlier work, and then we needed only to add a few more pieces to complete the task, and most of them can be handled with relative ease.

We presented the "ultimate" series of studies that can be done, knowing that there are always more and that most users will want to do less. Our hope has been to give you a menu and some confidence in your search for the truth about teachers' dispositions and your program's ability to help teachers acquire the skills-based (and standards-based) values they need to help children learn.

Story Starters

Starter #1:

Professor/Teacher Leevmeealon stomps into your office and says,

"We all know an enthusiastic, reflective, and moral teacher committed to social justice when we see one, so we don't need to check on any of this validity/reliability junk. That's just a bunch of statisticians being a pain in the butt. Nobody is going to challenge my decisions, much the less take me to court over a grade. If I want to kick a student/teacher out of here, I can do it based on my 45 years of experience. After all, I'm the pro! Obviously I can tell the difference between unacceptable, acceptable, and exemplary. Can't everybody?"

You say...

Starter #2:

Professor Dr. Neelbeformee, wearing a Harris Tweed jacket, scratches his beard and takes a drag from his pipe. There are funny-looking charts and graphs and pictures of the normal curve all over his office. He looks at you with a frown and says,

"Let's try some factor analysis and hierarchical linear modeling. I will tell you what you are measuring. It may or may not be all of these standards."

You say,

"Gee Doc, we have developed a specific assessment plan. Here's our checklist of the *exact analyses* we need, the *reports* we want, and an example of the way the results are *tabled and graphed*. Let's save the fancy stuff for the doctoral students."

THE END

DAATS STEP 5—WORKSHEET #5.1
Assessment Specifications

Explanation:

Fill in the cells in the right column based on the guidance in the chapter.

Content	Standards assessed:	
	Instrument types:	
	Use of multiple measures for decisions:	
Format	Components of each instrument:	
	Decision points/scale:	
Scoring	Computer or rater:	
	Personnel:	
	Exemplars and training:	

DAATS STEP 5—WORKSHEET #5.2

Analysis of Appropriateness of Decisions for Teacher Failures

Explanation:

Identify all of the teachers who were counseled out of the program because of dispositional problems. Summarize the results of their assessments and confirm that an appropriate decision was made to counsel them out of the program. Calculate the percentage of each protected population that was counseled out and determine whether it was more than 80% of the members of that population enrolled in your institution or district.

Year: _____

Name	Gender	Ethnicity	Handicap	Cumulative Data Summary	Correct Decision
					Yes No
					Yes No
					Yes No
					Yes No
					Yes No
					Yes No
					Yes No
					Yes No
					Yes No

Females: _____ Total enrolled _____ % Failed _____ yes _____ no 80% rule problem

Minorities: _____ Total enrolled _____ % Failed _____ yes _____ no 80% rule problem

Disabled: _____ Total enrolled _____ % Failed _____ yes _____ no 80% rule problem

DAATS WORKSHEETS

DAATS STEP 5—WORKSHEET #5.3
Analysis of Rehire Data

Explanation:

Identify all of the teachers who were not eligible for rehire. This includes those teachers who left for reasons other than personal reasons (moved, changed careers, had families). The reason in this case is typically "fired," but districts often cannot reveal the reasons. Calculate the percentage of teachers in each certification area (or by whatever categories you need) who were not eligible for rehire.

Year: _____

Teacher Name	Certification Area	District of Employment*	Eligible for Rehire

*Districts might want to substitute in-state/out-of-state, alternative/college-based certificate, graduating institution, or any other useful data.

DAATS STEP 5—WORKSHEET #5.4
Program Improvement Record

Explanation:

Record the mean rating for each item and make a determination about whether or not improvement is needed. Keep a running record of those improvements and faculty working on them. Record reasons for not working on items with low means.

Criterion	Mean Rating	Improvement Needed	Improvement Made/Date
		Yes No	
		Yes No	
		Yes No	
		Yes No	
		Yes No	
		Yes No	
		Yes No	
		Yes No	
		Yes No	

DAATS WORKSHEETS

DAATS STEP 5—WORKSHEET #5.5
Expert Rescoring

Explanation:

Record each rater's score, noting differences. If any raters are markedly different from their colleagues, discuss these differences with the rater, attempting to bring him or her into line with the others.

Instrument Name: _____

Item	Rater 1	Rater 2	Rater 3	Analysis of Differences

Conference Report

Date: _____

Rater: _____

Counselor: _____

Summary of Conversation: _____

_____

DAATS WORKSHEETS

DAATS STEP 5—WORKSHEET #5.6
Fairness Review

Explanation:

Each reviewer should complete a worksheet for each instrument.

Instrument: _____

Reviewer Name: _____

If the item is found to be offensive, please suggest modifications in the third column.

Item	Offensive	Suggested Modification
	Yes No	
	Yes No	
	Yes No	
	Yes No	
	Yes No	
	Yes No	
	Yes No	
	Yes No	
	Yes No	

DAATS WORKSHEETS

DAATS STEP 5—WORKSHEET #5.7

Analysis of Remediation Efforts and Equal Opportunity (EO) Impact

Explanation:

For each teacher from a protected population who required assistance, record the results of the remediation efforts. Then, make a judgment about whether improved remedial opportunities are needed.

Name	Gender/ Ethnicity	Handicap	Date	Problem and Remediation Efforts	Counseled Out
					Yes No
					Yes No
					Yes No
					Yes No
					Yes No
					Yes No
					Yes No

Remediation Efforts Sufficient?   _____ yes _____ no

Improvements Suggested: _____

_____

_____

Completer Name and Signature: _____

V̈

DAATS WORKSHEETS

DAATS STEP 5—WORKSHEET #5.8
Psychometric Plan Format

Explanation:

Complete each cell, based on the readings in the chapter.

Purpose and Use	
Construct Measured	Teacher Dispositions
Interpretation and Reporting of Scores	
Assessment Specifications and Content Map	
Assessor/Rater Selection and Training Procedures	
Analysis Methodology	
External Review Personnel and Methodology	
Evidence of Validity, Reliability, and Fairness	

DAATS WORKSHEETS

DAATS STEP 5—EXAMPLE #1
Logistic Ruler for Content Validity

Since most instruments do not have the same number of items and some are dichotomous and some have a rating scale, it would be difficult to rank order the tasks in terms of difficulty, based on teachers' total scores. A Rasch ruler, however, takes care of that, if one has an advance conceptualization of what to expect in terms of difficulty. The concept-mapping process provides a powerful tool to facilitate such a process. M. Wilson (2005) describes it well, highlighting that it provides "a coherent and substantive definition for the content" (p. 28) by creating a continuum for measuring both items and people.

In this example, we have listed items in order of expected difficulty or complexity, with the most difficult on top. Note that the items are clustered in categories. In the two example rulers that follow, the map on the right is aligned with the ordering and shows good coverage of the concept—no big gaps. It provides good evidence of validity. The map on the left shows gaps in coverage and problems with the ordering. Assessment designers need to rethink the map or look for problems causing some tasks to be easier than expected and others to be harder. For example, are there problems in the directions, rubrics, or judges' ratings?

Item 1	difficult
Items 2, 10	moderately difficult
Items 3, 6, 8, 9	moderately easy
Items 4, 5, 7	easy

```
TABLE 12.2 Sample Test for Rasch Demonstation ZOU855ws.txt Apr 16 15:17 2006

INPUT: 10 persons, 10 items MEASURED: 10 persons, 10 items, 2 CATS 3.57.2
```

Item Logistic Ruler with a Gap in a Critical Region of Measurement	Item Logistic Ruler with No Gap in a Critical Region of Measurement
persons MAP OF ITEMs	persons MAP OF ITEMs

```
      persons MAP OF ITEMs                  persons MAP OF ITEMs
          <more>|<rare>                        <more>|<rare>
    71            + Item2                 68          +T ITEM1
    70            +                       67     XX  +
    69     XX     +                       66          +
    68            +                       65          +
    67            +                       64          +
    66            +                       63          +
    65            +                       62          +
    64            +                       61          + ITEM10
    63          S+                        60          +
    62     X    +S                        59        S+S
    61            +                       58          +
    60            + ITEM1 ITEM3 ITEM5     57          +
    59            +                       56     X    + ITEM2
    58            +                       55          +
    57     X      +                       54          +
    56            +                       53          +
    55            +                       52          + ITEM9
    54            +                       51          +
    53            +                       50     X   M+M
    52     XX    M+                        49          + ITEM3 ITEM6
    51            +                       48          +
    50           +M                       47          +
    49            +                       46     XX   + ITEM8
    48            +                       45          +
    47            +                       44          +
    46            +                       43    XXX   + ITEM4 ITEM7
    45            +                       42          +
    44            +                       41        S+S
    43            + ITEM6 I0010           40     X    +
    42     XX     +                       39          +
    41          S+                        38          +
    40            +                       37          +
    39            + ITEM7 ITEM9           36          +
    38     XX    +S                       35          + ITEM5
    37            +                          <less>|<frequ>
    36            +
    35            +
    34            + ITEM4 ITEM8
       <less>|<frequ>
```

Items 3 and 5 are supposed to be easy!?! This is the hard end of the ruler.

In this important center region of the ruler, this set has **no items!** This means that the error for scores on people in the center region will be large– a problem for both validity and reliability.

This set has a dispersion of items in the center area of person difficulty which greatly improves the accuracy and precision of reported scores. It also validates the concept mapping, since the items are in the order predicted.

These items are too easy to be useful in terms of scaling, but they do help with certification.

DAATS EXAMPLES

DAATS EXAMPLES

DAATS STEP 5—EXAMPLE #2

Computation of the Lawshe (1975)
Content Validity Ratio (CVR)

The content validity ratio (CVR) can be used to quantify the extent to which a panel of expert judges think each task is critically important. In this example, 10 judges (a mixture of NBPTS teachers, school district supervisory personnel, and university faculty) were given an assessment instrument being considered for inclusion in the disposition assessment process. They were asked to rate each item as follows:

- Essential job function
- Useful but not essential job function
- Not necessary for the job

Results in this example: Our experts rated Item #1: "8 essential," "2 useful," "0 not necessary"

Here's how to calculate the CVR for this task: *ne = number of essential ratings.*

$$CVR = \frac{ne - (N/2)}{(N/2)} = \frac{8 - (10/2)}{10/2} = (8 - 5)/5 = .6$$

Conclusion: **Since a CVR that is greater than .50 is considered acceptable and the CVR on this task was .60, we can be comfortable using this task as one that is critical in our assessment system.**

Examples to Try

Here are some examples for you to practice computing. What would your decision be about the criticality of each item?

N (Number of Experts)	ne (Number of "Essential" Ratings)	Number of "Useful" Ratings	Number of "Not Necessary" Ratings	CVR
11	7	3	1	
20	18	1	1	
14	10	2	2	
10	7	0	3	
15	11	4	0	

*CVR answers = .27, .8, .42, .4, .53

DAATS STEP 5—EXAMPLE #3
Disparate-Impact Analysis

Checking for disparate impact is relatively simple using a variety of free online calculators. It helps to use these calculators, because the calculation is not as straightforward as it appears, and a statistical test of significance is helpful in decision making. The decision rule is based on what is called the "80% rule," which requires that protected populations succeed at a rate that is at least 80% of the success rate of the majority population. So, we have "percents of percents."

Protected populations include women, minorities, and disabled persons. In this example, we use an online calculator that is designed for employment selection, but the process works the same way for certification decisions. So that you can see behind the scenes the "percent of percent" calculations, we will work the numbers for you, first in word-processed tables and then show you the computer-generated output that does the chi-square analysis report for you. To help you find the "percent" on which the "80% percent rule" is to be calculated, we put it in bold italics.

We entered data for 111 teachers for the year 2005–2006, based on our definition of program "completers" and "non-completers" as follows:

- "Completers" included all teachers for whom an affirmative certification decision was made.

- "Non-completers" included all prospective teachers who were denied certification or dropped out of the program.

Gender

	Total		Completer		Non-Completer	
	#	%	#	%	#	%
Male	19	17	18	*95*	1	5
Female	92	83	87	95	5	5
Total	111		105		6	

Decision Rule: Males have a 95% certification rate; females should have 80% of that rate, or a 76% rate. Since 95% of the females were certified, the 80% rule was upheld.

(Continued)

(Continued)

Ethnicity

	Total		Completer		Non-Completer	
	#	%	#	%	#	%
Majority	99	89	99	**_100_**	0	0
Minority	12	11	6	50	6	50
Total	111		105		6	

Decision Rule: Majority population has a 100% certification rate; minorities should have 80% of that rate—still 80%. Since only 50% were certified, the 80% rule was *NOT* upheld.

Disability

	Total		Completer		Non-Completer	
	#	%	#	%	#	%
Nondisabled	109	98	103	**_95_**	6	5
Disabled	2	2	2	100	0	0
Total	111		105		6	

Decision Rule: The "nondisabled" population has a 95% certification rate; "disabled" should have 80% of that, or 76%—same as for gender. The certification rate is 100%, so the 80% rule is upheld.

Conclusion: Out of 111 students, 6 teachers were not certified, and all were minorities. This indicates a disparate impact that needs to be addressed. A chi-square statistical analysis confirms that the minority disparity is statistically significant.

The URL is in the public domain, and you can use it for your computations as well. We have reproduced the results in a screen shot from this URL: http://www.hr-software .net/EmploymentStatistics/DisparateImpact.htm

Chi-Square Report

Observed Expected	Selected	Not Selected	Row Totals
Males	18 17.973	1 1.027	19
Females	87 87.027	5 4.973	92
Column Total	105	6	111

Chi-Square = 0.0009
The value of the statistic is less than 3.841. This indicates that there is a 95% chance that these results have been obtained absent any form of bias. Therefore you may conclude that *these results fall within normal random variations and are not the result of bias.*

Observed Expected	Selected	Not Selected	Row Totals
Nonminorities	99 93.6486	0 5.3514	99
Minorities	6 11.3514	6 0.6486	12
Column Total	105	6	111

Chi-Square = 52.3286
The value of the statistic is greater than 6.635. This indicates that there is a less than 1% chance that these results would have been obtained absent any form of bias. Therefore *you may conclude that these results may have been the result of bias.*

Observed Expected	Selected	Not Selected	Row Totals
Nondisabled	103 103.1081	6 5.8919	109
Disabled	2 1.8919	0 0.1081	2
Column Total	105	6	111

Chi-Square = 0.1164
The value of the statistic is less than 3.841. This indicates that there is a 95% chance that these results have been obtained absent any form of bias. Therefore *you may conclude that these results fall within normal random variations and are not the result of bias.*

DAATS EXAMPLES

DAATS STEP 5—EXAMPLE #4

Computation of Cohen's (1960) Kappa Inter-Rater Reliability

Kappa is a statistic that can be used as a measure of inter-rater reliability. It ranges from 0 to 1.0, like all correlations. The usual expectation is that a kappa > .70 is desired for adequate reliability. In this example, two judges each rated 36 items on a 3-category rating scale (Exemplary, Acceptable, and Unacceptable). Here are the steps we go through to calculate kappa:

Step 1: Enter the raw data into a table by placing a tally mark into the cell that corresponds to the two judges' ratings. In the example, we will tally the ratings for nine examples only, skipping Items 8 to 34. After you finish placing all of the tally marks in the cell, count them and enter them into the table in Step 2.

Item Number:	1	2	3	4	5	6	7	(Items 8 to 34)	35	36
Rater # 1:	E	E	U	U	E	E	E	(Scores)	A	U
Rater # 2:	E	A	U	U	E	A	A	(Scores)	A	U

Rater #1 Across > Rater # 2 Down ∨	Exemplary	Acceptable	Unacceptable
Exemplary	‖		
Acceptable	‖‖	‖	
Unacceptable			‖‖

Step 2: Fill in the total counts per cell plus the row totals **(RT)** and column totals **(CT)**:

Rater #1 Across > Rater # 2 Down ∨	Exemplary	Acceptable	Unacceptable	Row Totals (RT) ∨
Exemplary	13 **(8.97)**	4	0	17
Acceptable	6	10 **(6.22)**	0	16
Unacceptable	0	0	3 **(.25)**	3
Column Totals (CT) >	19	14	3	**36** Grand Total (GT)

Step 3: Compute total number of rater agreements by summing the diagonal cells: 13 + 10 + 3 = 26

Step 4: Compute the expected frequencies (Ef) for each diagonal cell.

$$Ef(cell\ 11) = \frac{RT * CT}{GT} = \frac{17 * 19}{36} = 8.97$$

$$Ef(cell\ 22) = \frac{RT * CT}{GT} = \frac{16 * 14}{36} = 6.22$$

$$Ef(cell\ 33) = \frac{RT * CT}{GT} = \frac{3 * 3}{36} = .25$$

Step 5: Sum the expected frequencies (Ef): 8.97 + 6.22 + .25 = 15.44

Step 6: Compute kappa: $\kappa = \dfrac{\sum diagonal - \sum Ef}{N - \sum Ef} = \dfrac{26 - 15.44}{36 - 15.44} = .51$

Step 7: Since the obtained κ is less than .70, we decide that the inter-rater reliability is *not* good.

Conclusion: The news is not all bad, though! Our judges are in agreement about what constitutes unacceptable work, so we are comfortable with our cut score since it is based on that decision. In fact, we have 100% agreement ($\kappa = 1.0$) for the decision of certify/do not certify. Where we have a problem is in differentiating between acceptable and exemplary. Note that we have an equal amount of agreement and disagreement about the acceptable rating (10 the same and 10 different). This inconsistency is reflected in the kappa and calls for improvement in either the rater training or rubric refinement at the exemplary and acceptable levels.

Examples to Try

Here's a table of data filled in. You can calculate the kappa yourself and then reach some conclusions about your results:

Rater #1 Across > Rater # 2 Down $\vee\vee\vee$	Exemplary	Acceptable	Unacceptable	Row Totals (RT) $\vee\vee\vee$
Exemplary	44	5	1	
Acceptable	7	20	3	
Unacceptable	9	5	6	
Column Totals (CT) >>>				Grand Total (GT)
Categories = 3, N = 100				

You can go to http://faculty.vassar.edu/lowry/kappa.html and find a kappa calculator and this example.

DAATS EXAMPLES

DAATS STEP 5—EXAMPLE #5

Two Pearson Correlation Coefficients and Scatterplots: Disposition Scores Correlated With Praxis and Portfolio Scores

Disposition and Praxis Correlation Example

Suppose we had 10 students who were measured on a dispositions belief scale with raw scores from 0 to 50. They also took a Praxis test in elementary content. There is debate about whether these data are ordinal or interval, but technically they are ordinal and are probably not normally distributed. Therefore if they are not converted to interval-level data through Rasch, a Spearman's rho correlation should be calculated. Here, since we have converted the scores to a scaled score using Rasch, we do a Pearson correlation.

In this example, we see a correlation that is weak, $r = .122$, which provides evidence for our assessment system that dispositions is a different construct than knowledge. This is called "divergent validity."

Student	Rasch Measure	Praxis Score
Jane	39	190
Joe	76	170
Sam	54	176
George	77	188
Scarlett	60	189
Daryl	50	175
Anne	51	170
Mike	56	172
Bill	41	160
Tom	66	180

Spearman correlation matrix

	RASCH MEASURE	PRAXIS
RASCH MEASURE	1.000	
PRAXIS	0.122	1.000

Number of observations: 10

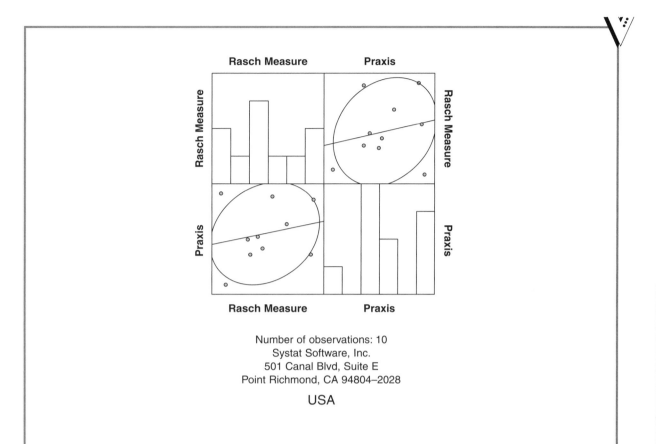

Number of observations: 10
Systat Software, Inc.
501 Canal Blvd, Suite E
Point Richmond, CA 94804–2028

USA

Disposition and Portfolio Correlation Example

Now suppose we had 100 teachers who were scored on a 3-point scale: Unacceptable = 1; Acceptable = 2; and Exemplary = 3. There were 12 criteria in the assessment instrument, a teacher portfolio of tasks. The total number of points would range from 12 to 36. We also administered the 50-item disposition belief scale to each student. All raw scores on both instruments were converted to interval measures using the Rasch model.

Both disposition measures and skill measures appear normally distributed. We can see that in the graphs in the upper-left and lower-right corners of the SPLOM plot below for dispositions score and portfolio score, respectively. The lack of correlation ($r = .04$), as evidenced in the other two boxes of the SPLOM plot, again indicates independence of skills and dispositions or evidence of divergent validity.

If the disposition instrument includes a lot of skill-based items (an error of construct validity), your correlations would be much higher, but misleading. If you have all teachers who are mostly high in both dispositions and skills, you will have a high correlation, because you are very lucky indeed!

(Continued)

DAATS EXAMPLES

(Continued)

Pearson correlation matrix

	DISPOSITION	PORTFOLIO
DISPOSITION	1.000	
PORTFOLIO	0.044	1.000

Number of observations: 100

Number of observations: 100
Systat Software, Inc.
501 Canal Blvd, Suite E
Point Richmond, CA 94804-2028

USA

DAATS STEP 5—EXAMPLE #6

Spearman Correlation Coefficient and Scatterplot: Disposition Scores Correlated With Principal Ratings

Suppose we had 10 beginning teachers who were scored on a 50-item disposition checklist, completed by supervisors during the teachers' preservice clinical internships. In the following year, as beginning teachers, each candidate was rated on a district teacher effectiveness scale of 20 items by the principal during the first semester of teaching. Ratings ranged from 1 to 5, with 5 representing "excellent" and 1 representing "poor." Five of the items were dispositional in nature and were analyzed separately, yielding a mean principal rating on dispositions. Because the data are clearly ordinal level this time, we use the Spearman rank order correlation (rho). In this example, we see a correlation that is good, $r = .834$, which provides predictive validity evidence for our assessment. It is predictive validity evidence because one instrument (the college-level disposition instrument) preceded the principals' ratings, which were administered once the teachers were working in the schools. A period of 1 year intervened.

We could recast this study in terms of another criterion validity study for teachers who are currently in the schools. In this case, we might have a mentor or peer teacher complete the disposition checklist and the principal complete the rating. In this case, we would be collecting evidence of both concurrent and convergent validity, since the two instruments were providing similar results on the same thing at the same time.

Either way, the data might look like this:

Student	Disposition Checklist Score	Principal's Rating
Jane	35	5
Joe	30	4.2
Sam	22	3.5
George	29	3.3
Scarlett	29	3.1
Daryl	18	2.1
Anne	31	4.2
Mike	30	4
Bill	28	3.1
Tom	32	3.6

(Continued)

(Continued)

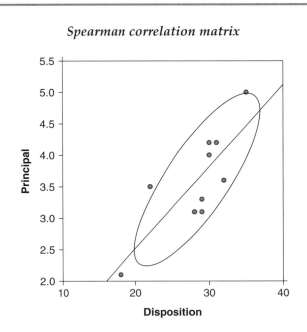

Spearman correlation matrix

Spearman correlation matrix

	PRINCIPAL	**DISPOSITION**
PRINCIPAL	1.000	
DISPOSITION	0.834	1.000

Number of observations: 10

Final Notes:

1. Although we do not illustrate this technique, if the principals' ratings were dichotomous—satisfied or not satisfied with the teachers' dispositions, the proper statistic to use would be the point-biserial correlation.

2. If you do not have any variability in your ratings, you will not have a good correlation. For example, if the principal rates everyone a 4 or a 5 on every item, don't bother to run the stats!

DAATS EXAMPLES

DAATS STEP 5—EXAMPLE #7

Correlation Matrix and Scatterplots for Knowledge, Impact, Dispositions, and Skills (KIDS)

Suppose we had 30 teachers who were scored on a series of assessments. Scores are reported here on a fictitious Rasch ruler, but they could also be summed raw scores. The framework is the INTASC Principles, where each instrument is organized by the type of evidence (we changed the traditional order to make a statement—but it is knowledge, skills, dispositions, and impact). A correlation matrix and set of scatterplots reveal relationships.

Name	Knowledge	Skills	Impact	Dispositions
Jerome	74.6	70.8	56.1	55.1
Jim	75.6	74.6	88.9	83.0
Jay	75.7	75.6	75.5	79.6
Judy	81.0	97.5	92.3	99.8
Fred	80	81.0	97.1	96.5
George	74.9	72.9	88.4	88.3
Henry	66.1	64.0	73.5	68.5
Ike	65.0	66.4	111	123.4
Jan	123.4	123.4	97.1	96.7
Karen	70.2	67.4	54.3	57.0
Lacey	64.6	64.4	74.9	76.5
Mike	100.5	102.4	80.9	81.5
Margaret	81.6	84.5	77.5	71.5
Nancy	95.8	89.5	66.1	64.8
Oprah	91.5	95.8	81.5	88.9
Paul	57.0	95.8	75.6	71.5
Quincy	84.5	89.5	66.1	60.5
Rita	81.5	95.8	74.0	71.1
Steve	123.4	115.7	57.0	63.5
Tom	81.5	89.5	80.1	81.5
Ulysses	111.6	123.4	96.5	97.6
Valerie	123.1	123.4	92.2	97.6
William	74.6	70.8	56.1	55.1
Xenia	75.6	74.6	88.9	83.0
Yianni	75.7	75.6	75.5	79.6

(Continued)

(Continued)

Name	Knowledge	Skills	Impact	Dispositions
Zach	81.0	97.5	92.3	99.8
Cathy	80.5	81.0	97.1	96.5
Debbie	74.9	72.9	88.4	88.3
Don	66.1	64.7	73.5	68.5
Ed	65.3	66.4	111.3	123.4
Angela	123.4	123.4	97.1	96.7

Pearson correlation matrix

	KNOWLEDGE	SKILLS	IMPACT	DISPOSITIONS
KNOWLEDGE	1.000			
SKILLS	0.876	1.000		
IMPACT	0.131	0.207	1.000	
DISPOSITIONS	0.177	0.230	0.948	1.000

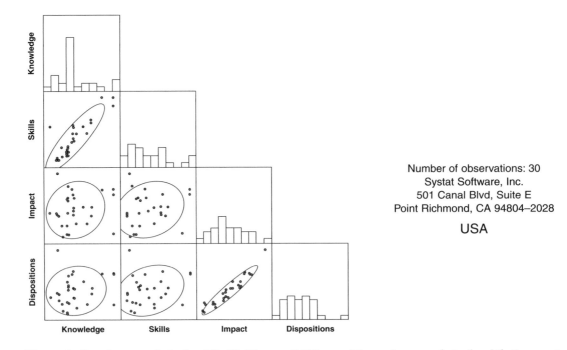

Number of observations: 30
Systat Software, Inc.
501 Canal Blvd, Suite E
Point Richmond, CA 94804–2028

USA

Knowledge is correlated with Skills, and Dispositions is correlated with Impact. This is revealed in the correlation coefficients in the table as well as in and the SPLOM scatterplots.

DAATS STEP 5—EXAMPLE #8

T-Test Comparing Dispositions of Mathematics and Science Teachers

Suppose we had 150 teachers, 75 in mathematics and 75 in science, who were scored on a series of assessments in a framework. Here, we want to see whether there is a significant difference in their overall dispositions, based on their mean scores. Group 1, the math teachers, has a higher mean score than Group 2, the science teachers, by approximately 5 points. The difference is significant at the .015 level. We can conclude, therefore, that math teachers are more consistent with the INTASC dispositions than are science teachers, and we can review instructional strategies and backgrounds to determine whether that accounts for the difference in scores.

```
Two-sample t-test on MEASURE grouped by GROUP against Alternative =
"not equal"
```

Group	N	Mean	SD
1	75	92.361	13.909
2	75	87.534	9.595

```
Separate variance:

Difference in means = 4.828

95.00% CI = 0.968 to 8.687

t = 2.474

df = 131.4

p-value = 0.015


Pooled variance:

Difference in means = 4.828

95.00% CI = 0.972 to 8.683

t = 2.474

df = 148

p-value = 0.014
```

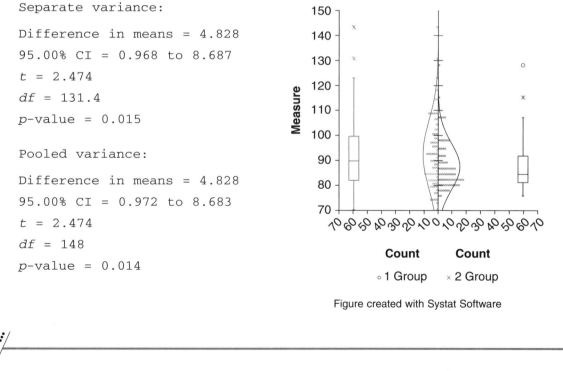

Count **Count**

∘ 1 Group ⨯ 2 Group

Figure created with Systat Software

(Continued)

(Continued)

Here are the item measures correlated from the first administration to the second, indicating stability on the ruler despite the different sample of people.

	ITEM1	ITEM2
ITEM1	1.000	
ITEM2	0.805	1.000

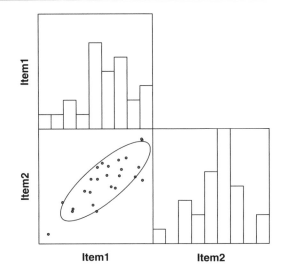

Number of observations: 25

DAATS STEP 5—EXAMPLE #9
DIF Analysis for Programs

Differential item functioning, or DIF, is a statistical process that seeks to determine whether there are meaningful differences in the way *subgroups* perform, particularly groups that are classified as protected—women and minorities. It is okay for the performance to be different, as long as it is not because of *problems in the construction or administration* of the assessment itself.

In this example, we look at the results of a DIF analysis on the belief scale of 75 items taken by 801 teacher candidates from three culturally and geographically diverse universities. DIF can reveal program and institution patterns that are useful for analysis and improvement. Even though the overall average dispositions of all three schools are similar, there are strengths and weaknesses that would be useful to examine.

We present a partial table of the results (Linacre, 2003), with some comments following each excerpt to explain the results. We list the results from the computer printouts, but we are not reporting levels of significance or fancy things here.

```
TABLE 30.2 DispositionScaleSRaschAnalysis ZOU638ws.txt Feb 17 18:40 2005
INPUT: 801 persons, 75 items MEASURED: 801 persons, 65 items, 8 CATS 3.49
--------------------------------------------------------------------------
          Positive DIF size is higher item difficulty measure
   +-------------------------------------------------------------+
   | person    DIF    DIF    item |
   | GROUP   MEASURE  S.E.   Number  Name                        |
```

Example #1

```
   | 1         16.37  2.84        1 BELIEF 1 HOME LIFE           |
   | 3         29.07  3.89        1 BELIEF 1 HOME LIFE           |
   | 2         25.64  5.11        1 BELIEF 1 HOME LIFE           |
```

Item: Agree or Disagree (Item Number 1):
"I usually think about children's home life and environment so that I can tell if something isn't right."

Analysis of Example #1:
Here, one institution (#1) has teachers showing **more** respect for family and home life than at the other two.
Institutions #2 and #3 are similar, while #1 is a whole logit (10 points on the scale) better.

(Continued)

(Continued)

Example #2

```
| 1        33.76 1.40        18 BELIEF 18 VOLUNTEER FOR PTA |
| 3        46.11 2.05        18 BELIEF 18 VOLUNTEER FOR PTA |
| 2        45.92 2.31        18 BELIEF 18 VOLUNTEER FOR PTA |
```

Item: Agree or Disagree (Item Number 18):
"I would likely volunteer to help the PTA improve the school yard."

Analysis of Example #2:
The teachers at Institution #1 are much **more** likely to volunteer for the PTA than at the other two.

Example #3

```
| 1        47.59 1.00        33 BELIEF 33 ART & MUSIC CREATIVITY |
| 3        55.20 1.76        33 BELIEF 33 ART & MUSIC CREATIVITY |
| 2        77.58 2.39        33 BELIEF 33 ART & MUSIC CREATIVITY |
```

Item: Agree or Disagree (Item Number 33):
The subject I teach doesn't focus on creativity or thinking skills, but I believe all students should be exposed to art and music while in school.

Analysis of Example #3:
Here, teachers at all three institutions differ in dispositions. Institution #1 is most consistent with INTASC Principles, #3 is the middle value, and institution #2 is the most inconsistent with INTASC. Compared to large samples, an average score of 77.58 on this scale is extreme and deserves investigation.

DAATS EXAMPLES

8

Using Teacher Scores for Continuous Improvement

*I*f you are really serious about using the data to make good decisions about individual teachers, individual items, criteria on your rubrics, and program quality, then this chapter is written for you. Here, we hope to provide you with the background you need in order to decide whether you want to use a modern measurement model to analyze your results.

In this chapter, we write about our preferred method of analysis, called the Rasch model of "item response theory" (IRT). The Rasch model is named for its developer, Georg Rasch (1960), a mathematician from the Danish Institute for Educational Research. It is the simplest of the IRT models and works well with small samples. IRT is a relatively new technique that differs greatly from "classical test theory" (a.k.a. CTT or "true score theory"). Most classical measurement is based on samples of data (called "norms") that are used to generate distributional statistics such as the mean, standard deviation, percentile rank, and standard scores such as SATs, IQs, and NCEs. Rasch is not sample dependent, does not rely on a normal distribution, and creates an interval scale better suited to statistical analysis.

> **Our Motto**
>
> **KISS—Keep it statistically simple!!!**

We recommend that those using the DAATS model choose the Rasch model for item analysis, reporting scores, and detecting rater effects, because it provides powerful statistics that are relatively simple to understand (if not to compute).

Our purpose in this book is to help you make some informed choices even if you do not want to do the computations yourself. We will not attempt to teach you everything you need to know to run the statistical software packages or read all of the printouts. Instead, our goals are (1) to help you understand what the model can do for you so that you can make informed choices, (2) to help you understand and use the results, and (3) to tell you what you can say to the statisticians about what you want (and don't want) if you ask someone else to crunch the numbers.

We ask you at this point to think back on the stories of Antoinette and Ruby at the end of Chapter 6, DAATS Step 4. There, we shared with you some anecdotes of how we have used statistics and reports produced with this model to diagnose teacher problems and initiate remediation.

Even if you are not interested in terms of measuring teacher competencies and dispositions, you may find this chapter useful when you deal with all those standardized tests that are now scored using IRT models. If you are a principal, your school is graded on a standardized test that almost assuredly is developed using one of the IRT models. We even use some of the examples in this chapter to teach undergraduate students about modern measurement.

We start with a list of seven reasons to use the Rasch model in this context. We continue with a demonstration of classical item analysis, so that you have the tools you need to stay with the classical approach, if you choose to do so. Next, we have a "getting started" section that tells you a little bit more about how the chapter is organized and begins to prepare you for working with your local statistician if you need to use one to implement Rasch techniques. We continue with a simple but technical discussion of how the model works and what it will do for you.

REASONS WHY WE USE THE RASCH MODEL

Here are seven reasons we can identify for using the Rasch model. If you find them to be intriguing and if they sound like what you want to do, then we think you will find this chapter useful:

1. *Valid Decisions About Individuals:* With Rasch, we can fine-tune the data to such an extent that we can be more confident than we can with classical models in our decisions for an individual teacher. Analyses conducted using Rasch tell us when the prediction is not valid or reliable for an individual person—not just the whole group (Smith & Cramer, 1989). *Stop and reread that sentence, please.* It does this through individual calculations of error and something called "fit," which replaces the standard error of measurement (SEM) in classical test theory (CTT). SEM works for the whole group but ignores individual *people* problems. If the teacher's answers are erratic or unpredictable, we know something is wrong with the way he or she answered or was rated. This is what happened with Ruby, in Chapter 6. Her score was not reliable because of her anxieties and was, therefore, not valid for her. Scores using the scale were valid for other people, just not Ruby! Armed with that knowledge, we

can do something about it. So, if you are interested in the individual, then this model is unparalleled in its power to help you. It is, for us, tops on the list. We like to say that *"Rasch puts the people back in the measurement process."*

2. ***Predictions and Diagnostics About Individuals:*** The Rasch model is robust in cases of missing data (Bayley, 2001). So, we can make *early* predictions, from a subset of our items or instruments, about whether a teacher is likely to be high or low on the disposition scale. This is not possible with CTT, which requires complete or relatively complete data. Rasch, therefore, gives us an early celebration (or warning) system. Again, if the individual teacher is of importance to you, the Rasch model is unparalleled.

3. ***Finding and Controlling Rater Effect:*** We can determine the harshness or leniency of raters, so that we can *adjust scores to make them more fair* and avoid excessive use of multiple raters to calculate inter-rater reliability statistics—which takes a lot of time. The need for multiple ratings is vastly reduced. Rasch helps you make *better decisions while spending less time and money.* Analyses conducted using the multifaceted Rasch model (MFRM) of IRT are sensitive to differences among individuals—not just the teachers assessed but also the judges doing the ratings (Myford & Wolfe, 2004). You can identify the raters who are too harsh or too lenient, along with other rater inconsistencies. This helps you have more confidence in the cut score—we are certifying people who should be certified and denying certification to those who shouldn't be certified, without being unduly influenced by rater issues. It also helps you give the benefit of the doubt (or the opposite) when a judge's ratings are too high or too low. You can estimate corrections to misjudged items on the computer, based on calculated rater error.

4. ***Item Analysis and Sensitivity:*** Analyses conducted using the Rasch model of IRT are sensitive to differences in items, making the job of identifying instruments or items that do not work well in practice easily identifiable for *replacement or editing* (Andrich & Wright, 1994).

5. ***Using All the Data—Even Dropouts:*** Since analyses conducted using the Rasch model are robust in cases of missing data, in situations where teachers do not complete all the instruments and drop out of the program, we have good numbers for comparison purposes. You could ask questions like "Did the teachers whose dispositions were inconsistent with INTASC Principles drop out, or am I losing the winners for some reason I need to fix?" This may be the most important information you can get for *predictive validity* studies down the road.

6. ***Research and Improvement:*** The Rasch model creates an interval score (Wright & Linacre, 1989). That helps not only with the decision-making process for individuals and groups but also for conducting other studies. We have a way of investigating important questions: for example, the relationship between dispositions and teacher retention. If we ever hope to do a *predictive validity study or anything longitudinal,* then this capacity is critically important. If you want to do any research on the quality of the program, you need to have measurement quality in the results that will help you do that. Some studies can be done with CTT scores; more and better studies can be done with Rasch measures.

7. ***Cost-Effectiveness:*** A single study using the Rasch model of IRT includes data that can *replace multiple complex statistical studies* when CTT is used as the approach. Because the Rasch model is not sample dependent, it is not necessary

to obtain normal distributions representing multiple demographics, which often takes lots of time and effort. Analyses conducted using the Rasch model of IRT provide evidence of both validity (construct unidimensionality) and reliability (precision).

THE CLASSICAL APPROACH

In both classical and modern approaches, item analysis procedures provide an empirical analysis of how difficult individual items were for the folks who took the test or completed the assessment. We can compare the empirical results with our expectations of how difficult the item or criterion should have been and make decisions about improvement in areas where they do not match in either model. In CTT, we base our decision about difficulty using sample-dependent proportions; in IRT, we use sample-independent conjoint probabilities. We show the proportions approach here.

In Box 8.1, let's start with a simple example for two items, using a simple scale (checklist approach) of "correct" or "incorrect" and addressing only two items from a larger set of items.

Box 8.1.   Example of What an Item Analysis Can Tell You Using Critical Thinking on a Belief Scale

Item 1: Students need to learn to think, and that is a goal that I have that is built into all my lessons. (Correct response is "agree")

Item 2: It's more important that the students learn to think and be creative than it is that they know the material covered by the lessons. (Correct response is "agree")

Expectations: More teachers will answer correctly for Item 1 than for Item 2 because the first item is at the "receiving" level. Those who agree know they should try to incorporate critical thinking (CT) into all lessons. For the second item, they must value CT enough to let it override memorization of content (valuing) or be ready to adapt their lessons to incorporate CT wherever possible (organization or characterization). We repeat the levels of the taxonomy here as a refresher in thinking about these two items.

- *Receiving*: attending, becoming aware of an idea, process, or thing
- *Responding*: makes response at first with compliance, later willingly with satisfaction
- *Valuing*: accepts worth of a thing, prefers it, consistent in responding, commitment
- *Organization*: organizes values, determines interrelationships, adapts behavior to value system
- *Characterization*: generalizes value into controlling tendencies, integrates these with total philosophy

Results: In fact, out of 1,123 students who responded to Item 1, 85% chose "agree." By comparison, out of 1,101 students who answered Item 2, 65% chose "agree." Clearly, Item 1 (at the receiving level) was easier than Item 2 (at the valuing level).

Conclusions and Decision: Teachers are responding consistently with the taxonomic classification of the items. This confirms the quality of the items and the validity of inferences about teachers but points toward the need for improved instruction in the area of valuing critical thinking.

To analyze difficulty if you have used a scale, as we recommended, you will need to be a little more creative in the CTT model. The easiest thing to do is to rank order the results, making sure that the item with the most unacceptable rating is the hardest (at the top) and the item with the most number of high scores is easiest (at the bottom). It doesn't matter which direction you go, but your analysis should logically explain why the items are in the order demonstrated, from easiest to hardest. Table 8.1 shows the example we provided in Step 4 (in Chapter 6). Here, though, we would not look at Professor Jones's class, but rather all sections over a period of time, say one year. In the original example, we had an interpretation about data aggregation, which still holds. Here, we write the explanation for item analysis. These are the same data, but resulting in different interpretations and uses.

Table 8.1. Results for a Group of Teachers on an Individual Assessment

Secondary Teachers' Results on the Belief Scale

$N = 50$

Criteria	Correct		Incorrect	
	#	%	#	%
I usually think about children's home life and environment so that I can tell if something isn't right.	10	20	40	80
I believe good teachers learn about the students' backgrounds and community so they can understand their motivations.	15	30	35	70
It is most important that I know and teach my subject well, regardless of the age and grade of students in my class.	20	40	30	60
If students complete all the lessons I teach and do all the assigned work, they will learn what they need to know.	25	50	25	50
Students need to learn to think, and that is a goal that I have that is built into all my lessons.	40	80	10	20

Interpretation: The most difficult items for these teachers relate to family and community life, age appropriate instruction, and regimentation. They performed very well on the question related to critical thinking. Many of the teachers are in an alternative certification program and have a prior military background, mostly officers.

Conclusion: The items are ordering by difficulty in a logical way.

If you are in a small department with minimal expectations regarding continued analysis and research, the process modeled above using CTT should work well for you.

A QUICK OVERVIEW OF WHERE RASCH FITS INTO THE GRAND SCHEME OF IRT MODELS

Know from the outset that IRT is a relatively recent development in measurement theory, getting started in the 1960s and taking more serious hold in the measurement community in the 1980s. All major test publishers now use IRT instead of (or in combination with) CTT, so if you have seen SAT, GRE, ACT, or SAT-9 scores recently, you have seen an IRT-based score. Even the states are moving in this direction for K–12 assessments. If nothing else, look at these next few pages as a professional development opportunity.

There are three major IRT models. The models calculate, and are identified by, the number of parameters that are estimated. All models estimate item difficulty, and it is not counted in the number of parameters in the model-naming conventions. In its simplest form, the one-parameter (1PL) model estimates the ability of people taking the test, in addition to the difficulty of test items. The 2PL model adds a discrimination parameter, and the 3PL model adds a guessing parameter. Explaining the differences, pros, and cons, is way beyond the scope of this book! Different folks use different models, depending on their needs and preferences. For example, most major test publishers write multiple-choice tests designed to sort people into normally distributed categories. They tend to prefer the 3PL model. States like Florida have also selected this model for K–12 testing. The 3PL model requires a sample size of at least 1,000, eliminating it from consideration for most of our readers no matter what your in-house statisticians tell you. It also precludes the test publishers from finding out about people problems (as Rasch does) and having to deal with them.

Other states prefer the 1PL model, or a version of it called the "Rasch model," because they are less concerned about discrimination and guessing statistics and want more stable estimates of ability and difficulty. The more parameters you add in, the fuzzier these numbers get. Texas has used the Rasch model for its K–12 tests (Texas Education Agency, 2005), as do the public schools for their classroom tests in Portland, Oregon (Ingebo, 1997), and the South Carolina High School Assessment Program (Wolfe & Mapuranga, 2004). It is also widely used outside the field of education, in various health sciences (Bezruczko, 2005). Because this is relatively technical stuff, we will provide some summaries for you as we go along.

> **QUICK SUMMARY**
>
> IRT is the current state of the art in measurement. It has three models. The Rasch model is a version of the simplest. It is widely used and growing rapidly. Classical test theory (CTT) is used less and less in the modern measurement world. Rasch is highly useful if you want to know about individuals as individuals—and not as members of a group—and if you are worried about raters and future research studies.

RASCH: THE BASICS

Here is the basic idea: The ability of individuals and the difficulty of items influence each other and are related. The standard discussion of Rasch talks about *ability*, and we will use that term here, but remember that the concept works for all traits— ability, dispositions, and consistency with INTASC Principles.

IRT models envision a continuum of ability (or dispositions or consistency) that can be placed on a ruler that measures a person's ability (or dispositions or consistency) along with item difficulty, without regard to a particular sampling. The units of measurement of difficulty and ability/disposition are called "logits" (Barnard, 2001), just as the units on the more familiar ruler are called "inches."

With the Rasch model of IRT, we answer questions like "Can a person lift a stone because the stone is light or because the person is strong" (Wright & Stone, 2004)? Obviously, the person's strength (or ability) and the weight of the stone (or difficulty) are related and influence each other. A weak person will not be able to lift a heavy stone, and a strong person will do so easily. What is easy for one person is difficult for another, so talking about a stone's weight by itself does not tell you who will be able to lift it. The Rasch model works because we put both ability and difficulty on the same interval scale, so we can make predictions about one from the other. This is called "conjoint measurement." The conceptual appeal is so clear that we have to pause to ask why it took us so long to figure this out. The answer to that question is that it took a very creative mathematician in Denmark to make it work.

If you are familiar with Lexiles (Stenner, 1996), a scale for reading, then you have heard of this model. When we estimate the ability of a reader and the difficulty of a reading passage using Lexiles, we acknowledge that the *probability* of a reader understanding what he or she has read is dependent on two things: how good a reader he or she is and how hard the passage is. The two work together, which is really common sense. It stands to reason that your assessment process will have some instruments that are more difficult and some teachers who are less disposed, just as some people are stronger and lift heavier stones and others are better readers and can read more difficult passages. We all know that there are some teachers who are more dedicated, enthusiastic, and caring than other teachers. Rasch addresses the fundamental question: "What are the odds (probability) that this person can read this passage or this teacher can do this task well or this teacher will spend more time planning or go the extra mile for a child?"

The description of the model from the Rasch Unidimensional Measurement Model (RUMM, 2003) Laboratory Web site is useful:

> **QUICK SUMMARY**
> Ability and difficulty are related, and that relationship can be used to measure both together. What is easy for one person might be difficult for another. Rasch puts ability and difficulty on the same scale, making the relationship between the two explicit. The same can be said for dispositions or consistency with the INTASC Principles. The method creates a "ruler" of abilities (or dispositions or consistency) and difficulties. People and items are placed on the ruler based on probabilities or odds of success. This psychometric ruler will have measurement units on it (called "logits"), just like a wooden ruler has inches on it.

> Rasch analysis can be applied to assessments in a wide range of disciplines, including health studies, education, psychology, marketing, economics and social sciences. . . . The Rasch model is the only item response theory (IRT) model in which the total score across items characterizes a person totally. . . . The aim of a Rasch analysis is analogous to helping construct a ruler, but with the data of a test or questionnaire. (See http://www.rummlab.com.au/)

Now that you're armed and ready for meeting and greeting your friendly local statistician (just kidding), you might want to know just a little so you can teach him or her a thing or two. You can expect some arguments. Most statisticians and measurement folks will try to sway you toward classical test theory because that is what they studied in graduate school. If they are familiar with IRT, they will probably try to push you toward the 2PL or 3PL models, because that, too, is what they studied. To end the debate, remember these things about Rasch:

1. Rasch is the model of choice for fit statistics about people (not just items); the others address fit statistics for items only and don't put the people back into the measurement process. If there were ever a place where people counted, it would be dispositions!

2. Rasch is the only IRT model that allows you to look systematically at rater effect.

3. Rasch is not sample dependent, does not require a large sample of people, and does not make assumptions about the normality of the distribution. It also works really well with missing data.

4. Rasch is easier to compute and understand, which will reduce your future dependency and debating time.

Here's your start. Take the statement in Box 8.2 to the statistician, and read it to him or her (with conviction!).

Box 8.2.   Gaining Control of the Local Statistician: What You Say

I have selected the Rasch model because I am implementing an assessment process targeted at measuring consistency with INTASC disposition indicators. My expectation is that eventually almost all teachers will successfully complete all instruments and be certified. I have only 100 teachers in my program, so my sample size will be small. They will not be normally distributed; I will have data that have extreme negative skew—with most teachers showing high consistency. I am not interested in measuring the utility of my process in discriminating between high and low performers, and guessing is not a factor. I am very interested, though, in locating and helping teachers who have scores with unexplained or unusual anomalies (misfitting scores) and identifying and correcting for rater effect. I also want to make use of data on non-completers, so I need a model that is powerful with missing data. Rasch is the only measurement model that provides the fit statistic I need for diagnostic purposes and allows me to estimate and correct for rater effect. I want to use the Rasch model for those reasons. Thank you very much for expressing your concerns. I will be happy to help you obtain some of the references I have read about and purchase some software for you. [End of discussion]

GETTING STARTED

Do you remember your first statistics course? We would wager that at some point during the course, the professor said to you something like the following:

In this course, you are going to do some statistical analysis that will generate some tables (probably in SPSS or SAS). You will not understand every number on every table. Don't worry about it. I'll tell you what you need to know.

If your statistics professor didn't tell you that, it may be too late to ask for your money back, but you should have done so at the time. Approach this chapter with that caveat in mind. You will see some tables with lots of numbers on them because the best way to learn about this method is to read a little about it and then look at some actual output from some fake data sets. That is what we will do here. You may not understand every number, and that is fine. At a minimum, you will be able to converse intelligently about the model and what it can do for you. We will guide you through what you need to know to make an informed decision about whether this is something worth doing in your department. Skip the rest.

We note one more thing. For demonstration purposes, in the examples that follow, we will use data based on a correct/incorrect (right/wrong) response set—often the result of a Thurstone agreement scale. We add in rating scales later, just as we did in the classical example, to keep it statistically simple. Everything we present in the beginning is equally relevant to rating scales and performance assessments. The numbers are a bit easier to follow with dichotomous (right/wrong) data, though.

We start with a very big hurdle that we have to jump over: the difference that item writers can make. Like test takers, some are skilled, and some are not. The way the item is written influences how difficult it is.

Differences That Item Writers Make

Now imagine Jo. Jo is smart and caring, and she would be a good teacher. She completes a 10-item survey. (We know, that's too short, but it is easy to draw on our picture.) Her score, though, can be influenced by the difficulty of the test. In the example for valuing critical thinking, above, she might answer correctly on the first item and incorrectly on the second item. If all items were easy, her score would be higher. Few individuals would disagree with the statement "Planning is important." Less would agree with "I would rather plan a lesson than eat a fine meal."

Now let's imagine two sets of item writers—the tough group and the easy group. If Jo takes the survey from the tough group, she gets a score of 2. If she takes the survey from the easy group, she gets a score of 8. With the first survey, she is scheduled for counseling; with the second, she is cleared to move forward.

Remember now, Jo is Jo—same person, just a different survey. Only the people who wrote the items were different. Her dispositions are a constant; the item writers' abilities vary. Now look at Figure 8.1 on page 212, which shows where Jo would be placed on the survey without taking into account the difficulty of the survey items (and the skill/brains of the writers). Note also that we have symbolized her answers with "1's" and "0's."

Assessment will always be misleading with sample-dependent scores. Counting the number of items right is not measuring, but measurement occurs when you know where both the items and the people fall on the ruler (Wright & Stone, 1979).

Guttman Scaling

We looked at Jo's scores in Figure 8.1 on just two different assessments, noting which items she had right and which ones she had wrong, using 1's and 0's. A theoretical model exists (Guttman, 1944) that says people have a certain ability level and they will get items right (on a perfect test) until this ability level (or dispositions) falls off. Then, they start getting items wrong when items become too difficult for them. Of course, there is no such thing as a perfect test or survey, but we can use this theory

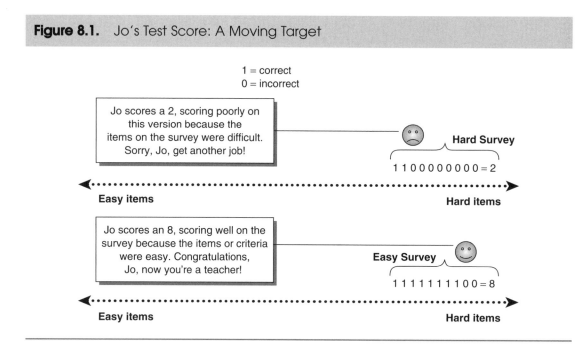

Figure 8.1. Jo's Test Score: A Moving Target

1 = correct
0 = incorrect

Jo scores a 2, scoring poorly on this version because the items on the survey were difficult. Sorry, Jo, get another job!

Hard Survey

1 1 0 0 0 0 0 0 0 0 = 2

Easy items   Hard items

Jo scores an 8, scoring well on the survey because the items or criteria were easy. Congratulations, Jo, now you're a teacher!

Easy Survey

1 1 1 1 1 1 1 1 0 0 = 8

Easy items   Hard items

to establish some expectations, or probabilities, that people will get certain items right and certain items wrong, based on their abilities, and we can figure out where they are likely to make the transition to "not able" or "inconsistent with standards-based dispositions." If a survey works well, we can see a pattern of 1's up to the point that their abilities trail off; then we see 0's. Usually, there is a mix of 1's and 0's in between. Remembering that there is no perfect test and no perfect testing situation for an individual, we allow for deviations in the pattern. This pattern is at the core of the Rasch model because it looks at the ability of the people and the difficulty of the items together.

Figure 8.2 on the page opposite is a Guttman scalogram of 10 people taking a 10-item survey. Remember that "1" stands for right and "0" stands for wrong. This is our first computer-generated data. We are using a software program called Winsteps (Linacre, 2003).

The items are in order from easiest to hardest. The item numbers are at the top (third and fourth row), beginning with Item 4 and ending with Item 2. Item 10 takes two rows to print. Item 4 (first column; read down) is the easiest because all 10 persons taking the survey answered the item correctly (all 1's). Item 2 is the hardest (last column), and only one student got it right. Putting items and people in the same analysis is called "conjoint measurement," previously mentioned, which is a special characteristic of the Rasch model. Notice also that there is a diagonal that runs through the data from top to bottom: Most of the 1's are to the left, and most of the 0's are to the right of the diagonal.

You can also see that Steve, Roy, and Judy had the highest scores, with nine right answers. Pink was the lowest, with two right answers. Pink is at the bottom. Let's talk about Steve and Judy first. Steve has a perfect Guttman pattern (as does Roy). He would; he wrote most of this chapter. Judy, on the other hand, is a bit weird, according to her scalogram, of course. She got Item 10 wrong and was the only person to get Item 2 right. If she had an ideal Guttman pattern, she would have answered Item 10 correctly, too, but then she might conclude that she had a better attitude than Steve, and he did create the data in this chapter.

Figure 8.2. Example Guttman Scalogram of Responses to a 10-Item Survey

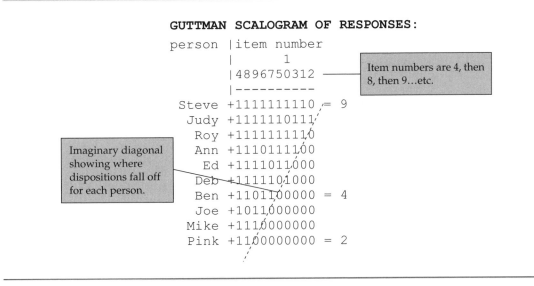

There are other deviations from the Guttman pattern in the test, but it is not really about being "Guttman perfect." We said already that the pattern is theoretical, just like the normal curve. Ben and Joe, for example, also have an item wrong in the "right" zone, but we're all human, and the survey items are not perfect. We will revisit these later and see whether they are something to worry about. For now, let's focus on the fact that the data are pretty close to a perfect Guttman scale. We're ready to see how they would look on a Rasch ruler.

A Sample Rasch Ruler

In the graphic in Figure 8.3, we show a Rasch ruler that places our 10 items and 10 people on the same scale. You can see that Item 4, our easiest item, is to the far left and Item 2, our hardest item, is to the far right. For simplicity's sake, we did not put all 10 people on the ruler, just 3—Steve, who was at the top of our Guttman scale; Pink, who was the bottom; and Ben, who was in the bottom half. Notice that the

Figure 8.3. Sample Logistic Ruler of 10 Survey Items Calibrated on a Ruler—User-Friendly Version

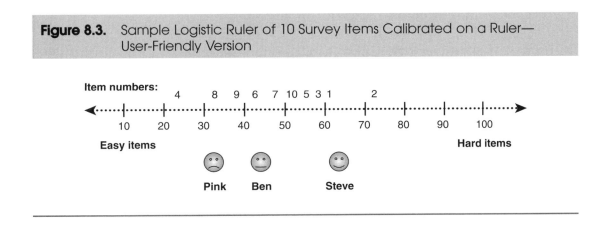

distance between the items is not equal. That is because the difference in difficulty between the items is not the same. That's a sure sign that we are converting to interval data, not ordinal data. The same would be true with the people—different distances because of differing abilities. Item 4 is a lot easier than Item 8, but Item 5 has little difference in difficulty from Item 3. The process of calculating the amount of difficulty in these items is called "calibration."

We write items that we believe represent the construct and *calibrate* them where they fall on the ruler, with equal intervals (from 10 to 100). In CTT, item difficulty is based on the *proportion* of people who answer correctly. In IRT, difficulty is based on the *probability* that people will get the item correct. Some pretty basic and logical expectations follow:

- At your ability level, you have a 50% chance of being right on items with the same difficulty level as your ability (same logit value for ability and difficulty). In practical terms, because Guttman scaling is not precise—no perfect people and no perfect surveys—there is a gray area of items where people get some right and some wrong, but this is where your ability starts to fall off, so it makes sense that you have only a 50–50 chance of being right. It's the "coin toss zone."

- For items that are "harder than you are able," you are less likely to answer correctly. The higher up they are on the ruler, the more difficult they are and the less likely you are to get them right. You reach a point where it makes no sense for you to get them right; they are much harder than you are able—unless you looked at somebody else's survey or had a sudden flash of inspiration.

- For items that are "easier than you are able," you are more likely to get them correct. So, again, the further away they are from you (lower down on the ruler), the more likely you are to get them right! You reach a point where it makes no sense for you to get them wrong unless you fall asleep during the test or are off one on the bubble sheet all the way down the page.

- The more frequently you correctly answer questions that are too hard for you and/or you are wrong for items that are easier than your ability level, the more peculiar your total score is. You are not responding according to the mathematical odds. When this happens, if it happens just to you—most everybody else is responding as expected in terms of the odds—then we know that something went wrong for you! Were you really nervous?

- This is what we meant by "putting the people back into the measurement process." We look at the score for each person as an individual and see whether they responded according to the odds.

Let's go back to our example. Probabilistically speaking, Pink should get items easier than her ability correct (in this case, Items 4 and 8). Ben should get Items 4, 8, and 9 correct, but not 1, 2, or 3.

From Pictures to Numbers

If we are presenting a report to someone over the age of 10, we probably should lose the smiley faces. In this section, we will provide some real computer printouts for our fake data. Remember the advice we gave you at the beginning: You don't have to understand all of the numbers! In the charts and tables that follow, we will first convert the smiley faces to a graph (Figure 8.4), generated again from the Winsteps (Linacre, 2003) software. We call it "The Ruler"; some people, including Linacre, call it the "variable map." It is the same thing.

Figure 8.4. Sample Logistic Ruler of 10 Survey Items Calibrated on a Ruler—Grown-Up Version

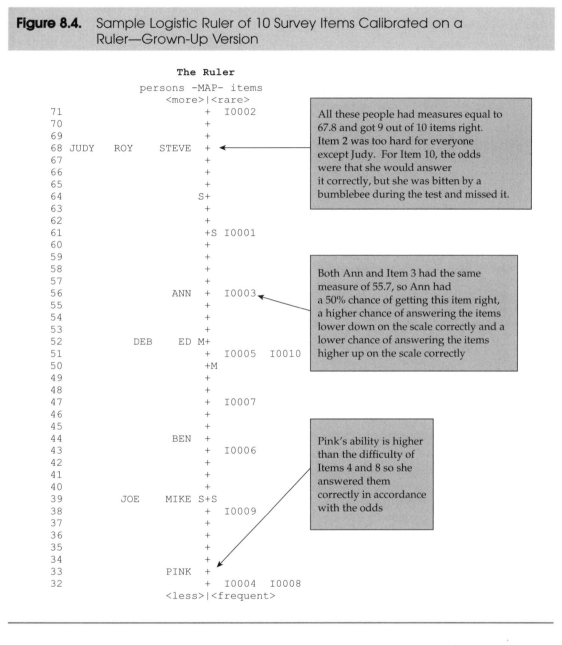

From the raw scores, the "measure" of each person and item can be calculated. Although it is a scale score, we use the term "measure" in Rasch because there are many types of scale scores. The "measure" is described in logits, which, as mentioned, are the psychometric version of inches. We can label the scale to any set of values we want, so you will see logistic rulers that have positive and negative numbers that range from 0 to 100, from 0 to 10, or from 200 to 1,600. The default is –3.0 to 3.0, with a mean of 0 and a logit of 1. Our sample ruler has a mean of 50 and a logit of 10. The mean and standard deviation are indicated by "M "and "S."

Now, in Figure 8.5, we will look at a table from the Winsteps output that provides the data for the people. There will be the same kind of table for items. This makes sense, because Rasch is using conjoint measurement to measure people and items at the same time on the same scale. So, two tables are needed: one for people and one for items. Actually, the tables are split into two parts, and we will explain them separately. First—the people, of course!

Figure 8.5. Rasch Output for Sample Data—People

```
+--------------------------------------------------------------------------------+
|ENTRY    RAW                     MODEL|   INFIT   |  OUTFIT   |PTMEA|         |
|NUMBER  SCORE  COUNT  MEASURE   S.E. |MNSQ  ZSTD|MNSQ  ZSTD|CORR.| PERSON|
|-----------------------------------------+----------+----------+-----+-------|
|    4      8      9     67.8    6.8| .28  -.9| .10   1.3| .61| Steve  |
|    5      8      9     67.8    6.8|2.64  1.6|3.33  1.9| .10| JUDY   |
|    7      8      9     67.8    6.8| .28  -.9| .10   1.3| .61| Roy    |
|    3      6      9     55.7    4.7|1.23   .6|1.80   .9| .54| Ann    |
|    2      5      9     51.6    4.5| .89  -.1| .59   .0| .70| Ed     |
|   10      5      9     51.6    4.5| .57 -1.1| .36  -.3| .77| Deb    |
|    8      3      9     43.6    4.7|1.12   .4| .72   .5| .68| Ben    |
|    1      2      9     39.0    5.1|1.37   .8| .79  1.0| .62| Joe    |
|    9      2      9     39.0    5.1| .41 -1.2| .22   .7| .79| Mike   |
|    6      1      9     32.9    6.1| .47  -.8| .17  1.7| .73| Pink   |
|-----------------------------------------+----------+----------+-----+-------|
| MEAN    4.8    9.0    51.7    5.5| .93  -.2| .82   .9|     |        |
| S.D.    2.6     .0    12.4    1.0| .68   .9| .97   .7|     |        |
+--------------------------------------------------------------------------------+
```

We can order the output in different ways. In Figure 8.5 it is ordered on the basis of difficulty, with the people with the highest disposition scores on top. Steve, Judy, and Roy are first, all with the same measure of 67.8. During data entry, they were the fourth, fifth, and seventh persons entered. Names are in the last column. We could have had the output in other orders—problems or misfits, order of data entry, and so forth. The table is divided into eight columns, as follows:

1. "Entry number" is the number assigned to the person as the data were entered into the computer.

2. "Raw score" is the number of items correct. When calculating the score (or measure), Rasch eliminates all of the items that everyone got right or wrong, because they do not contribute to the calculation. That's a bitter pill to swallow, but we are looking for variability, so it works. Item 4 was excluded from this analysis because everyone got it right. In Steve's case (first row), his score is 8.

3. "Count" tells you how many items Steve answered. Since Item 4 was eliminated, there were only nine items used to calibrate this survey.

4. "Measure," in boldface, is the set of scores on the logistic ruler. Steve's score is 67.8 in our scale. Remember that we chose to label "50" as our midpoint.

5. "Model S.E." is the standard error for Steve's score. We could be off by 6.8 scale points, so if Steve were retested, he would probably score between 61 and 74.6. On our map, a logit equals 10 points, so 6.8 points is two thirds of a logit. Notice that the error is different for everyone who took the survey. This is a major difference from CTT, where we do not differentiate for any individual. Scores are more precise (less error) for people in the middle, like Ed, for whom the standard error is only 4.5.

6. "Infit" is in the next column, and it is divided into two subcolumns. The first, mean square (MNSQ) tells us how accurate the measure is for Steve. Remember Guttman and the idea that no survey or person is perfect? The fit statistic tells us how far off of the pattern we are—how well the odds worked for each person. We expect (and want) some difference, typically between .5 and 2.0. If the fit statistic is less than .5, the odds were just too perfectly met. More than 2.0, we're not so sure what we've got—we call it a lot of "noise." The person did not respond as expected based on the probabilities. In these data, only Judy was in that range. Remember, she got one wrong that she wasn't expected to get wrong. It's tough to make big decisions about fit with small numbers of people and items, but that is basically how it works. The standardized z score is a significance test for the value of the MNSQ, and typically, we look for values over 2.0 as indicating suspicious scores, but the sample size and the possibility of type I error mean that we don't automatically assume anything until we investigate.

7. "Outfit" works a lot like infit except it takes into account whether the items that were not answered as predicted were on the high or low end of the scale. Infit focuses more on the midrange. In practice, infit is sensitive to "organized misfit," such as marking everything as answer "B." Outfit is more sensitive to "random misfit," such as test anxiety.

8. "PTMEA CORR." is the point-biserial correlation. In classical test theory, you might recognize this as a measure of item discrimination. It's a little hard to think of what this means in terms of people, but we could say that it means that the people's scores are helping to differentiate between easy and hard items. Talk about role reversal!

9. "Persons" are people—you probably guessed that one.

At the bottom of the table are means and standard deviations (SD). Yes, they are what you think they are. The most important new number is the mean for "INFIT ZSTD," which is expected to be 0.0 with an SD of 1.0. INFIT ZSTD is a standardized unweighted statistical test of the disturbances in the data as reflected in the fit of the data to the underlying construct. Here the values are −.2 and .9. We are where we should be with Guttman.

Figure 8.6 (Part II of the table in Figure 8.5), is the summary table for people. It starts by repeating the last two rows of the previous table. We include the table only because of the bottom part. Remember that we said earlier that a perk of using Rasch is that you get reliability as a bonus. Well, this is where you get it. For 10 items and 10 people, a Cronbach's alpha of .82 is pretty respectable!

Figure 8.6. Rasch Output for Summary Statistics on the 10 Persons Measured

```
+--------------------------------------------------------------------+
|          RAW                    MODEL      INFIT        OUTFIT      |
|          SCORE    COUNT   MEASURE ERROR   MNSQ  ZSTD   MNSQ  ZSTD   |
|--------------------------------------------------------------------|
| MEAN      4.8      9.0     51.68  5.50    .93   -.2    .82    .9    |
| S.D.      2.6       .0     12.39   .96    .68    .9    .97    .7    |
| MAX.      8.0      9.0     67.81  6.80   2.64   1.6   3.33   1.9    |
| MIN.      1.0      9.0     32.91  4.46    .28  -1.2    .10   -.3    |
|--------------------------------------------------------------------|
| REAL RMSE   6.36 ADJ.SD  10.64  SEPARATION 1.67  person RELIABILITY .74 |
|MODEL RMSE   5.58 ADJ.SD  11.07  SEPARATION 1.98  person RELIABILITY .80 |
| S.E. OF person MEAN = 4.13                                         |
+--------------------------------------------------------------------+
          person RAW SCORE-TO-MEASURE CORRELATION = 1.00
      CRONBACH ALPHA (KR-20) person RAW SCORE RELIABILITY = .82
```

The Rasch model gives estimates of reliability of the test items and the persons taking the test at the same time.

In Figure 8.7, you see Item 4 being dropped out of the analysis. We mentioned it earlier in the "people table" (Figure 8.5). Rasch is labeling it "minimum estimated measure." If everyone got it wrong (and it was dropped), it would have been "maximum estimated measure." Either way, it does not contribute to the variability of scores.

All of the columns work the same way. You can see what Judy did to Item 10—the one she was likely to get right until the bumble bee bit her. Outfit was 3.03, which is above our ceiling of 2.0. It is showing up as outfit because she was a top-scoring person, not a middle-range person. Again, though, we would need more people and items to be very worried about this. We probably would take a look at it, though, as part of our validation and evaluation efforts, and then put an ice cube on the bee bite.

Figure 8.7. Rasch Output for Sample Data—Items

```
                    ITEM STATISTICS:  MEASURE ORDER
+------------------------------------------------------------------------+
|ENTRY   RAW                    MODEL|  INFIT   |  OUTFIT  |PTMEA|        |
|NUMBER  SCORE  COUNT  MEASURE   S.E. |MNSQ  ZSTD|MNSQ  ZSTD|CORR.| ITEM  |
|------------------------------------+----------+----------+-----+------- |
|   2      1     10    71.4      5.8| .90   .0| .31   1.9|  .43| I0002|
|   1      3     10    60.6      5.1| .23  -1.5| .15    .0|  .85| I0001|
|   3      4     10    55.7      4.9| .44  -1.1| .23   -.4|  .86| I0003|
|   5      5     10    51.2      4.7| .56   -.9| .29   -.5|  .84| I0005|
|  10      5     10    51.2      4.7|1.36   .8|3.03   1.5|  .58| I0010|
|   7      6     10    46.9      4.7| .98   .1| .56    .1|  .73| I0007|
|   6      7     10    42.6      4.7|1.50  1.0|1.76   1.0|  .48| I0006|
|   9      8     10    38.0      4.9|1.03   .2| .53   1.0|  .54| I0009|
|   8      9     10    32.3      5.9|1.25   .6| .51   2.0|  .34| I0008|
|   4     10     10    24.9      9.4| MINIMUM ESTIMATED MEASURE |  I0004|
|------------------------------------+----------+----------+-----+------- |
| MEAN    5.8   10.0   47.5      5.5| .92   -.1| .82    .7|     |       |
| S.D.    2.6    .0    13.0      1.4| .41   .8| .90    .9|     |       |
+------------------------------------------------------------------------+
```

In Rasch, we make every effort to fix items rather than tossing them if they are problematic, because we found the item critical when we put it on the assessment. We start with a reason for putting each item on the survey, so we need to salvage them. Items and people are measured together and stay together. This is the measurement version of the Equal Rights Amendment. This is a different philosophy than the classical or traditional approach, in which items are randomly representative of a domain of skills and a bit more expendable. We can't just toss out items in conjoint measurement, or we would have to shoot some people, too. The Rasch model is a conceptual approach to measurement as much as it is a statistical method (see Figure 8.8).

Figure 8.8. Rasch Output for Summary Statistics on the 10 Items Measured

```
          SUMMARY OF 10 MEASURED (EXTREME AND NON-EXTREME) items
+----------------------------------------------------------------------+
|           RAW                          MODEL       INFIT      OUTFIT  |
|           SCORE    COUNT    MEASURE     ERROR    MNSQ  ZSTD  MNSQ  ZSTD|
|----------------------------------------------------------------------|
| MEAN       5.8     10.0      47.49      5.48                          |
| S.D.       2.6       .0      13.00      1.38                          |
| MAX.      10.0     10.0      71.41      9.42                          |
| MIN.       1.0     10.0      24.92      4.69                          |
|----------------------------------------------------------------------|
| REAL RMSE  5.90  ADJ.SD  11.58  SEPARATION 1.96  item  RELIABILITY .79|
|MODEL RMSE  5.66  ADJ.SD  11.71  SEPARATION 2.07  item  RELIABILITY .81|
| S.E. OF item MEAN = 4.33                                              |
+----------------------------------------------------------------------+
```

The Winsteps "person reliability" is equivalent to the traditional "test" reliability. Low values indicate a narrow range of person measures, or a small number of items. To increase person reliability, test persons with more extreme abilities (high and low) or lengthen the survey. Improving the survey targeting may help slightly. The Winsteps "item reliability" has no traditional equivalent. Low values indicate a narrow range of item measures, or a small sample. To increase item reliability, survey more people (Linacre, 2003).

The Fit Statistic

In our example above, we noticed how the score for Judy had a potential problem called "misfit," because she answered one question incorrectly when the probability was that she would be correct on that question. We also noted that we do not make too big a deal out of one item, and we gave her an ice cube to cure the bee sting. Let's see what happens when the response pattern is really fouled up.

In the following example, we will change the results and have Ann doing some really bizarre things. In fact, her responses are all backwards; she gets wrong what she should get right (easy stuff) and right what she should get wrong (hard stuff). The Guttman scalogram is repeated in Figure 8.9, with the data for Ann changed. We follow that with our "people table."

Figure 8.9. Guttman Scalogram With Ann's Data Manipulated for Misfit Demonstration

```
                    GUTTMAN SCALOGRAM OF RESPONSES:

                    person |item number
                           |    1
                           |4896750312
                           |----------
                    Steve +1111111110
                     Judy +1111110111
                      Roy +1111111110
                      Ann +0010111111  (instead of 1110111100)
                       Ed +1111011000
                      Deb +1111101000
                      Ben +1101100000
                      Joe +1011000000
                     Mike +1110000000
                     Pink +1100000000
                           Easy    Hard
```

Ann's score (7) is the same, but we've caused Ann to miss some easy items while getting some hard items correct. Remember that we said we could print out the tables in various orders. Figure 8.10 shows the "person table" printed in misfit order. This quick process allows users to identify very quickly the teachers for whom the data are highly suspect (i.e., not reliable and not valid.)

Figure 8.10. Rasch Output in Misfit Order Showing Ann on Top With the Most Misfitting Score (Not Reliable and Not Valid)

PERSON STATISTICS: MISFIT ORDER

ENTRY NUMBER	RAW SCORE	COUNT	MEASURE	MODEL S.E.	INFIT MNSQ	INFIT ZSTD	OUTFIT MNSQ	OUTFIT ZSTD	PTMEA CORR.	PERSON
3	*7*	*10*	*57.4*	*4.7*	*1.34*	*.8*	*8.53*	*2.5*	*A .39*	*ANN*
5	9	10	69.5	6.8	2.60	1.6	2.86	1.9	B .09	JUDY
8	4	10	45.5	4.5	.93	.0	.59	.3	C .69	BEN
1	3	10	41.5	4.5	.93	.0	.59	.7	D .62	JOE
2	6	10	53.3	4.5	.88	-.1	.51	-.1	E .73	ED
10	6	10	53.3	4.5	.57	-1.0	.33	-.4	e .80	DEB
9	3	10	41.5	4.5	.54	-1.0	.31	.5	d .72	MIKE
6	2	10	37.3	4.7	.51	-1.3	.26	1.0	c .63	PINK
4	9	10	69.5	6.8	.28	-.9	.09	1.4	b .66	STEVE
7	9	10	69.5	6.8	.28	-.9	.09	1.4	a .66	ROY
MEAN	5.8	10.0	53.8	5.2	.89	-.3	1.42	.9		
S.D.	2.6	.0	11.8	1.0	.65	.9	2.49	.9		

Now, Ann is at the top of this list. Her OUTFIT is much higher than the normal value we expect (MNSQ > 2), so we need to look at Ann's survey and responses carefully to see what's going on. This type of analysis is very sensitive to unusual patterns in students and can be used to detect carelessness, guessing, cheating, anxiety, clerical errors, response sets, and bias (Linacre, 2003).

Gain Scores—Real or Imagined?

One of the biggest advantages of using the Rasch model and calibrating items and people on the same interval scale is that we can make mathematical statements that make sense. We can talk about an item being twice as hard as another item or a person being twice as able or enthusiastic or committed in a scientific way. That allows us to measure growth accurately. In the data we have just fabricated, we could make the following mathematical computations and conclusions:

Steve (67.8) – Ben (43.6) = 24.3
Ben (43.6) – Pink (32.9) = 10.7

"Steve is twice as far ahead of Ben as Ben is ahead of Pink."

We can make this statement because we have scientifically based data on the difficulty of the items. One of the most common problems in using gain scores in the classroom context, such as the Teacher Work Sample Methodology, is that we reach conclusions about what students learned or did not learn on the basis of tests that have items of different difficulty that have not been calibrated scientifically. While we could use CTT to calculate difficulty in one sense (the proportion of students responding correctly), that is dependent on the sample we happen to be working with, so the difficulty of the items is still not calibrated correctly. This makes faking possible.

Ratings and Raters

One of the biggest challenges faced in assessment is ensuring that ratings are valid and reliable. We dedicated much attention in this book to the creation of good rating scales, including the definition of proficiency levels for each item rated. With Rasch, we have the opportunity to obtain empirical evidence of whether or not the ratings are working as we intended. Given the certification context, we expect that there will be very few unacceptable ratings. Depending on how we define "upper levels of disposition"—acceptable and beyond—we need to know whether our raters are using the scales in meaningful ways. Rasch output helps us make these judgments. Two examples are shown in Figures 8.11 and 8.12. Both examples use three categories: high, medium, and low (so we don't argue about the descriptors!) As in all analysis, we need to compare our results with our expectations.

In the first example, Figure 8.11, where rating categories are 0, 1, and 2, if we expect to see a distinction of categories in our ratings, this graph would be appropriate. In the second example, Figure 8.12, we see a problem. If we expect our raters to use the rating of "2"—the middle ground—we see that they are not doing so. This can be a useful diagnostic tool. We see this when categories or rubrics are not clear (i.e., 1 = bridging, 2 = emerging, 3 = improving).

Figure 8.11. Rasch Output Showing Distinct Rating Categories

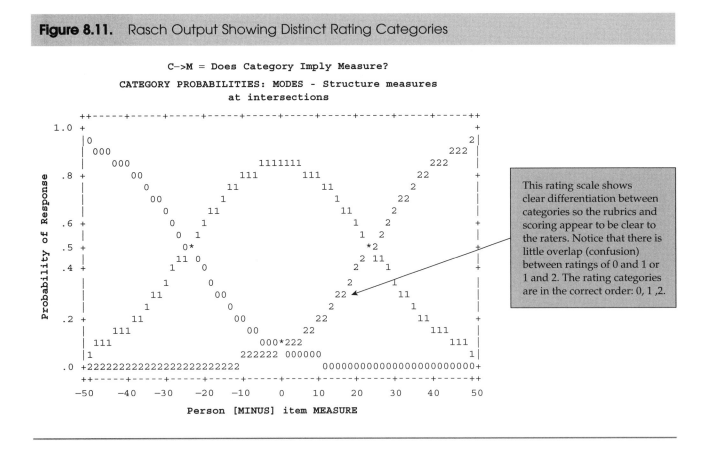

Figure 8.12. Rasch Output Showing Rater Confusion—No Middle Category

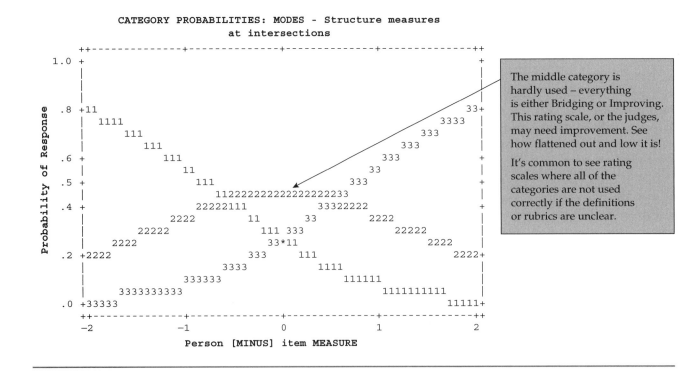

You may be thinking that you can obtain that information just from looking at the frequency counts of ratings, and this is partially correct. There are two major problems with that logic. First, we have already suggested that sometimes rating categories are unclear or misjudged. Second, ratings are not equal intervals; the distance from 1 to 2 is not always the same as the distance from 2 to 3. The Rasch model reveals category confusion and also puts the ratings on an equal-interval ruler.

Here is a final example, Figure 8.13. Sometimes rating scales have too many categories and people get confused determining the difference between a score of 2 or 3 or 4. In this example, the rating scale has seven categories in the original items.

Figure 8.13. Rasch Output Showing Rater Confusion—Too Many Categories

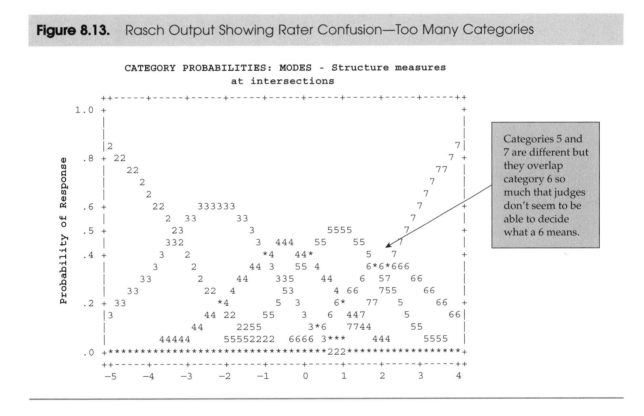

You can see that some categories aren't used and others are confused where there is a mixture of 5, 6, and 7 ratings. There are several solutions for this, but many people never realize the problem with their rating categories so they simply report misleading results.

Probably one of your greatest concerns, though, is the extent to which you can count on the raters to rate consistently. Everybody loves a good inter-rater reliability study! A special case of the Rasch model called the multifaceted Rasch model (MFRM), previously mentioned, is useful at detecting rater errors such as leniency/severity, central tendency, randomness, halo, and restriction of range effects (Myford & Wolfe, 2004). MFRM allows us to put judges on a ruler, just like items and respondents. We can see who is the harshest, who is the most lenient, and whether we should adjust teacher scores to report a fair measure.

All of our analyses to date have used the Winsteps software. We now turn to another software package, FACETS, also from Linacre (2003) to demonstrate how to analyze rater effect. This time, we will also show you something real even though it is competency based rather than dispositions based. Our example in Figure 8.14 is from a study Braun (1988) did for the Educational Testing Service on the ratings of essays on the Advanced Placement English test. To this point, we have put two things on the same ruler, item difficulty and person ability. We now add the raters, whom we often refer to as "judges." They are the "readers" in this study. The session is also calibrated on the same ruler. We can add other things, too, depending on our need, with this tool.

Figure 8.14. FACETS (MFRM) Output for Rater Consistency Analysis

```
           AP English Essays (College Board/ETS)  04-10-2006 22:46:48
              Table 6.0  All Facet Vertical "Rulers". (Braun, 1988)

      Vertical = (1*, 2A, 3A, 4A) Yardstick (columns, lines, low, high)= 0,
                                  10, -2, 1
 ---------------------------------------------------------------------------
 |Measr|+examinee|-Essay|-Reader          |-Session              |Scale|
 ---------------------------------------------------------------------------
 +   1 +         +       +                 +                      + (9) +
 |     | *       |       |                 |                      | --- |
 |     | *       |       |                 |                      |     |
 |     |         |       |                 |                      |     |
 |     | ***     |       |                 |                      |  6  |
 |     | *       |       | 1               |                      |     |
 |     | *       |       |                 |                      |     |
 |     | ****    |       |                 |                      | --- |
 |     | ***     |       | 3   6           |                      |     |
 |     | *       | B     | 5               |                      |  5  |
 *   0 * **      * A     * 10  11          * day 1 time 1     *   |     |
 |     | **      | C     | 12  2   7   9   |                      |     |
 |     |         |       | 4               |                      | --- |
 |     | **      |       | 8               |                      |     |
 |     | *       |       |                 |                      |     |
 |     | **      |       |                 |                      |     |
 |     | ***     |       |                 |                      |  4  |
 |     | *       |       |                 |                      |     |
 |     |         |       |                 |                      |     |
 |     | *       |       |                 |                      | --- |
 +  -1 + *       +       +                                        +     +
 |     |         |       |                                        |     |
 |     | *       |       |                                        |     |
 |     |         |       |                                        |  3  |
 |     |         |       |                                        |     |
 |     |         |       |                                        |     |
 |     | *       |       |                                        |     |
 |     |         |       |                                        |     |
 |     |         |       |                                        | --- |
 |     |         |       |                                        |     |
 +  -2 +         +       +                 +                      + (1) +
 ---------------------------------------------------------------------------
 |Measr| * = 1   |-Essay|-Reader          |-Session              |Scale|
```

This essay reader (#1) is too harsh as a judge compared to most judges. Can you see that reader #8 is lenient?

This analysis had 12 raters scoring three essays (ABC). The three essays are at about the same difficulty, but the readers who scored the essays differed a whole logit depending on their leniency/severity as a judge.

In Figure 8.14, the first column is labeled "Measr," for "measure." It is the logit value we use to create our ruler. In this case, the ruler is labeled from –2 to 1. The tabled values follow the ruler for some of the columns.

The second column, "Examinee," shows the students who wrote essays in response to one of three prompts. Each student is represented by an asterisk:*. More highly rated essays are at the top, and lower-rated essays are at the bottom. These tables are not produced here.

In the third column, "Essay," each essay question is calibrated. This tells us that the essay questions are of approximately the same difficulty. B is slightly harder than A, which is slightly harder than C on the rulers. By examining the tabled values below, it looks like B is .15 logits harder than A, which is −.9 logits harder than C.

In the fourth column, "Reader" is the rating of the readers by harshness/leniency. You can see that some readers are different from others on the rulers. The "Session" column could be used to determine whether a particular time or day influenced the scores, but it is not used here. The "Scale" column is the raw rating scale for the essays, which could be scored from 1 to 9 (with higher being better) now aligned with the ruler.

While there is a lot of detail here, we show it to get to the following point. It is possible to identify differences in raters and then adjust teachers' scores to account for those differences. It can be easier to change the scores than the raters! In Figure 8.15, that is just what we do—adjust the scores to make them fair.

In Figure 8.16 on page 226 we look at how the raters' decisions can be adjusted based on their leniency or harshness. You can see that each judge scored 96 essays, with Reader #1 awarding 392 points total, while Reader #8 awarded 508 points. Reader #1 was too harsh by almost half a logit (.45); Reader #8 was too lenient by about one third of a logit (−.30); and Reader #10 was in the middle (0.0). Facets can be used to provide a fair average to correct for this, but we won't do that here.

Figure 8.15. FACETS (MFRM) Output for Adjusting Scores to Make Them Fair—Essay-Adjusted Average Score

```
AP English Essays (College Board/ETS)   04-14-2006 23:48:07
Table 7.2.1  Essay Measurement Report  (arranged by mN).
-------------------------------------------------------------------------------
| Obsvd  Obsvd  Obsvd  Fair-M|        Model | Infit     Outfit    |Estim.|
| Score  Count Average Avrage|Measure S.E. | MnSq ZStd  MnSq ZStd|Discrm| N Essay
-------------------------------------------------------------------------------
|  1762   384     4.6   4.51|   .13   .04 |  .98 -.2   .99 -.1| 1.03 | 2 B
|  1854   384     4.8   4.76|  -.02   .04 |  .80 -3.0  .79 -3.3| 1.21 | 1 A
|  1913   384     5.0   4.92|  -.11   .04 | 1.20  2.7 1.18  2.5|  .76 | 3 C
-------------------------------------------------------------------------------
|  1843.0 384.0   4.8   4.73|   .00   .04 | 1.00 -.2   .99 -.3|      | Mean (Count:3
|    62.1    .0    .2    .17|   .10   .00 |  .16  2.4  .16  2.4|      | S.D.
-------------------------------------------------------------------------------
RMSE (Model)  .04 Adj S.D.   .09 Separation  2.28 Separation Reliability   .84
Fixed (all same) chi-square: 18.5  d.f.: 2  significance (probability): .00
Random (normal) chi-square: 2.0  d.f.: 1  significance (probability): .16
-------------------------------------------------------------------------------
```

Figure 8.16. FACETS (MFRM) Output for Adjusting Scores to Make Them Fair—Rater-Adjusted Average Score

```
AP English Essays (College Board/ETS)   04-14-2006 23:48:07
   Table 7.3.1  Reader Measurement Report   (arranged by mN).
```

Obsvd Score	Obsvd Count	Obsvd Avrage	Fair-M Avrage	Measure	Model S.E.	Infit MnSq	ZStd	Outfit MnSq	ZStd	Estim. Discrm	Exact Agree. Obs %	Exp %	Nu Reader
392	**96**	4.1	4.00	**.45**	.08	.79	-1.5	.79	-1.5	1.23	19.7	19.8	**1 1**
433	96	4.5	4.43	.18	.08	1.06	.4	1.03	.2	.99	27.8	21.8	3 3
434	96	4.5	4.44	.17	.08	1.04	.3	1.06	.4	.93	38.9	21.9	6 6
444	96	4.6	4.55	.11	.08	.85	-1.1	.84	-1.1	1.14	36.1	22.0	5 5
461	96	4.8	4.73	.00	.08	.71	-2.3	.71	-2.2	1.31	42.4	21.9	10 10
466	96	4.9	4.79	-.04	.08	1.14	.9	1.11	.8	.81	30.6	21.9	11 11
470	96	4.9	4.83	-.06	.08	1.40	2.6	1.37	2.4	.63	27.8	22.0	12 12
473	96	4.9	4.86	-.08	.08	1.06	.5	1.06	.4	.93	20.8	21.7	2 2
479	96	5.0	4.93	-.12	.08	1.13	.9	1.13	.9	.83	28.8	21.7	7 7
484	96	5.0	4.99	-.15	.08	1.02	.1	1.01	.0	.97	24.1	21.6	9 9
485	96	5.1	5.00	-.16	.08	.52	-4.2	.53	-4.1	1.48	21.2	21.7	4 4
508	96	5.3	5.26	**-.30**	.08	1.23	1.6	1.21	1.4	.75	20.8	20.4	**8 8**
460.8	96.0	4.8	4.73	.00	.08	1.00	-.1	.99	-.2				Mean (Count: 12)
29.5	.0	.3	.32	.19	.00	.23	1.8	.22	1.7				S.D.

```
RMSE (Model)  .08 Adj S.D.   .17  Separation  2.17  Separation (not inter-rater) Reliability  .82
       Fixed (all same) chi-square: 66.2  d.f.: 11  significance (probability): .00
       Random (normal) chi-square: 10.9  d.f.: 10  significance (probability): .36
Rater agreement opportunities: 384  Exact agreements: 108 = 28.1%  Expected: 82.6 = 21.5%
```

Well, why not? That's probably your big question now. Why take us this far? The reason is simple. This technique is used frequently in high-stakes testing to adjust examinees' scores when they fall just below the cut score. In the case of dispositions assessment, we do not need to do that. What we do need to do, though, is keep track of the degree to which our raters are scoring differently, yielding big differences in our decisions about teacher dispositions. Remember that in the data shared above, these are highly trained raters on a very high-stakes test. Being a little off is a dangerous thing.

In our work in teacher education, we may be doing less training and monitoring than ETS, but we may be in more danger of over- or underrating. An analysis such as this can help us make midcourse corrections, with a gentle prompt to our raters to be tougher or harsher in their decisions! And that is only fair to our teachers and their students.

If this is something you feel the need to do, it may be far less expensive in the long run to hire your friendly statistician to run the numbers than to do lots of Cohen's kappas and retraining of all of your faculty.

LEARNING MORE ABOUT RASCH

If you want to know more, here is a list of useful texts from beginning to advanced:

- *Applying the Rasch Model,* by Bond & Fox (2001): This is a good beginner's book for anyone interested in learning the Rasch model.
- *Rating Scale Analysis Rasch Measurement,* by Wright & Masters (1981): An excellent early explanation of rating scale development.
- *Constructing Measures,* by Mark Wilson (2005): This is a step-by-step process and explanation for creating a test with the Rasch model. Contains a CD.
- *Making Measures,* by Wright & Stone (2004): A short and easy-to-read explanation of major Rasch concepts.
- *Probability in the Measure of Achievement,* by Ingebo (1997): This work is from the Portland, Oregon, schools and describes their experience building tests.
- *Introduction to the Rasch Model,* by Smith & Smith (2004): A set of overview articles and applications for the Rasch model.
- *Best Test Design Rasch Measurement,* by Wright & Stone (1979): This is a classic text, but it has excellent explanations, and basic statistical concepts are illustrated.
- *Item Response Theory for Psychologists,* by Embretson & Reise (2000): A good overview of IRT, including the Rasch model along with others.
- *Item Response Theory* (2nd ed.), by Baker & Kim (2004): A serious mathematical explanation of IRT models, including Rasch. Contains a CD.
- *Rasch Measurement in Health Sciences,* by Bezruczko (2005): A collection of application articles of the Rasch model.

The online issues of *Rasch Measurement Transactions* (RMT) are also useful and readily available at the http://www.rasch.org/rmt/ Web site. A recommended journal is the *Journal of Applied Measurement.* An activity to help you sort out the pros and cons of IRT and CTT is provided at the end of the chapter.

V WRAP-UP

Classical test theory (CTT) is viable, but it will be limited in how far you can take it in terms of analyzing items and scores and conducting research. Rasch is a powerful technique that works well with small groups and has many advantages. The software is a little cumbersome, so you may need the help of a statistician if this is not something you enjoy doing. It is our method of choice if you

- want to find and fix teachers who were not assessed accurately.
- want to find and adjust for rater error.
- want one analysis that gives you lots of information, including empirical evidence of validity and reliability.
- expect to do statistics to look for gain scores or longitudinal growth.
- need to report validity, reliability, or fairness of your assessments.

You can use other methods, but here is our last comparison of the alternatives that are available to you:

Parting Words of Wisdom

KISS—Keep it statistically simple!!!

- If you want a competitive instrument to determine the best teacher(s), some classical statistics work better.
- If you want to search for constructs such as personality, the 2PL or 3PL IRT methods work well, too.
- If you want to assess standards-based, complex performance with rating scales, Rasch is the best.

DAATS CHAPTER 8—ACTIVITY #1

A Decision-Making Tool for Measurement

List the pros and cons of both measurement theories. Then, select the one you prefer to use for each analysis you need to make.

Classical Test Theory		Item Response Theory (Rasch Model)	
Pros	Cons	Pros	Cons

9

Legal and Psychometric Issues

The Return of the Pied Piper

They wrote the story on a column,
And on the great church-window painted
The same, to make the world acquainted
How their children were stolen away,
And there it stands to this very day.

—Robert Browning

In this chapter, we write an adaptation of a story we told in an article titled "Portfolios, The Pied Piper of Teacher Certification: Legal and Psychometric Issues" (Wilkerson & Lang, 2003).[1] In that article, we raised the ugly image of potential lawsuits that had not yet happened in the world of standards-based teacher competency assessment. By doing so, we hoped to redirect institutions in ways that could make their work safer by aligning more closely with the standards, attending to issues of validity and reliability, and ensuring due process.

Now, we raise that ugly image one more time, this time with regard to dispositions, which are typically assessed without specific alignments to standards—a very different context. In this chapter, we adapt the scenario we wrote in the "Pied Piper" article about "Mary Beth JoAnne" (MBJ). In 2003, she sued "XYZ University" over a competency-based decision regarding her portfolio, in a context in which the standards were not well applied. She won in various scenarios. In 2007, the dispute is about dispositions, and the linkage to standards is even more vague. Again, she wins in various scenarios. This time, as in the real world, her costs are supported by an independent organization; she is no longer on her own financially.

We then adapt some of our earlier work on legal issues and precedents, adding three recent legal cases on dispositions, supported by the Foundation for Individual Rights in Education (FIRE) and the American Civil Liberties Union (ACLU). We conclude with yet another version of the MBJ story, one that is standards aligned and one that we suspect would have a happier ending for XYZ University and the children she might have taught but won't.

WHY NOT PORTFOLIOS?

When we wrote the "Pied Piper" article, we were thinking about the manner in which portfolios have been viewed as a kind of panacea to the "assessment problem" faced by institutions and districts seeking to provide educational programs leading to the credentialing of teachers. We provided much advice in that article about how to avoid legal complaints through credible assessment (psychometric integrity), and much of the work was reprinted in our companion CAATS book that followed (Wilkerson & Lang, 2007). Even now, as we write, there are institutions seeking to use portfolios as a vehicle to assess dispositions as well as competencies. Faculty and administrators hope that teachers' dispositions will just leap off the pages with compelling indications that the teacher values what the institution values.

> **REMINDER**
>
> Portfolios should not be a one-stop-shopping approach. Most of us own more than one pair of shoes. We wear tennis shoes to play tennis and dress shoes to go out. The shoe, like the assessment method, has to fit the occasion.

Although we all have learned over the years that some assessment methods fit some forms of learning while others do not, we seem to be forgetting that lesson here and reverting back to a bad habit. We would not think of determining whether a person could play the piano through a multiple-choice test; many of us rail at the thought of a Saturday morning test to certify teachers. Yet in terms of our own accountability, we seem to be engaged in a one-stop-shopping approach to teacher assessment. In real estate, the most important thing is "location, location, location." In professional assessment, the most important thing is "validity, validity, validity."

WHY THE PIED PIPER?

Why, then, the "Pied Piper"? We remembered the story of Hamlin, where a panacea turned into "Pandora's Box." For those who have forgotten the fable (Browning, 1888), we summarize it here. Yes, we reduce a great story to a series of bullets, in keeping with our style, ruining the style of the original but breaking up all this long text!

- The small town of Hamlin was plagued by rats.
- The mayor hired the famed Pied Piper to play his magic flute to lure them away.

- The Pied Piper did his job.
- The mayor refused to pay the bill.
- The piper led all the children out of town.
- The children were never seen again*

*Modern version: "All Children Left Behind."

Box 9.1. The Message of the Pied Piper

The unstated (albeit morbid) analogy we were drawing was that for those who hope to manage the requirements imposed by the accountability movement, with portfolios or any other assessment devices, there is a need to pay the piper—the piper who plays the flute called psychometric integrity. If we fail to pay this piper, he, too may lead all the children (our teacher candidates) away through loss of program approval or accreditation or, worse, terribly costly litigation from the disgruntled teacher who was denied graduation and/or credentialing.

WHAT IF?? A LEGAL SCENARIO: MARY BETH JoANNE SUES XYZ UNIVERSITY

MBJ Helps Us to Understand the Convergence of Psychometrics and Legal Requirements

In Chapter 7 of this book, as well as Chapter 7 of our competencies book, we discussed how to collect evidence of validity, reliability, and fairness. To this point, we have attempted to convince our readers of the moral imperative of doing it right. For both competencies and dispositions, we have argued that if we fail to adequately assess a teacher, the teacher may harm children. Children may not learn important material, or worse, they may learn to hate a subject like math. Teachers make a difference that lasts a lifetime, including their transference of affect, creativity, and success (Torrance, 1981).

Here, in this chapter, with the help of Mary Beth Joanne (nicknamed MBJ), we introduce some of the potential legal consequences of not doing it right, drawing heavily on our *Education Policy Analysis Archives* (EPAA) article, but switching our focus to dispositions. We will use the same basic scenarios as before and the same disgruntled teacher candidate—MBJ. This time, her legal fees are paid jointly by the Foundation for Individual Rights in Education (FIRE) and the American Civil Liberties Union (ACLU)—both of which have a recent history of backing such claims.

Background "Facts"

Mary Beth Joanne is a fictitious student who attends XYZ University, which is located in our home state of sunny Florida, where teacher education programs must certify that their graduates have demonstrated all 12 of the Florida Educator Accomplished Practices (FEAPs). The FEAPs are very similar to the INTASC Principles. Florida has added two Practices, one on ethics and one on technology, which are embedded within the INTASC Principles. Florida does not require the measurement of dispositions in its standards.

Here are the facts about XYZ:

- XYZ candidates must have the required GPA, pass the state teacher certification exam, and successfully complete the portfolio and the final internship to graduate. If they successfully pass the state's background check, they are awarded a five-year professional certificate, renewable every five years thereafter.

- The XYZ University portfolio is digital, using a national commercial software package designed for standards-based assessment. The portfolio includes 12 sections, one for each FEAP. Institution-specified artifacts are required for each Practice, and XYZ has ensured that all important aspects of the Practices are covered in the artifacts. (Bravo!! They decided to do this after reading the Pied Piper article.) Some evidence serves a dual purpose, addressing two Practices.

- The teacher candidates must include a reflection on each of the Practices, explaining how they have demonstrated the Practices and what their improvement plans are. These reflections are used as evidence of the Practice on Continuous Improvement (FEAP #3). They are the primary source of grading the portfolio, since specific pregraded artifacts are now required.

- For accreditation purposes, XYZ includes its assessment of dispositions in the portfolio requirements through a review of the reflections in the portfolio. Faculty review of the reflections incorporates an attempt to ascertain the degree of commitment to the Practices and the values of the institution.

- The portfolios are reviewed during internship, although artifacts are gathered and stored throughout the program. Candidates cannot write their reflections until all work is completed, since they are required to analyze their work and status at the time of graduation. The portfolio is, therefore, an exit requirement.

- XYZ uses a scoring rubric for the portfolios. The rubric requires at least one linkage to the relevant FEAP per artifact and at least one area for improvement to be identified. The minimum length is specified as one-half page, double-spaced, 12-point font. If students meet these minimum requirements, they receive an acceptable rating for the Practice. If they make more than one linkage per artifact or identify more than one improvement area, they receive a target rating for the Practice. If they miss a linkage or the improvement, the reflection is scored as unacceptable for the Practice. If any reflection is unacceptable, the candidate must redo the reflection. Two opportunities to remediate are provided. If the candidate is still unable to fix the problem, a grade of F is assigned and the candidate does not complete the state-approved program for certification.

- To ensure reliability, the portfolios are double-scored—once by the cooperating teacher and once by the university supervisor.

- The requirements are properly documented in the XYZ portfolio materials, the catalog, and an advising sheet provided to students upon admission to the program.

Here are some more detailed "facts" about MBJ:

- Mary Beth JoAnne is 35 years old, is a single mother of three, works 20 hours a week at TarMart, and has typically enrolled in 15 to 18 credit hours per semester. She wants to get her teaching degree as quickly as possible so she can leave TarMart.

- MBJ has a GPA of 4.0 on a 4.0 scale—all A's. She has successfully completed all requirements of the internship except the portfolio requirement. All required assessments for the portfolio were scored as "A" work. All ratings on her internship evaluation form are 5's on a 5-point scale. She appears to be doing a good job in the classroom, according to her cooperating teacher.

- From the cooperating teacher, MBJ has received six acceptable and six target ratings (all 2's or 3's on a 3-point scale) on all reflections. None of her reflections were found to be unacceptable (rating of 1) by the cooperating teacher. The cooperating teacher correctly applied the rubric, rating half of the Practices "target" because MBJ identified two improvements in each of them. The scores result in a "satisfactory" summative score for internship, which is graded "S/U."

- MBJ has an attitude. She is a loner who has fought in every university class about working in groups. She interrupts her colleagues, professors, and teachers in her internship school when they are speaking. She openly admits that she wants to work in a high-socioeconomic-status school and does not like working with poor minority children, although she is careful to mask this feeling when teaching. (She calls equally on all children of all races and socioeconomic backgrounds, using a chart of free-lunch students and easily meeting the internship requirements.) She has been overheard complaining about the workload and says she is going to use only the materials the district gives her, although she has introduced new materials from the Web in her internship teaching. It is pretty obvious to her instructors that she will be the kind of teacher who is home by 3:30, puts quick check marks on every child's work without looking at it (after watching *Oprah* at 4:00 p.m.), and will be asleep by 9:00 p.m.

- On April 14, MBJ shows up in Senior Seminar in a shirt with an American flag imprinted on it, an American flag draped over her shoulders, a very short skirt with her underwear showing, and body jewelry (in her nose and tongue). She makes a peace sign with her fingers and proclaims, "Free at last; soon I'm outta of this ____ place!" (expletive deleted). She then makes a profane comment about her flag attire. She is feeling liberated because she is so near the end of her university experience.

- Dr. Jack, MBJ's University Supervisor, is furious and tells her that she is going to receive a grade of U in Internship, based on an unsatisfactory rating on FEAP #11—Role of the Teacher (the Florida professionalism standard) in her portfolio. Dr. Jack tells MBJ that she cannot dress that way or speak that way. It is both unprofessional and un-American. He tells her that the reflections in her portfolio are shallow and do not reflect the attitudes of a professional teacher, resulting in a grade of D on the portfolio. He advises her to change her major to Liberal Studies to graduate.

- MBJ responds, telling Dr. Jack that he is mean and unfair because this will prevent her from receiving her transcript endorsement from XYZ and, therefore, her teacher certification in the State of Florida. He concludes by telling her that she "can appeal the grade if she wants to waste her time."

- This is the chance XYZ has have been waiting for! MBJ finally showed her true colors!!

- MBJ appealed the decision. She appeared before the Academic Regulations Committee in a black two-piece business suit with a white blouse buttoned at the neck. No body jewelry. The Committee supported Dr. Jack's judgment about her values with regard to the standard on Role of the Teacher (FEAP #11) because of her comments in class, her appearance, and the shallow nature of her reflections. Those were their official reasons. After all, she was known around the halls as "Ms. Paininthebutt." Her appeal was denied.

- MBJ contacts the nonpartisan ACRE organization. Her case is taken by a group of a team of three of their finest lawyers, all of whom have graduated from Ivy League law schools.

Scenario #1

MBJ is Hispanic; her father is from Cuba, and her last name is Gonzalez. She files a claim under Titles VI and VII of the 1964 Civil Rights Act. The results follow and are outlined in the steps used by the courts in such cases:

- Step 1: MBJ's lawyers analyze the results of the portfolio evaluations, and a smaller percentage of Hispanics (70%) passed than non-Hispanic Caucasians (95%). The 80% disparate-impact criterion is 76%. The court determines that there is disparate impact for Hispanics (biased results) with this result. The court notes that XYZ did not conduct its own studies of disparate impact.

- Step 2: The burden of proof shifts to XYZ. MBJ claims that the reflections in the portfolio could not provide valid evidence of her potential to perform in the classroom (i.e., to be certified), since teachers do not have to write reflections about their work in the classroom. Reflections are not job related. The lawyers cite Chapter 14 of the AERA, APA, and NCME *Standards* (1999). XYZ claims that the evidence is valid because the portfolio requirements were developed in direct response to the NCATE and state requirements. They ensured the validity of the artifacts through a content validity study. The court finds as follows:

  - The court upholds MBJ. The judge's opinion notes that the state places a heavy emphasis on teachers' ability to impact K–12 learning, and this is documented in both State Statute and State Board of Education Rule. XYZ has failed to demonstrate that reflections aligning teacher products to standards have a scientifically proven impact on K–12 learning. While reflections on teaching and assessment that should be changed to improve student scores would have a valid basis, the university has failed to provide evidence of a job-relatedness study showing that reflections linking teacher products to teacher competency standards are valid based on the job-relatedness criterion. The court further notes that "shallowness" is not an objective criterion and was not part of the published procedure.

  - The court also finds that the institution has not used any research-based techniques to assess candidates' dispositions. MBJ's lawyers presented research on the use of scales, questionnaires, focus groups, behavior checklists, and apperception tests as the methods used for decades to measure dispositions. The inference is, therefore, not valid, since an inappropriate methodology was used.

- The court finds that instructional validity is also limited, since the writing of the reflections was extracurricular and not graded at the time of the creation of the assignments. There was no specific instruction provided on how to write adequate reflections. Since the reflections were not graded until the end of MBJ's internship, MBJ did not have adequate opportunity to learn the skills needed to prepare a portfolio, and she was given inadequate opportunity to remediate. These are also issues related to fairness and due process.

- The court finds that the reliability of the decision is questionable, since the cooperating teacher found that all requirements were met, properly applying the criteria established and published by XYZ.

- Step 3: Not applicable, since MBJ prevails at Step 2. Step 3 addresses MBJ's rights to alternatives, and it is addressed below in Scenario #2.

Scenarios #2, #3, and #4

In Scenario #2, all of the contextual elements are the same; however, MBJ's lawyers do not know about the AERA, APA, and NCME *Standards*. They do not make an effective case on all the aspects related to validity and reliability. Consequently, this time, XYZ prevails at Step 2. The trial moves to Step 3, and MBJ must prove that she was denied any reasonable alternatives. Remember Dr. Jack? He did not offer her any alternatives. He did not tell her she could rewrite the reflections to meet his standards, and he did not provide any alternative assessments for her. MBJ now asserts that she should have been allowed to substitute some other way of demonstrating that she had the correct dispositions to teach, since it is clear to her that XYZ is determined to find fault with her reflections. In this scenario, MBJ prevails again. XYZ is unable to show that it had made any alternatives to the portfolio reflections available to her.

In Scenario #3, all of the contextual elements are the same as in Scenario #1; however, MBJ is a non-Hispanic Caucasian. Although females are a protected class, she knows that the statistics would not support a discrimination claim under Titles VI and VII. She does, however, have a due process claim under the Fourteenth Amendment. She asserts that the bachelor's degree in elementary education is a property right of which she has been deprived without procedural due process. The court finds that the procedural due process claim introduces new problems for XYZ. The court finds in MBJ's favor again on procedural due process because

MBJ Wins in Scenario #1

- Job-relatedness (construct validity)
- Unpublished subjective criterion (reliability and fairness)
- No research-based techniques (construct validity)
- No opportunity to learn or remediate (instructional validity)
- Different results from teacher and professor (inter-rater reliability)

MBJ Wins in Scenario #2

The main legal and psychometric issue is a lack of opportunity to learn or remediate (instructional validity and Title VII). This would have been a reliability issue (equivalent forms) if XYZ had used a different assessment that was not checked.

MBJ Wins in Scenario #3

The main legal and psychometric issue is a due process failure (fairness and Fourteenth Amendment).

> **MBJ Wins in Scenario #4**
>
> The main legal and psychometric issue is a due process failure (fairness and First Amendment).

XYZ had no published policy related to a dress code or the use of dispositions as a deciding factor in graduation. Dr. Jack's decision was upheld by the XYZ Academic Regulations Committee, but both decisions were determined by the court to be unfair.

In Scenario #4, all of the contextual elements are the same as in Scenario #3; however, MBJ makes a First Amendment claim on freedom of speech. She claims that her failing grade was the result of her verbal and nonverbal communication about the flag, her attire, and her comment to Dr. Jack. She wins again.

PSYCHOMETRIC ISSUES AND LEGAL CHALLENGES IN THE REAL WORLD

We have raised the specter of legal challenges. These challenges are based upon the convergence of federal law and psychometric properties. It is difficult, if not impossible, to separate the two. A review of the research written about legal challenges indicates that there are four basic legal issues in employment testing: two challenges under the 1964 Civil Rights Act (Title VI and Title VII) and two challenges under the Fourteenth Amendment to the U.S. Constitution (due process and equal protection). Title VI supplements Title VII by reinforcing the prohibition against discrimination in programs or activities that receive federal funding, which includes most teacher preparation programs through grants and financial aid (McDonough & Wolf, 1987; Mehrens & Popham, 1992; Pascoe & Halpin, 2001; Pullin, 2001; Sireci & Green, 2000). We have also introduced a small scenario about the First Amendment above, since a dispositions lawsuit based on that amendment was just won by the plaintiff at the end of 2006.

> **DISCLAIMER**
>
> The authors hold degrees in measurement, not law. We express here our opinions and analyses as measurement experts and researchers, not lawyers.

Precedent-setting cases come from a variety of employment situations, both within and outside the field of education. Many challenges introduce psychometric issues, the chief of which is validity. The applicable guidelines and standards governing the psychometric properties of the test and the decisions made using the test, whether it be in the field of education or not, are based in educational psychology and measurement as well as employment guidelines. The two most influential resources that provide operational direction for these legal decisions are the 1999 AERA, APA, and NCME *Standards for Educational and Psychological Testing* and the 1978 *Uniform Guidelines on Employee Selection Procedures* (Pascoe & Halpin, 2001). Perhaps you now see why we have pounded away at those AERA, APA, and NCME *Standards* throughout this book!

Box 9.2. Applicable Laws and Guidelines

- First and Fourteenth Amendments of the U.S. Constitution
- Titles VI and VII of the Civil Rights Act
- 1999 AERA, APA, and NCME *Standards for Educational and Psychological Testing*
- 1978 *Uniform Guidelines on Employee Selection Procedures*

Regarding the Civil Rights Act of 1964, Titles VI and VII forbid not only intentional discrimination on the basis of race, color, or national original but also practices that have a disparate impact on a protected class. Courts use a three-step process, in which the burden of proof shifts back and forth from the plaintiff to the defendant. We used these three steps in our analysis of the MBJ case. In the first step, the plaintiff must prove discrimination. The discrimination could be either intended or coincidental, but it is clearly the responsibility of the institution to ensure that unintended discrimination (disparate impact) does not occur. This is why the results changed from scenario to scenario, dependent on MBJ's ethnic background. She was a member of a minority group that was less successful than the majority population in the first scenario. In DAATS Step 5, we showed you how to monitor for disparate impact in Example #3.

If discrimination has occurred, the defendant (SCDE or district) must demonstrate that the test was valid and is necessary, and this is most often linked to the job-relatedness (or the "business necessity") of the test. This second step is where the legal and psychometric issues converge (Scenario #1 of MBJ). If the defendant proves in court that the test is valid, the plaintiff has one more chance to prevail. If he or she can prove that the defendant could have used an alternative test with equivalent results, the defendant will lose (Scenario #2).

> **Validity vs. Reliability**
>
> Validity trumps reliability. Lawyers and measurement folks agree. As scary as that may be to all of us, it means you can't skip validity in favor of inter-rater reliability!

There are two basic requirements in the U.S. Constitution's Fourteenth Amendment that apply to this context: equal protection and due process. For a plaintiff to win under the equal protection claim, it must be shown that there was intent to discriminate. This is difficult and, therefore, rarely used. If Dr. Jack had said something about MBJ's Hispanic heritage, she would have had a claim on intent, but he did not do so.

The due process provisions have become relatively common. They forbid a governmental entity from depriving a person of a property or liberty interest without due process of law. The *Debra P. v. Turlington* (1984) case established the diploma as a property right. There are two kinds of these claims: substantive and procedural due process. Substantive due process requires a legitimate relationship between a requirement and the purpose. This is much easier to establish than the business necessity require-

> "But as for the guilders, what we spoke, Of them, as you very well know, was in joke."
>
> —Robert Browning

ment of the Civil Rights Act. Procedural due process requires fairness in the way things are done, and this includes advance notice of the requirement, an opportunity for hearings/appeals, and the conduct of fair hearings. Psychometric properties are excluded from this claim. MBJ prevailed on the latter type of due process in Scenario #3 (Mehrens & Popham, 1992; Sireci & Green, 2000).

Thus the linkage between legal rights and psychometric properties can occur in two places, opening the Pandora's Box of validity, reliability, and fairness. First, it can occur within the context of Step 2 of a discrimination claim under Titles VI and/or VII of the Civil Rights Act in which there is intended discrimination or disparate impact on a protected class. Second, it can occur within the context of a lack of a legitimate relationship between a requirement (e.g., a test) and a purpose (e.g., protecting the public from unsafe teachers) that constitutes a violation of substantive due process rights as ensured by the Fourteenth Amendment of the U.S. Constitution.

240 ASSESSING TEACHER DISPOSITION

LEGAL ISSUES AND PRECEDENTS

Lemke (2001) reviewed court decisions concerning the dismissal of college students from professional programs and determined that courts upheld school decisions when the institution followed its own published processes and the students' rights had been observed. If students are told what is expected of them in clear terms, colleges are safer. But Lemke also found that there is a lack of information about what the judicial system finds to be appropriate and inappropriate admissions and dismissal procedures. She looked at the decision of *Connelly v. University of Vermont* (1965), in which the federal district court ruled that it is within the purview of academic freedom for faculty to make decisions about students' progress. Faculty and administrators were described as uniquely qualified to make these decisions. In those days, though, certification was still the purview of the state. Lemke also reviewed eight cases of students filing against institutions. In these cases, the institutions had the right to make decisions about a student's academic fitness as long as it followed its advertised processes. Reasons for dismissals that were upheld included the use of subjective assessments in clinical experiences, time requirements for program completion, comparison of test scores between the plaintiff and peers, GPA, and absenteeism.

Educators in Florida have seen that the K–12 system is not so safe either. The groundbreaking *Debra P. v. Turlington case* (1984) reduced the level of comfort. This was a diploma sanction case in which the court ruled that a diploma is considered a property right and one must show some evidence of curricular/instructional validity, or what is also called "opportunity to learn" or "adequacy of preparation." In this case, both due process and the equal protection clauses of the Fourteenth Amendment were found to be violated by Florida officials who were using a basic skills test for diploma denial at the high school level. In appeals, additional issues were raised about whether the test covered material that was adequately covered in Florida's classrooms, and this has become the major precedent for looking at "instructional or curricular" validity. (Mehrens & Popham, 1992). In the MBJ case, XYZ required candidates to write their reflections outside of their regular courses and late in the program, thereby increasing their risk of challenge based on the principle of "opportunity to learn" and "opportunity to remediate."

McDonough and Wolf (1987) identified five issues around which litigation against educational testing programs occurs: (1) the arbitrary and capricious development or implementation of a test or employee selection procedure, (2) the statistical and conceptual validity of a test or procedure, (3) the adverse or disproportionate impact of a testing program or selection procedure on a "protected group," (4) the relevance of a test or procedure to the identified requirements of the job (job-relatedness), and (5) the use of tests of selection procedures to violate an individual's or group's civil rights (McDonough & Wolf, 1987).

The California Basic Education Skills Test (CBEST) was challenged in 1983 under Tile VII by the Association of Mexican American Educators. The state won the case based on a job-relatedness study (Zirkel, 2000). In 1984, Florida lost a challenge to Florida Performance Measurement System (FPMS) (an observation assessment) when the question of the validity of the decision about a teacher's certificate removal was successfully raised (Hazi, 1989). In this case, the issue at hand was dispositional in nature because enthusiasm was the attribute being measured! Georgia's Teacher Performance Assessment Instrument (TPAI) challenge was won by the plaintiff, based on due process and validity challenges (McGinty, 1996). This system was also observation- and portfolio-artifact based.

As far as teacher educators are concerned, Pullin (2001) notes that the courts generally have been reluctant to second-guess educators' judgments of educational performance that are based on subjective evaluations. Many college administrators believe that academic freedom will protect their decisions about denying admission or graduation to teacher candidates (Milam, 2006). As long as the context is academic freedom, Milam (2006) asserts that almost any criteria deemed important by faculty or the institution can be used for admission, grading, or completion requirements, including physical-motor skills (*Southeastern Community College v. Davis*, 1979), disabilities (*Ohio Civil Rights Commission v. Case Western Reserve University*, 1996), interaction with instructors (*Richmond v. Fowlkes*, 2000), inability to interact (*Lunde v. Iowa Board of Regents*, 1992), maturity (*Van De Zilver v. Rutgers University*, 1997), cooperation (*Stretten v. Wadsworth Veterans Hospital*, 1976), lack of judgment (*Regents of University of Michigan v. Ewing*, 1985), personality (*Kirsch v. Bowling Green State University*, 1996), harmony (*McEnteggart v. Cataldo*, 1972), and even personal hygiene (*Board of Curators of the University of Missouri v. Horowitz*, 1978)!

But what about three cases that have occurred just recently? We describe them next.

THREE LANDMARK DISPOSITIONS CASES IN TWO YEARS

There are some recent challenges in which academic freedom appears to provide less of a safety net than it used to provide (R. Wilson, 2005). In Matter of *McConnell v. Le Moyne College* (2006), the appellate court ordered readmission of Mr. McConnell after he had been dismissed from the program for having values inconsistent with those of the college. He believed in corporal punishment and disavowed multiculturalism. He wrote about his beliefs in a classroom management plan. Although college officials contended that it was their expert opinion that he did not have what it takes to be a teacher, despite his high grades, the college did not have a standards-based process to assess him, nor did they have policies and procedures in place to tell him they were measuring his values and that he could challenge their decisions. The court held that Le Moyne had violated his rights to due process and had to take him back and let him graduate.

> **McConnell v. Le Moyne College**
>
> McConnell won in New York State with legal aid from the Foundation for Individual Rights in Education (FIRE).

The second landmark dispositions case is that of Edward Swan, a Washington State University education student who was threatened with expulsion after failing a formal dispositions assessment. The instrument was not aligned with standards and can be found on the FIRE Web site: (http://www.thefire.org/pdfs/c3abc758b8c5a4b8fe4547728beb260f.pdf). Swan allegedly opposed affirmative action and gay adoption and believed in traditional ideas about the roles of men and women in the family. One professor wrote him up for writing "Diversity is perversity" on his textbook, while another wrote that Swan was a White supremacist because he used the term "wetback" in a paper in which he was explaining the use of the term. Swan is the father of four Mexican American children. He was given a choice between being expelled or submitting to sensitivity training. This training included

Swan v. Washington State University

Swann won in Washington State with legal aid from FIRE.

Thompson v. Southeastern Louisiana University

Thompson won in Louisiana with legal aid from the ACLU.

doing certain assigned (presumably sensitizing) projects and agreeing to greater-than-usual supervision as a student teacher. Swan responded by contacting FIRE. In February 2006, Washington State University revised the criteria used to evaluate Swan, creating a standards-aligned process (see http://www.thefire.org/pdfs/092f5e84bfeb9f7332fa6decde3d73b0.pdf).

In October 2006, in the *Thompson vs. Southeastern Louisiana University* case, the court ordered reinstatement of Ms. Thompson, who had received a failing grade in internship because she reported forced school prayer in a public school. Upon reporting to her university supervisor this violation of the laws related to separation of church and state, the university supervisor took out a prayer book and prayed for her. Then, the supervisor failed her. Ms. Thompson was represented by lawyers from the American Civil Liberties Union (ACLU) and won her case, based on a violation of her First Amendment rights.

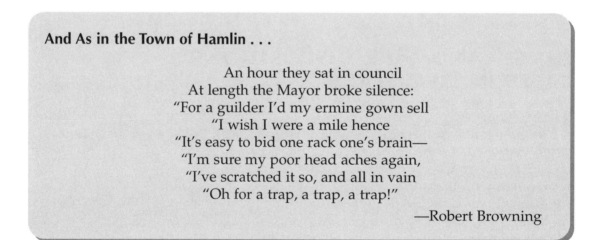

And As in the Town of Hamlin . . .

An hour they sat in council
At length the Mayor broke silence:
"For a guilder I'd my ermine gown sell
"I wish I were a mile hence
"It's easy to bid one rack one's brain—
"I'm sure my poor head aches again,
"I've scratched it so, and all in vain
"Oh for a trap, a trap, a trap!"

—Robert Browning

TIDE CHANGING IN NCATE

In Chapter 1, we reviewed some of the confusion in the language of the NCATE *Standards* regarding dispositions. We noted that in some places, institutions are directed to use the INTASC Principles, while in others, they are directed toward the NEA Code of Ethics. NCATE has long had a strong focus on diversity, which we support. We also support ethical behavior! NCATE has been encouraging institutions to focus on social justice issues. We support social justice. However, this encouragement has met with criticism and accusations that NCATE was engaging in "groupthink" (Leo, 2005), with negative publicity not only in the education community (*Chronicle of Higher Education,* Wasley, 2006) but also in the popular media (*U.S. News and World Report*).

Only after agreeing to soften its advocacy for institutional commitments to "social justice" as part of the accreditation process could NCATE continue to have its own federal approval as an accreditation agency. Wasley (2006) described the opposition to the use of the social justice theme as a vehicle to weed out would-be teachers based on their social and political beliefs. She noted that several teacher candidates, in fact, have complained recently about education professors who seemed more interested in students' political views than in their classroom performance:

> At a hearing of the U.S. Department of Education's National Advisory Committee on Institutional Quality and Integrity, Arthur E. Wise, president of NCATE, called the criticisms of the standards "unwarranted" but announced that the organization would drop "social justice" from the guidelines, "lest there be any misunderstanding about our intentions." (Wasley, 2006, p. A13)

As strong advocates for the measurement of dispositions as the ethical and moral thing to do, we hope to help reverse the fears that have grown out of this turn of events. It is time to start thinking of dispositions in a standards-based way so that we can diagnose and remediate in cases in which that is appropriate. We also need to have a system that has the teeth to counsel students out of teaching, if that is warranted.

STANDARDS ARE THE VANGUARD!

By combining the use of stated and accepted professional standards as the basis for a measurement system, the provision of opportunities to learn and to remediate, and the accessibility of a hearing that can challenge decisions, an institution or district can feel more secure if challenged on due process. We live at a time and in a country in which standards are at the forefront of public demands for accountability. It is only common sense that standards can be used to achieve a sustainable system of disposition assessment. If we want to measure commitment to social justice, let us do it in ways that are aligned with standards, using appropriate methodologies consistent with the AERA, APA, and NCME *Standards for Educational and Psychological Testing* and the INTASC Principles.

We predict that institutions will prevail in cases of academic freedom when they can support the expert judgment of faculty on valid and reliable instruments that yield decisions regarding students within the accountability framework of standards. The creation of such instruments is the end product of working through a process such as the one proposed in DAATS. Without such evidence, losing may become a foregone conclusion. Imagine the forensic expert who claims there is evidence of the guilty party but cannot describe the evidence or the process of collecting the evidence. In writing about the Le Moyne College case, we concluded (Wilkerson, 2006)

> If the data collected have the potential to provide useful information to advise, diagnose and remediate, it is clearly well worth the time and resource investment for colleges of education to develop good measurement devices from which solid decisions about candidates' skill-based values surface. The colleges can prevail in court, be accredited, and produce better teachers at the same time.

MBJ REVISITED

MBJ v. XYZ University

MBJ loses.

XYZ and the children of Florida win.

We wonder what would have happened at XYZ University with Mary Beth JoAnne if XYZ had a disposition assessment system in place that made use of a series of six instruments, the first five of which had been tested for validity, reliability, and fairness. Box 9.3 shows the imaginary results for MBJ in our assessment system.

Box 9.3. Assessing MBJ With Validity, Reliability, and Fairness in Mind

1. **Belief Scale:** MBJ's belief scale score was 49, two standard deviations below the mean, with incorrect answers clustering on items aligned with standards on professionalism (INTASC Principle #10), communication (INTASC Principle #6), and continuous improvement (INTASC Principle #9).

2. **Teacher Questionnaire:** MBJ received an unacceptable rating on Question #2 of the teacher questionnaire. She wrote, "I do not like to work with colleagues because they slow me down. I'm smarter." This question provided evidence of a lack of valuing of professional relationships (INTASC Principle #10).

3. **Focus Group:** A group of five of MBJ's internship students were asked whether she appeared to be listening to them. The children were unanimous in their responses that she shortchanged their ideas and cut them off while they were talking, often sneering at what they had to say (INTASC Principle #6 on Communication and also INTASC Principle #5 on Motivation/Learning Environment).

4. **Behavior Checklist:** The cooperating teacher provided a frequency rating of "rarely" on an item related to positive interactions with colleagues. In the "Notes" section, the cooperating teacher wrote that MBJ frequently cut off her colleagues and made snide remarks to them (INTASC Principle #6 on Communication and INTASC Principle #10 on Professionalism).

5. **Thematic Apperception Test:** In the simulation reflection assessment, MBJ was shown a picture of a scantily clad teacher and was asked to talk about the teacher. She admired the clothing, unlike 95% of the other teacher candidates who pointed out the unprofessional nature of the attire (INTASC Principle #10 on Professionalism). She was also shown a picture of a lesson plan that was scratched in poor handwriting and limited in content. She admired the teacher's ability to plan quickly (INTASC Principle #7 on planning). Most (97%) of the respondents recognized that the lesson was not well planned and was likely not to be effective.

6. **Disposition Event Report:** There are four reports in MBJ's file. Documented incidents include cursing at a professor, slapping a colleague, making a disparaging remark about Vietnamese children, and tearing up a graded report in class (INTASC Principle #10 on Professionalism and INTASC Principle #3 on Diversity). For each incident, there was documentation of a meeting between MBJ and professor completing the form, a remediation plan, and a record of a formal apology to the offended parties.

V END NOTE

We end this work with a parting note about planning. We teach our students day after day that they should never enter a classroom without a lesson plan, a unit plan, and a classroom management plan. There's always a plan. Sometimes we call it something else, like a "concept map." We would never hire a builder without an architect or try to put together a computer desk without a plan or set of instructions. Yet somehow, many of us have deluded ourselves into thinking that planning is less important in our world of teacher assessment—and worse, that we don't have to practice what we preach.

> **In case you have been wondering:**
>
> - V is for Validity.
> - V is for Values.
> - V is for Victory.
> - V is for the Five-Step Model (Roman numeral version).
>
> The three dots are for Validity, Reliability, and Fairness.

In this book, we have attempted to demonstrate how solid planning for the assessment of dispositions not only gives us the data we need in a systematic way, but it gets us there safely. We hope that you have found our discussions useful, our model informative, and our worksheets invaluable. But even more important, we hope that we have convinced you that failure to measure standards-based dispositions systematically and with integrity will surely leave some children behind.

We hope we have given you some of the tools you need to make good assessment happen. For all of our sakes, Hamelin *must* be just a medieval fairytale village.

P.S. Here's one for the road:

Story Ender

We're down to just one:

Your boss, Dr. Nohaydinero (find a Spanish-speaking friend if you don't get this one), says: "We just need to keep the Board, the State Department, and NCATE out of our hair. This Wilkerson and Lang DAATS model is just too darned expensive and too much work. Cut the junk, and just do the minimum. Give 'em a reflection to write, stick it in their portfolios, and be done with it."

You say...

NOTE

1. The authors thank the editor of *Education Policy Analysis Archives* for permission to adapt portions of material previously printed as an article in the journal, an open-access, refereed education journal available at http://www.epaa.asu.edu.

Resource A

INTASC Principles and Disposition Indicators

Principle #1: The teacher understands the central concepts, tools of inquiry, and structures of the discipline he or she teaches and can create learning experiences that make these aspects of subject matter meaningful for students

1.1 The teacher realizes that subject matter knowledge is not a fixed body of facts but is complex and ever-evolving. He or she seeks to keep abreast of new ideas and understandings in the field.

1.2 The teacher appreciates multiple perspectives and conveys to learners how knowledge is developed from the vantage point of the knower.

1.3 The teacher has enthusiasm for the discipline(s) he or she teaches and sees connections to everyday life.

1.4 The teacher is committed to continuous learning and engages in professional discourse about subject matter knowledge and children's learning of the discipline.

SOURCE: The authors thank the Council of Chief State School Officers for permission to reproduce the INTASC standards in our discussion.

AUTHORS' NOTE: The original version of these Principles does not number the indicators. The numbering system has been added by the authors.

Principle #2: The teacher understands how children learn and develop, and can provide learning opportunities that support their intellectual, social, and personal development

2.1 The teacher appreciates individual variation within each area of development, shows respect for the diverse talents of all learners, and is committed to help them develop self-confidence and competence.

2.2 The teacher is disposed to use students' strengths as a basis for growth, and their errors as an opportunity for learning.

Principle #3: The teacher understands how students differ in their approaches to learning and creates instructional opportunities that are adapted to diverse learners

3.1 The teacher believes that all children can learn at high levels and persists in helping all children achieve success.

3.2 The teacher appreciates and values human diversity, shows respect for students' varied talents and perspectives, and is committed to the pursuit of "individually configured excellence."

3.3 The teacher respects students as individuals with differing personal and family backgrounds and various skills, talents, and interests.

3.4 The teacher is sensitive to community and cultural norms.

3.5 The teacher makes students feel valued for their potential as people, and helps them learn to value each other.

Principle #4: The teacher understands and uses a variety of instructional strategies to encourage students' development of critical thinking, problem solving, and performance skills

4.1 The teacher values the development of students' critical thinking, independent problem solving, and performance capabilities.

4.2 The teacher values flexibility and reciprocity in the teaching process as necessary for adapting instruction to student responses, ideas, and needs.

Principle #5: The teacher uses an understanding of individual and group motivation and behavior to create a learning environment that encourages positive social interaction, active engagement in learning, and self-motivation

5.1 The teacher takes responsibility for establishing a positive climate in the classroom and participates in maintaining such a climate in the school as a whole.

5.2 The teacher understands how participation supports commitment, and is committed to the expression and use of democratic values in the classroom.

5.3 The teacher values the role of students in promoting each other's learning and recognizes the importance of peer relationships in establishing a climate of learning.

5.4 The teacher recognizes the value of intrinsic motivation to students' lifelong growth and learning.

5.5 The teacher is committed to the continuous development of individual students' abilities and considers how different motivational strategies are likely to encourage this development for each student.

Principle #6: The teacher uses knowledge of effective verbal, nonverbal, and media communication techniques to foster active inquiry, collaboration, and supportive interaction in the classroom

6.1 The teacher recognizes the power of language for fostering self-expression, identity development, and learning.

6.2 The teacher values many ways in which people see to communicate and encourages many modes of communication in the classroom.

6.3 The teacher is a thoughtful and responsive listener.

6.4 The teacher appreciates the cultural dimensions of communication, responds appropriately, and seeks to foster culturally sensitive communication by and among all students in the class.

Principle #7: The teacher plans instruction based upon knowledge of subject matter, students, the community, and curriculum goals

7.1 The teacher values both long-term and short-term planning.

7.2 The teacher believes that plans must always be open to adjustment and revision based on student needs and changing circumstances.

7.3 The teacher values planning as a collegial activity.

Principle #8: The teacher understands and uses formal and informal assessment strategies to evaluate and ensure the continuous intellectual, social, and physical development of the learner

8.1 The teacher values ongoing assessment as essential to the instructional process and recognizes that many different assessment strategies, accurately and systematically used, are necessary for monitoring and promoting student learning.

8.2 The teacher is committed to using assessment to identify student strengths and promote student growth rather than to deny students access to learning opportunities.

Principle #9: The teacher is a reflective practitioner who continually evaluates the defects of his or her choices and actions on others (students, parents, and other professionals in the learning community) and who actively seeks out opportunities to grow professionally

9.1 The teacher values critical thinking and self-directed learning as habits of mind.

9.2 The teacher is committed to reflection, assessment, and learning as an ongoing process.

9.3 The teacher is willing to give and receive help.

9.4 The teacher is committed to seeking out, developing, and continually refining practices that address the individual needs of students.

9.5 The teacher recognizes his or her professional responsibility for engaging in and supporting appropriate professional practices for self and colleagues.

Principle #10: The teacher fosters relationships with school colleagues, parents, and agencies in the larger community to support students' learning and well-being

10.1 The teacher values and appreciates the importance of all aspects of a child's experience.

10.2 The teacher is concerned about all aspects of a child's well-being (cognitive, emotional, social, and physical) and is alert to signs of difficulties.

10.3 The teacher is willing to consult with other adults regarding the education and well-being of his or her students.

10.4 The teacher respects the privacy of students and confidentiality of information.

10.5 The teacher is willing to work with other professionals to improve the overall learning environment for students.

Resource B

Glossary

Alignment

Alignment is a judgmental process by which we analyze two sets of like elements (e.g., standards) and position together the ones that are similar. Because it is a judgmental process, not all people will agree on every alignment. It is here that we can use standards to provide strength and credibility to locally defined values. For example, social justice can be aligned with diversity.

> *Guiding Question: "Does the standard I am reading have a lot in common with my local values or conceptual framework?"*

Anchor examples

These are model responses selected as examples of each level in the scoring process. They are used to develop rubrics, train raters, and serve as reminders during the scoring process.

> *Guiding Question: "What does a response at the ___ level look like?"*

Behavior checklist

The list of attributes, traits, or behaviors that are observed over time. Someone who has special knowledge of the teacher (e.g., principal, mentor, supervising professor, parents) evaluates the teacher on the basis of experience over time. Typically a yes/no checklist is used, but a rating scale can be used as well.

> *Guiding Question: "What can we tell over time about the teacher's beliefs?"*

Conceptual framework

The conceptual framework is the content and philosophy that guide teaching and assessment. It is drawn from standards, research, professional experience, and vision.

> *Guiding Question: "What do I want to include in my system? Any standards?"*

Construct

The concept or characteristic that a test or assessment system is designed to measure. In this work, we name it "teacher performance."

> *Guiding Question: "What's the big-picture idea of what we are assessing?"*

Construct-irrelevant variance

Construct-irrelevant variance is any extraneous factor that distorts the meaning or interpretation of a score. A common form of this variance is measuring the wrong thing.

> *Guiding Question: "Have I mixed some other stuff that's not useful into the decision I am trying to make?"*

Construct underrepresentation

Construct underrepresentation occurs when we do not have enough data to make a decision about the construct because we haven't sampled well.

> *Guiding Question: "Do I have enough stuff to make a confident decision?"*

Content

The content is the set of topics or matter with which we are going to work. Content includes, at a minimum, the standards for teaching, as well as any locally defined expectations. The content defines precisely what material will be assessed and requires good sampling procedures once defined.

> *Guiding Question: "What will we assess?"*

Content domains

Content domains consist of each grouping of standards that have been aligned because they are similar and convey the same basic set of ideas. In the case of disposition assessment, they might include indicators from INTASC and indicators of locally defined values.

> *Guiding Question: "Does this set of standards and indicators hang together to form a logical body of content that can be assessed?"*

Content validity

Content validity is a form of validity evidence that ensures that the test measures the construct comprehensively and appropriately and does not measure another construct instead of, or in addition to, the construct of teacher performance on the job.

> *Guiding Question: "How do I know that the decisions I will make about teachers will be based on adequate coverage of the construct of teacher performance and nothing else?"*

Context

The context defines and describes the conditions that surround us and influence our work. They may be institutional, state, or national. Some contextual factors are helpful, and some are not.

> *Guiding Question: "What are the factors that will help or hinder implementation of the envisioned assessment system?"*

Credibility

Believability.

> *Guiding Question: "Is there any evidence that this stuff is right?"*

Data aggregation

Data are compiled in ways to make different decisions for individual teachers and programs. Percents and frequencies are most common, but sophisticated analyses using item response theory are also possible.

> *Guiding Question: "How can I combine data to make a decision about a teacher or program or a unit?"*

Dichotomous response

Two choices only!

> *Guiding Question: "Yes or no?" "Right or wrong?"*

Differential item functioning (DIF)

DIF is a statistical process that seeks to determine whether there are meaningful differences in the way subgroups perform, particularly groups that are classified as protected—women and minorities. It is okay for the performance to be different, as long as it is not because of problems in the construction or administration of the assessment itself.

> *Guiding Question: "Are minorities and women doing worse on the assessments because they are minorities and women?"*

Differential person functioning (DPF)

DPF is a statistical process that seeks to determine whether there are meaningful differences in the way item subsets perform, particularly patterns that are classified as a certain type—representing a subconstruct. It is okay for the performance to be different, as long as it is not because of problems in the persons such as anxiety, cheating, guessing, or test strategy.

> *Guiding Question: "Do any item patterns demonstrating a person's score need individual interpretation?"*

Directions

Statements that tell someone precisely how to work or respond. These should be written for both the teacher and the person asking questions.

Guiding Question: "How do I do it: step-by-step, please?"

Disposition

We will use the word "disposition" in this book to mean teacher affect—attitudes, values, and beliefs that influence the application and use of knowledge and skills. We will aim at determining whether or not the teacher has reached the "valuing" level in the Bloom and Krathwohl taxonomy. Our focus will be on standards-based, skill-related values, aligned with the INTASC Principles.

Guiding Question: "What does the teacher believe to be important about teaching and being a good teacher? How is he or she likely to act?"

Dispositional baseline

This is the bottom line for dispositions. If teachers are below the baseline, they probably should not be teachers.

Guiding Question: "How poor can the values be before we deny a license?"

Empirical evidence

Evidence based on numbers and scores that the assessment is credible.

Guiding Question: "What do the numbers tell us about credibility?"

Fairness

Fairness ensures that rights are protected and that people are not penalized because they are members of a protected group, because they don't have adequate opportunities to learn and succeed, because the criteria and tasks have language or contexts that are offensive to them, or because their rights to due process were violated.

Guiding Question: "Do all teachers have an equal opportunity to complete the tasks successfully, regardless of gender, ethnicity, or handicapping condition, and is there an appeals process in place?"

Focus group

Meetings of five to seven persons designed to put respondents at ease in talking about important issues. Prompting questions cause the group to respond and interact with each other, building consensus or difference among group members to give a truer picture than would be available from working with one person at time.

Guiding Question: "What do the kids say their teacher believes and values?"

Frameworks

Frameworks are two-way grids that help one conceptualize a balanced and appropriate set of assessments.

> *Guiding Question: "What do I have in my system that helps me chart out my stuff in an organized way so I can check to see whether I have everything I need where I need it?"*

Indicators

Indicators are statements or subparts that give specific examples or meanings to standards. We would call them "substandards," but that might be misinterpreted!

> *Guiding Question: "What are the details of the standards that help me visualize what the standard is intended to mean?"*

Inference levels

Inference levels are controlled by the level of difficulty in making a decision or judgment. They range from no judgment (low inference), as in a correct/incorrect response, to extensive judgment requiring professional expertise to interpret a response.

> *Guiding Question: "How hard will it be to make a decision about the teacher's level of commitment, or how much subjectivity is there in this decision?"*

Instrument

The paper designed to elicit responses. This could be a survey, a questionnaire, or a test.

> *Guiding Question: "What is the device that is designed and created to scientifically measure the construct?"*

Inter-rater reliability

Inter-rater reliability is an index of consistency across raters calculated using correlations. Raters' scores should consistently go up or down across students. When one rater rates a student high, the other rater should rate him or her high. Low ratings should also be consistent across raters. If some raters score students high and the other raters score the same students as low, then the ratings are not consistent or reliable.

> *Guiding Question: "Are scorers consistent in their ratings?"*

Interview

A set of questions typically asked orally of one person at a time.

> *Guiding Question: "How can I find out what he or she believes using interactive communication?"*

Item

The statement or question posed.

Guiding Question: "What's the question?"

Item analysis

An analysis of each item to see whether it is functioning as expected—consistently with other items, difficult or easy.

Guiding Question: "Is this item good?"

Item response theory

A measurement method that maximizes the information obtained about each item so that decisions can be made at the item level, not just the instrument level.

Guiding Question: "How good is each item and each score?"

Job analysis

A job analysis requires that we identify all the important things a teacher is expected to value to be able to perform the job well.

Guiding Question: "What does a teacher have to believe to be important to work effectively in today's schools?"

Judgmental evidence

Judgmental evidence relies on expert opinion rather than numbers.

Guiding Question: "What do the experts say?"

Likert

A scale that is typically four or five points and asks respondents to "agree" or "disagree" or to do so "strongly." The midpoint may be "neutral" or may be missing; missing is preferred.

Guiding Question: "How much do respondents agree or disagree on an item?"

Maintenance system

The maintenance system is the set of procedures and plans used to keep the system going and to make updates and changes as needed.

Guiding Question: "How will I know what needs to be changed, when, and by whom?"

Management or tracking system

The management or tracking system is the process used to keep track of scores in the system so that reports can be generated for decision making. It may be kept by hand or on a computer.

Guiding Question: "What procedures and materials do I need to have in place to store and retrieve data?"

Observation

Watching someone for specific traits or behaviors.

Guiding Question: "Can I see them doing what they should be doing?"

Proposition

Propositions are what we believe to be true that influences the way we will develop and use the assessments. They are the agreed-upon "givens" we hold to be self-evident. They are based on our values and beliefs about teaching and assessment.

Guiding Question: "What are the fundamental truths about teaching and assessment that guide our thinking?"

Psychometric

Psychometric is a big word that refers to the measurement of aspects of people such as knowledge, skills, abilities, or personality.

Guiding Question: "What do the data tell me about validity, reliability, and fairness in this test?"

Psychometric integrity

Psychometric integrity, like other forms of integrity, is about doing what is right—in this case, when we assess teachers. It is all about making sure people (children and teachers) don't get hurt by design.

Guiding Question: "Will I be able to sleep at night if I make these decisions?"

Purpose

The purpose is the reason for establishing an assessment system. It is the end (not the means).

Guiding Question: "Why are we assessing our teachers?"

Questionnaire

A set of questions to be answered in writing.

Guiding Question: "What does so-and-so think?"

Recording form or protocol

The structured form and process used to gather data.

> *Guiding Question: "How can I organize my work so it is neat and looks the same for every interview or focus group and provides consistent information?"*

Reliability

Reliability is the degree to which test scores are consistent over repeated applications of the process and are, therefore, dependable or trustworthy.

> *Guiding Question: "If a student took the same test again under the same conditions (or a similar version of the test), would he or she score the same score?"*

Rubric

A rubric is a set of scoring guidelines that facilitate the judgment-making process. They typically include a set of criteria and a mechanism (rating scale or checklist) to determine and record levels of quality.

> *Guiding Question: "How will I decide whether teachers did the task well or not?"*

Sampling plan

There are bunches of things a teacher could do to provide evidence of dispositions. The sampling plan selects the most important indicators from the domains being assessed. It must include a representative sample from each domain. It would not be a good sampling plan if the teacher had to answer 30 questions during an interview on only 3 of 15 indicators or 6 of 10 standards.

> *Guiding Question: "What items and instruments will I pick to cover all of the standards?"*

Scoring key

The answers.

> *Guiding Question: "May I have a cheat sheet, please?"*

Tally

Counting and making little sticks on a paper to keep track. Typically, there are four vertical sticks and then a horizontal stick crossing through them so we can count by five.

> *Guiding Question: "How many times did you see it?"*

Thematic apperception test (Our version: Situation reflection assessment)

A projective technique that allows for a wide range of possibility and interpretation in how the examinee responds to stimulus cards and the examiner interprets the results. This technique is useful to find patterns of response that surface without direct prompting.

> *Guiding Question: "What does this person believe or feel that he or she is not directly saying or doesn't know how to say?"*

Thurstone Agreement Scales

A scale similar to a Likert except that respondents are forced to "agree" or "disagree" only. There is no place for "strongly" or "neutral." This is often called "forced choice." It is easier to interpret.

> *Guiding Question: "Do they agree or disagree with a statement without copping out with a 'don't know' response?"*

Use

The use of the system is the decision or set of decisions to be made about teachers. It defines what will be done with the data collected.

> *Guiding Question: "What decisions will we make with our data?"*

Utility

"Utility of data" refers to usefulness. There's no point in collecting a bunch of stuff to fill a filing cabinet if you have no expectation of using it.

> *Guiding Question: "Will the data I collect give me useful information so I can have better teachers and programs?"*

Validity

Validity is the extent to which assessment measures are truthful about what they say they measure or the degree to which evidence and theory support the interpretations and use of a test or assessment process.

> *Guiding Question: "Does this test really measure what it says it measures? Does the assessment system provide adequate coverage of the standards?*

References

Adams v. State of Florida Professional Practices Council, 406 So 2nd 1179 Florida 1st DCA (1981).

American Educational Research Association, American Psychological Association, and National Council of Measurement in Education. (1999). *Standards for educational and psychological testing.* Washington, DC: American Educational Research Association.

Anderson, L. W. (1988a). Attitudes and their measurement. In J. P. Keeves (Ed.), *Educational research, methodology, and measurement: An international handbook* (pp. 421–426). Oxford, England: Pergamon.

Anderson, L. W. (1988b). Guttman scales. In J. P. Keeves (Ed.), *Educational research, methodology, and measurement: An international handbook* (pp. 428–430). Oxford, England: Pergamon.

Anderson, L. W. (1988c). Likert scales. In J. P. Keeves (Ed.), *Educational research, methodology, and measurement: An international handbook* (pp. 427–428). Oxford, England: Pergamon.

Anderson, L. W., & Krathwohl, D. (Eds.). (2001). *A taxonomy for learning, teaching, and assessment: A revision of Bloom's taxonomy of educational objectives.* New York: Longman.

Andrich, D., & Wright, B. D. (1994). Rasch sensitivity and Thurstone insensitivity to graded responses. *Rasch Measurement Transactions, 8,* 382.

Baker, F. B., & Kim, S. (2004). *Item response theory: Parameter estimation techniques* (2nd ed.). New York: Marcel Dekker.

Baldridge National Quality Program. (2006). *Education criteria for performance excellence.* Gaithersburg, MD: Author. Retrieved December 11, 2006, from http://www.quality.nist.gov/PDF/2006_Education_Criteria.pdf

Barnard, G. A. (2001). "Logit," "log," and "log-odds." *Rasch Measurement Transactions, 14,* 785.

Bayley, S. (2001). Rasch vs. tradition. *Rasch Measurement Transactions, 15*(1), 809.

Bezruczko, N. (2005). *Rasch measurement in health sciences.* Maple Grove, MN: JAM Press.

Bloom, B. S., & Krathwohl, D. R. (1956). *Taxonomy of education objectives: The classification of educational goals, by a committee of college and university examiners.* New York: Longman, Green.

Board of Curators of University of Missouri v. Horowitz, No. 76–695, Supreme Court of the United States, 435 U.S. 78; 98 S. Ct. 948; 55 L. Ed. 2d 124; 1978 U.S. LEXIS 64, Argued November 7, 1977, March 1, 1978.

Bond, T. G., & Fox, C. M. (2001). *Applying the Rasch model: Fundamental measurement in the human sciences.* Mahwah, NJ: Lawrence Erlbaum.

Braun, H. I. (1988). Understanding score reliability: Experiments in calibrating essay readers. *Journal of Educational Statistics, 13,* 1–18.

Briggs, C., & Wilson, M. (2004). An introduction to multidimensional measurement using Rasch models. In E. V. Smith & R. M. Smith (Eds.), *Introduction to Rasch measurement* (pp. 322–341). Maple Grove, MN: JAM Press.

Browning, R. (1888). *The Pied Piper of Hamelin.* London: Frederick Warne.

Cannell, C. F., Miller, P. V., & Oksenberg, L. (1981). Research on interviewing techniques. In S. Leinhardt (Ed.), *Sociological methodology* (pp. 389–437). San Francisco: Jossey-Bass.

Cohen, J. (1960). A coefficient of agreement for nominal scales. *Educational and Psychological Measurement, 20,* 37–46.

Columbia Encyclopedia Online, Sixth Edition. (2001–2005). Ethics. Retrieved November 26, 2006, from http://www.bartleby.com/65/

Connelly v. University of Vermont and State Agricultural College, 244 F. Supp. 156 (D. Vt., 1965).

Council of Chief State School Officers. (1992). *Model standards for beginning teacher licensing, assessment, and development: A resource for state dialogue.* Washington, DC: Author. Retrieved April 24, 2005, from http://www.ccsso.org/projects/Interstate_New_Teacher_Assessment_and_Support_Consortium/Publications

Darling-Hammond, L. (2000). Teacher quality and student achievement: A review of state policy evidence. *Education Policy Analysis Archives, 8*(1), 1–50. Retrieved April 21, 2005, from http://www .epaa.asu.edu/epaa/v8n1/

Debra P. v. Turlington, 730 F.2d 1405 (11th Cir., 1984).

Diez, M. E. (2006). Assessing dispositions: Five principles to guide practice. In H. Sockett (Ed.), *Teacher dispositions: Building a teacher education framework of moral standards* (pp. 49–68). Washington, DC: American Association of Colleges of Teacher Education.

Dottin, E. S. (2006). A Deweyan approach to the development of moral dispositions in professional teacher education communities: Using a conceptual framework. In H. Sockett (Ed.), *Teacher dispositions: Building a teacher education framework of moral standards* (pp. 27–47). Washington, DC: American Association of Colleges of Teacher Education.

Elder, C., McNamara, T., & Congdon, P. (2004). Rasch techniques for detecting bias in performance assessments: An example comparing the performance of native and non-native speakers on a test of academic English. In E. V. Smith & R. M. Smith (Eds.), *Introduction to Rasch measurement* (pp. 419–444). Maple Grove, MN: JAM Press.

Embretson, S. E., & Reise, S. P. (2000). *Item response theory for psychologists.* Mahwah, NJ: Lawrence Erlbaum.

Flores, J. G., & Alonso, C. G. (1995). Using focus groups in educational research. *Evaluation Review, 19*(1), 84–101.

Groves v. Alabama State Bd. of Educ., Civil Action No. 88-T-730-N, U.S. District Court for the Middle District Of Alabama, Northern Division, 776 F. Supp. 1518; 1991 U.S. Dist. LEXIS 14890, October 3, 1991, Decided, October 3, 1991, Filed.

Guttman, L. (1944). A basis for scaling qualitative data. *American Sociological Review, 9,* 139–150.

Haladyna, T. M., & Downing, S. M. (1989). A taxonomy of multiple-choice item-writing rules. *Applied Measurement in Education, 1,* 37–50.

Hazi, H. M. (1989). Measurement versus supervisory judgment: The case of *Sweeney v. Turlington. Journal of Curriculum and Supervision, 4,* 211–229.

Holt-Reynolds, D. (1991). *The dialogues of teacher education: Entering and influencing preservice teachers' internal conversations* (Research report). East Lansing: Michigan State University National Center for Research on Teacher Learning. Retrieved April 26, 2005, from http://www.ncrtl.msu.edu/ http/rreports/htlm/rr914.htm

Hopkins, K. D. (1998). *Educational and psychological measurement and evaluation.* Boston: Allyn & Bacon.

Ingebo, G. S. (1997). *Probability in the measure of achievement.* Chicago: MESA Press.

Ingersoll, G. M., & Scannell, D. P. (2002). Performance-based teacher certification: Creating a comprehensive unit assessment system. Golden, CO: Fulcrum.

Interstate New Teacher Assessment and Support Consortium. (1992). *Model standards for beginning teacher licensing, assessment, and development: A resource for state dialogue.* Washington, DC: Author. Retrieved November 30, 2006, from http://www.ccsso.org/content/pdfs/corestrd.pdf

Interstate New Teacher Assessment and Support Consortium. (1995). *Next steps: Moving toward performance-based licensing in teaching.* Washington, DC: Council of Chief State School Officers.

Jacobson, J. (2006, January). Court orders college to readmit education student it had expelled for advocating corporal punishment. *Chronicle of Higher Education.* Retrieved October 9, 2006, from http://www.chronicle.com/daily/2006/01/20060120tn.htm

Johnson, E. M. (1999). An examination of person misfit in five affective measures. *Rasch Measurement Transactions, 12,* 4.

Katz, L. (1993). *Dispositions as educational goals.* Urbana, IL: ERIC Clearinghouse on Elementary and Early Childhood Education [ED363454]. Retrieved November 30, 2006, from http://www .chiron.valdosta.edu/whuitt/files/edoutcomes.html

Kirsch v. Bowling Green State University, No. 95API11–1476, 1996 Ohio App. LEXIS 2247 (Ohio C. App. May 30, 1996).

Krathwohl, D., Bloom, B., & Masia, B. (1956). *Taxonomy of educational objectives. Handbook II: Affective domain.* New York: McKay.

Krathwohl, D. R., Bloom, B. S., & Masia, B. B. (1964). *Taxonomy of educational objectives, Book 2: Affective domain.* New York: Longman.

Lang, W. S. (2005, February). *Analysis of disposition measures of consistency with INTASC principles: Results of an initial study. Measuring teacher dispositions with credibility: A multi-institutional perspective* (J. Wilkerson, Chair). Symposia presented at the Annual Meeting of the American Association of Colleges of Teacher Education, Washington, DC.

Lang, W. S., & Wilkerson, J. R. (2004, February 7). An assessment framework: Designing and using standards-based rubrics to make decisions about knowledge, skills, critical thinking, dispositions, and K–12 impact (Preconference workshop handouts). 2004 Conference of the Association for the American Association of Colleges for Teacher Education, Chicago.

Lang, W. S., & Wilkerson, J. R. (2006, February). *Measuring teacher dispositions systematically using INTASC principles.* Paper presented at Annual Meeting of the American Association of Teacher Educators, San Diego, CA.

Lawshe, C. H. (1975). A quantitative approach to content validity. *Personnel Psychology, 28,* 563–575.

Lemke, J. C. (March, 2001). Preparing the best teachers for our children. *No Child Left Behind: The vital role of rural schools.* Annual Conference Proceedings of the American Council on Rural Special Education (ACRES), Reno, NV.

Leo, J. (2005, October 24). Class(room) warriors. *U.S. News & World Report.* Retrieved October 9, 2006, from http://www.townhall.com.opinion/columns/johnleo/2005/10/17/171490.html

Likert, R. (1932). A technique for the measurement of attitudes. *Archives of Psychology, 140,* 55.

Linacre, J. M. (1994). *A user's guide to FACETS.* Chicago: MESA Press.

Linacre, J. M. (2003). *A user's guide to Winsteps and Ministep: Rasch-model computer programs.* Chicago: Winsteps.

Lunde v. Iowa Bd. of Regents, 92–365, Supreme Court of the United States, 506 U.S. 940; 113 S. Ct. 377; 121 L. Ed. 2d 288; 1992 U.S. LEXIS 6643; 61 U.S.L.W. 3301, October 19, 1992.

McConnell v. Le Moyne College, CA 05–02441, Supreme Court of New York, Appellate Division, Fourth Department , 2006 NY Slip Op 256; 25 A.D.3d 1066; 808 N.Y.S.2d 860; 2006 N.Y. App. Div. LEXIS 330, January 18, 2006, Decided, January 18, 2006.

McDonough, M., Jr., & Wolf, W. C., Jr. (1987). Testing teachers: Legal and psychometric considerations. *Educational Policy, 1,* 199–213.

McEnteggart v. Cataldo, Supreme Court of the United States, 408 U.S. 943; 92 S. Ct. 2878; 33 L. Ed. 2d 767; 1972 U.S. LEXIS 1985, June 29, 1972.

McGinty, D. (1996). The demise of the Georgia Teacher Performance Assessment Instrument. *Research in the Schools, 3*(2), 41–47.

McMillan, J. (2003). *Classroom assessment* (3rd ed.). Boston: Allyn & Bacon.

Mehrens, W. A., & Popham, W. J. (1992). How to evaluate the legal defensibility of high-stakes tests. *Applied Measurement in Education, 5,* 265–283.

Merriam-Webster Online Dictionary. (2006). Dispositions. Retrieved November 28, 2006, from http://www.merriamwebster.com/dictionary/dispositions

Milam, S. (2006, February). *Legal issues in assessment of dispositions.* Paper presented at the Annual Meeting of the American Association of Colleges of Teacher Education, San Diego, CA.

Miller, P. V., & Cannell, C. F. (1982). A study of experimental techniques for telephone interviewing. *Public Opinion Quarterly, 46,* 250–269.

Myford, C. V., & Wolfe, E. W. (2004). Detecting and measuring rater effects using the many-facet Rasch measurement: Part I and Part II. In E. V. Smith & R. M. Smith (Eds.), *Introduction to Rasch measurement* (pp. 460–574). Maple Grove, MN: JAM Press.

National Board for Professional Teaching Standards. (1986). *Five core propositions.* Arlington, VA: Author. Retrieved January 14, 2007, from http://www.nbpts.org/the_standards/the_five_core_propositio

National Commission on Excellence in Education. (1983). *A nation at risk.* Retrieved November 15, 2006, from http://www.ed.gov/pubs/NatAtRisk/index.html

National Commission on Teaching and America's Future. (1997). *Doing what matters most: Investing in quality teaching.* New York: Author. Retrieved September 9, 2006, from http://www.nctaf.org/documents/DoingWhatMattersMost.pdf

National Commission on Teaching and America's Future. (2003). *No dream denied: A pledge to America's children.* New York: Author. Retrieved April 24, 2005, from http://www.ecs.org/html/Document.asp?chouseid=4269

National Council for Accreditation of Teacher Education. (2002). *Professional standards for the accreditation of schools, colleges, and departments of education.* Washington, DC: Author. Retrieved November 4, 2004, from http://www.ncate.org/2000/unit_stnds_2002.pdf

Ohio Civil Rights Commission, et al. v. Case Western Reserve University, 666 N.E. 2nd 1376, 1386 (Ohio 1996).

Pascoe, D., & Halpin, G. (2001, November 13–16). *Legal issues to be considered when testing teachers for initial licensing.* Paper presented at the Annual Meeting of the Mid-South Educational Research Association, Little Rock, AR.

Perkins, D., Jay, E., & Tishman, S. (1989). *Beyond abilities: A dispositional theory of thinking.* Project Zero, Harvard, Cambridge, MA. Retrieved November 15, 2006, from http://www.learnweb.harvard.edu/alps/thinking/docs/Merrill.pdf

Phillips, J. L. (1988). Semantic differential. In J. P. Keeves (Ed.), *Educational research, methodology, and measurement: An international handbook* (pp. 430–432). Oxford, England: Pergamon.

Popham, J. W. (2004). All about accountability: Why assessment illiteracy is professional suicide. *Educational Leadership, 62*(1), 82–83.

Pullin, D. C. (2001). Key questions in implementing teacher testing and licensing. *Journal of Law and Education, 30,* 383–429.

Rasch, G. (1960). *Probabilistic models for some intelligence and attainment tests.* Copenhagen: Danish Institute for Educational Research; Chicago: University of Chicago Press. (Expanded edition with foreword and afterword by B. D. Wright, 1980)

Ray, J. W. (1974). Projective tests can be made more reliable: Measure need for achievement. *Journal of Personality Assessment, 38,* 303–307.

Rebell, M. A. (1991). Teacher performance assessment: The changing state of the law. *Journal of Personnel Evaluation in Education, 5,* 227–235.

Regents of University of Michigan v. Ewing, No. 84–1273, Supreme Court of the United States, 474 U.S. 214; 106 S. Ct. 507; 88 L. Ed. 2d 523; 1985 U.S. LEXIS 149; 54 U.S.L.W. 4055, October 8, 1985, Argued, December 12, 1985, Decided.

Richmond v. Fowlkes, No. 99–4162, U.S. Court of Appeals for the Eighth Circuit, 228 F.3d 854; 2000 U.S. App. LEXIS 24822, June 15, 2000, Submitted, October 2, 2000, Filed.

Ricker, K. L. (2003). *Setting cut scores: Critical review of Angoff and modified-Angoff methods.* Center for Research in Applied Measurement and Evaluation. Retrieved November 15, 2006, from http://www.education.ualberta.ca/educ/psych/crame/files/RickerCSS2003.pdf

Rudner, L. M. (2002). *Measurement decision theory.* Retrieved May 28, 2004, from http://www.edres.org/mdt/home3.asp

RUMM. (2003). *Rasch unidimensional measurement models.* Duncraig, Western Australia: RUMM Laboratory.

Salzman, S. A., Denner, P. R., & Harris, L. B. (2002). *Teacher education outcomes measures: Special study survey.* Washington, DC: American Association of Colleges of Teacher Education.

Sandman, W. (1998, November). *Current cases on academic freedom.* Paper presented at the Annual Meeting of the National Communication Association, New York.

Schulte, L., Edick, N., Edwards, S., & Mackiel, D. (2004, Winter). The development and validation of the Teacher Dispositions Index. *Essays in Education, 12.* Retrieved April 15, 2005, from http://www.usca.edu/essays/v0112winter2004.html

Shulman, L. (1998). Teacher portfolios: A theoretical activity. In N. Lyons (Ed.), *With portfolio in hand* (pp. 23–37). New York: Teachers College Press.

Sireci, S. G., & Green, P. C., III. (2000). Legal and psychometric criteria for evaluating teacher certification tests. *Educational Measurement: Issues and Practice, 19*(1), 22–24.

Smith, E. V., & Smith, R. M. (2004). *Introduction to Rasch measurement.* Maple Grove, MN: JAM Press.

Smith, R. M. (2004). Detecting item bias with the Rasch model. In E. V. Smith & R. M. Smith (Eds.), *Introduction to Rasch measurement* (pp. 391–418). Maple Grove, MN: JAM Press.

Smith, R. M., & Cramer, G. A. (1989). Response pattern analysis with supplemental score reports. *Rasch Measurement Transactions, 2*(4), 33–40.

Sockett, H. (2006). Character, rules, and relations. In H. Sockett (Ed.), *Teacher dispositions: Building a teacher education framework of moral standards* (pp. 9–25). Washington, DC: American Association of Colleges of Teacher Education.

Southeastern Community College v. Davis, 442 U.S. 397, 99 S. Ct. 2361, 2371 (1979).

Southern Association of Colleges and Schools, Commission on Colleges. (2001). *Principles of accreditation: Foundations for quality enhancement.* Decatur, GA: Author.

Stalling, J. A., & Mohlman, G. G. (1988). Classroom observation techniques. In J. P. Keeves (Ed.), *Educational research, methodology, and measurement: An international handbook* (pp. 469–173). Oxford, England: Pergamon.

StatSoft, Inc. (2006). *Electronic statistics textbook.* Tulsa, OK: Author. Retrieved November 30, 2006, from http://www.statsoft.com/textbook/stathome.html

Stefanakis, E. (2002). *Multiple intelligences and portfolios.* Portsmouth, NH: Heinemann.

Stemler, S. E. (2004). A comparison of consensus, consistency, and measurement approaches to estimating interrater reliability. *Practical Assessment, Research, Evaluation, 9*(4). Retrieved April 16, 2006, from http://www.PAREonline.net/getvn.asp?v=9&n=4

Stenner, A. J. (1996, February). *Measuring reading comprehension with the Lexile framework*. Paper presented at the Fourth North American Conference on Adolescent/Adult Literacy, Washington, DC.

Stenner, A. J., & Wright, B. (2004). Uniform reading and readability measures. In B. D. Wright & M. H. Stone (Eds.), *Making measures* (pp. 79–114). Chicago: Phaneron.

Stevens, S. S. (1946). On the theory of scales of measurement. *Science, 103,* 667–680.

Stiggins, R. (1997). *Student-centered classroom assessment.* Upper Saddle River, NJ: Prentice Hall.

Stiggins, R. (2000). *Specifications for a performance-based assessment system for teacher preparation.* Washington, DC: National Council for Accreditation of Teacher Education. Retrieved June 15, 2004, from http://www.ncate.org/resources/commissioned%20papers/stiggins.pdf

Stretten v. Wadsworth Veterans Hospital, No. 75–2309, U.S. Court of Appeals for the Ninth Circuit, 537 F.2d 361; 1976 U.S. App. LEXIS 11283, May 18, 1976.

Teitel, L., Ricci, M., & Coogan, J. (1998). Experienced teachers construct teaching portfolios: Culture of compliance vs. a culture of professional development. In N. Lyons (Ed.), *With portfolios in hand* (pp. 143–155). New York: Teachers College Press.

Texas Education Agency. (2005). *Technical digest for the academic year 2004–2005.* A collaborative effort of the Texas Education Agency, Pearson Educational Measurement, Harcourt Educational Measurement and Beck Evaluation and Testing Associates. Retrieved April 15, 2006, from http://www.tea.state.tx.us/student.assessment/resources/techdig05/index.html

Thompson, S., & Cobb-Reiley, L. (2003, June 23). *Using electronic portfolios to assess learning at the University of Denver.* Presentation at 2003 AAHE Assessment Conference, Seattle, WA.

Thurstone, L. L. (1927a). A law of comparative judgment. *Psychological Review, 34,* 273–286.

Thurstone, L. L. (1927b). The method of paired comparisons for social values. *Journal of Abnormal and Social Psychology, 21,* 384–400.

Thurstone, L. L. (1928). Attitudes can be measured. *American Journal of Sociology, 33,* 529–554.

Thurstone, L. L. (1929). *The measurement of attitude: A psychophysical method and some experiments with a scale for measuring attitude toward the church.* Chicago: University of Chicago Press.

Toldson, I., & Jacobs, R. (2005, February). Analyses and interventions with candidates identified as having dispositional deficits at an HBCU. *Measuring teacher dispositions with credibility: A multi-institutional perspective* (J. Wilkerson, Chair). Symposia presented at the Annual Meeting of the American Association of Colleges of Teacher Education, Washington, DC.

Torrance, E. P. (1981). Predicting the creativity of elementary school children (1958–80) and the teacher who "made a difference." *Gifted Child Quarterly, 25*(2), 55–61.

Trochim, W. (2000). *The research methods knowledge base* (2nd ed.). Cincinnati, OH: Dog Atomic Publishing. Retrieved August 10, 2006, from http://www.trochim.human.cornell.edu/kb/index.htm

U.S. Department of Education. (2004, March). *Overview: Fact sheet on the major provisions of the conference report to H.R. 1, the No Child Left Behind Act.* Washington, DC: Author. Retrieved March 24, 2006, from http://www.ed.gov/nclb/overview/intro/factsheet.html

Usher, D., Usher, M., & Usher, L. (2003, November 17–19). *Nurturing five dispositions of effective teachers.* 2nd National Symposium on Educator Dispositions, Eastern Kentucky University, Richard, KY.

Van de Zilver v. Rutgers Univ., Civil Action No. 97–806, U.S. District Court for the District of New Jersey, 971 F. Supp. 925; 1997 U.S. Dist. LEXIS 11213, August 1, 1997, Decided, August 1, 1997, Original Filed.

Vega, C., & Blankenship, V. (2006). *Using the Rasch model to increase the reliability of the Picture Story Exercise.* Retrieved February 2, 2006, from http://www.jan.ucc.nau.edu/~shuster/REU%20Home%20Page_files/REU%20abstracts/2003_program_abstracts.ht

Velasquez, M., Andre, C., Shanks, S. J., & Meyer, M. J. (2006). *What is ethics?* Markkula Center for Applied Ethics, Santa Clara University. Retrieved November 15, 2006, from http://www.scu.edu/ethics/practicing/decision/whatisethics.html

Vestal, S. (2005, October 22). WSU takes hit on free speech; disposition assessment for teachers draws criticism. *Spokesman Review.* Retrieved November 30, 2006, from http://www.thefire.org/index.php/article/6368.html

Walsh, J. J. (1988). Projective testing techniques. In J. P. Keeves (Ed.), *Educational research, methodology, and measurement: An international handbook* (pp. 432–436). Oxford, England: Pergamon.

Wasicsko, M. M. (2004, October). The 20-minute hiring assessment: How to ensure you're hiring the best by gauging educator dispositions. *The School Administrator.* Retrieved January 15, 2007, from http://www.aasa.org/publications/saarticledetail.cfm?ItemNumber=1133&snItemNumber=950&tnItemNumber=1995

Wasley, P. (2006). Accreditor of education schools drops controversial "social justice" language. *Chronicle of Higher Education, 52*(41), A13.

Watson, H. O., & Rayner, R. (1920). Conditioned emotional reactions. *Journal of Experimental Psychology, 3*(1), 1–14.

Wikipedia, The Free Encyclopedia. (2006). Ethics. Retrieved November 26, 2006, from http://www.en.wikipedia.org/wiki/ethics

Wikipedia, The Free Encyclopedia. (2006, October 1). Morality. Retrieved November 26, 2006, from http://www.en.wikipedia.org/w/index.php?title=Morality&oldid=78896254

Wilkerson, J. R. (2005, February). *Building progressive measures of teacher dispositions. Measuring teacher dispositions with credibility: A multi-institutional perspective* (J. Wilkerson, Chair). Symposia presented at the Annual Meeting of the American Association of Colleges of Teacher Education, Washington, DC.

Wilkerson, J. R. (2006, April 20). Measuring teacher dispositions: Standards-based or morality-based. *Teachers College Record.* Retrieved October 9, 2006, from http://www.tcrecord.org/content.asp?/contentid=12493

Wilkerson, J. R., & Lang, W. S. (2003, December 3). Portfolios, the Pied Piper of teacher certification assessments: Legal and psychometric issues. *Education Policy Analysis Archives, 11*(45). Retrieved February 14, 2004, from http://www.epaa.asu.edu/epaa/v11n45/

Wilkerson, J. R., & Lang, W. S. (2005, February). *Measuring dispositions with practicality, utility, validity, and reliability in mind* Workshop for Annual Meeting of the American Association of Teacher Educators in Washington, DC.

Wilkerson, J. R., & Lang, W. S. (2006, February). *Measuring dispositions with practicality, utility, validity, and reliability in mind.* Workshop for Annual Meeting of the American Association of Teacher Educators in San Diego, CA.

Wilkerson, J. R., & Lang, W. S. (2007). *Assessing teacher competency: Five standards-based steps to valid measurements using the CAATS model.* Thousand Oaks, CA: Corwin Press.

Wilson, M. (2005). *Constructing measures: An item response modeling approach.* Mahwah, NJ: Lawrence Erlbaum.

Wilson, R. (2005). We don't need that kind of attitude. *Chronicle of Higher Education, 52*(17), 8.

Wise, A. (2006, June 16). A message from Arthur E. Wise. *NCATE News.* Retrieved June 20, 2006, from http://www.ncate.org/public/0616_MessageAWise.asp?ch=150

Wolf, R. M. (1988a). Questionnaires. In J. P. Keeves (Ed.), *Educational research, methodology, and measurement: An international handbook* (pp. 496–500). Oxford, England: Pergamon.

Wolf, R. M. (1988b). Rating scales. In J. P. Keeves (Ed.), *Educational research, methodology, and measurement: An international handbook* (pp. 478–481). Oxford, England: Pergamon.

Wolfe, E. W., & Mapuranga, R. (2004). *South Carolina High School Assessment Program (HSAP) 2003 field test evaluation: A report to the Education Oversight Committee.* Retrieved April 15, 2006, from http://www.sceoc.org/PDF/HSAPFinalReport.pdf

Wright, B. D., & Linacre, J. M. (1989, November). Observations are always ordinal; Measurement, however, must be interval. *Archives of Physical Medicine and Rehabilitation, 70*, 857–860.

Wright, B. D., & Masters, G. N. (1981). *Rating scale analysis.* Chicago: MESA Press.

Wright, B. D., & Stone, M. H. (1979). *Best test design.* Chicago: MESA Press.

Wright, B. D., & Stone, M. H. (2004). *Making measures.* Chicago: Phaneron.

Yancey, K. B., & Weiser, I. (Eds.). (1997). *Situating portfolios: Four perspectives.* Logan: Utah State University Press.

Zirkel, P. (2000). Tests on trial. *Phi Delta Kappan, 8*(10), 793–794.

Index